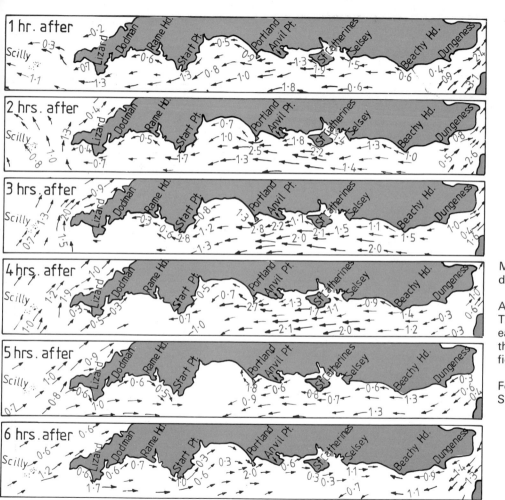

Mean rate of tidal streams in the Channel during the six hours after HW DOVER.

Arrows indicate direction of the stream. The figures give average rate in knots at each point. For Spring rate, add one-third. At Neaps, subtract one-third of the figures shown on each chart.

For greater detail, see Admiralty Tidal Stream Atlases or relevant charts.

The Shell Pilot to the English Channel

1. Harbours on the South Coast of England

Ramsgate to the Scillies

K. Adlard Coles

Revised and edited by

Captain J. O. Coote, Royal Navy

with plans by
James Petter

A Shell Guide

faber and faber
LONDON · BOSTON

First published as *Sailing on the South Coast*
Reissued 1939
by Faber and Faber Limited
3 Queen Square London WC1N 3AU
Second edition, with new title, 1950
Pocket Pilot for the South Coast
Third edition 1962
Fourth edition, wholly revised, 1968
Reprinted, with new title, 1971
The Shell Pilot to the South Coast Harbours
Interim edition, with correction pages, 1973
Fifth edition, wholly revised, 1977
Sixth edition, wholly revised, 1982
Interim edition, with correction pages and new title, 1985
The Shell Pilot to the English Channel
1. Harbours on the South Coast of England : Ramsgate to the Scillies

Filmset and printed in Great Britain by
BAS Printers Limited, Over Wallop, Hampshire
All rights reserved

British Library Cataloguing in Publication Data

Coles, K. Adlard
   Shell pilot to the English Channel.
   Pt. 1 : Harbours on the South Coast of England
   1. Pilot guides—English Channel
   2. Harbours—England
   I. Title
   623.89′2916336   VK841

ISBN 0-571-13540-4

To
GERALD POTTER
for whom the rocks did not move

It is regretted that neither the book's sponsor, nor its author
nor the publisher can accept responsibility for errors or
omissions, especially those brought about by changes made by
harbour and navigation authorities after the time of going to
press.

The Shell symbol and the name 'Shell' are both trademarks.

AMENDMENTS

This list of errata includes only the main ones affecting the text of this book. For a full list of corrections, consult Notices to Mariners. Amendments appear in *italic* type.

p. 34   Anvil Head. Add *VHF Lt Ho Call sign AL* (see p. 14).

p. 38   Add after Admiralty chart No. 442 *1267*.

p. 45   Ramsgate. First para. Delete 'planned' and substitute *under construction 0.35 miles to the SE from shore (1984)*.

p. 46   Line 2 should read 'Ch 16 or *14*'.

p. 57   Rye. *New leading lights on Co. 300° established* on east side of the fairway near the entrance. Both are *Oc W 10s 6M*.

p. 68   Littlehampton. Characteristics of Winter buoy are now *Q(6)+LFl 15s*.

p. 72   Chichester Harbour. *Water tower on Thorney Island has been demolished.*
Drying area W. side of Chichester Bar now extends to seaward to a point close SW of the Bar buoy.

p. 73   2nd para, 3rd sentence, delete *The square tower . . . right ahead.*

pp. 80–1   NW corner of Hayling Island now has *2FG lights*. Amend chart and last sentence of p. 81 accordingly.

p. 84   Portsmouth Harbour. Add after Admiralty chart Nos. *2629*.

p. 85   New small craft channel in harbour entrance. *Boats under 20m must use a channel running from the W of No. 4 buoy, passing within 50m of Fort Blockhouse. Boats under power may enter Portsmouth Harbour by hugging the E side of the main entrance.*

p. 91   Bembridge. Caption to picture 55. Delete *to be left to port.*

p. 92   Substantial dredging and extra alongside berths provided have enhanced its appeal as a port for visiting yachts. *Cut out new chart on p. 6 and paste over the existing one.*

p. 127   Poole. There have been so many changes to the buoyage in Poole Harbour that it is advisable to acquire a new chart 2611 corrected up to date. The channels themselves have not changed significantly. *The RO/RO terminal at Hamworthy has been extended 600m to the W on reclaimed land, with a least depth of 5m6 off it extending across the main channel.*

p. 128   Chart. *No. 31 buoy* immediately before the entrance to the Poole Harbour Marina is now *FIG 5s*.

p. 146   Bridport. Chart. Main Lt over the HM office is now *Iso R.*

p. 152   Exmouth. Lts at S extremity of Town Dock changed from *2FR to 2FG.*

p. 156   Teignmouth. Chart. Delete note *Occasl* on all leading lights. *Sector lt on Training Wall* NW of The Ness *is now OcR 5.5s* and all-round.
At the bend of the channel off Ferry Point on the edge of drying area *add an FG light.*
Add *2FG lts (vert)* on the end of the pier.
Leading lights at New Quay are now both *F Bu.*

p. 159   Torquay. The outer harbour has been extensively dredged and furnished as a major marina. *Cut out chart below the dotted line on p. 6 and paste over the bottom part of the existing chart.*

p. 165   Dartmouth. Chart. The buoy close SE of Dartmouth Castle (Checkstone) has been *moved 80m SE* and *now has a lt Fl(2)R 5s.*

pp. 171–2 Salcombe. The QWR lt off Blackstone Rock at the entrance has the following sectors: *R 218°–048° W 048°–218°.* Chart and text should be amended accordingly.

p. 181   Plymouth. Chart. Off Mount Batten pierhead the West Mallard W-cardinal buoy has been substituted by a *G conical starboard-hand buoy* with *QG light. The Asia N-cardinal buoy has been replaced by a R can port-hand buoy.*

p. 186   Looe. Delete *fog signal at pierhead.* Insert one on *Nailzee Point* with characteristics *Siren (2) 30s (Occasl).*

p. 199   Falmouth. Chart. Delete *FOr lt* at root of E pier forming Docks Basin.

p. 207   Helford. Chart. Add *E-cardinal buoy 0.1M ESE of Dennis Head. Bn 0.35M E of Bosahan Pt replaced by a N-cardinal buoy.*

p. 230 *et seq.* Amendments to List of Agents for Admiralty Charts and Hydrographic Publications

Avonmouth	W F Price & Co. Ltd	24 Gloucester Road
Bangor	A M Dickie & Sons	36 Garth Road
Brighton	Marina Watersports of Brighton	Marine Centre
Cardiff	T J Williams & Son Ltd	15–17 Harrowby Street
Chatham	Gransden Marine	Pier Chambers, Medway Street
Dartford	Lilley & Reynold	165a Heath Lane (Upper)
Emsworth	Castlemain (Marine Ltd)	Emsworth Yacht Harbour, Thorney Road

Fort William	Corpach Chandlers and Sailing School	Corpach, Fort William
Ipswich	Ipswich Marina Ltd	The Strand, Wherstead
London	Kelvin Hughes	31 Mansell Street, EC3
London	Stanfords International (Map Centre)	12–14 Long Acre, WC2
London	Brown & Perring Ltd	Redwing House, 36–44 Tabernacle Street, EC2
Manchester	International Marine	Manchester Marina, Trafford Road
Ramsgate	Seagear (Ramsgate) Ltd	10 Military Road
Sheffield	Peter Copley Marine Ltd	125–129 London Road
Southwick	A O Muggeridge Ltd	141–143 The Gardens
Tobermory, Isle of Mull	Seafare	Royal Buildings
West Mersea	The Mersea Chandlers	110 Coast Road

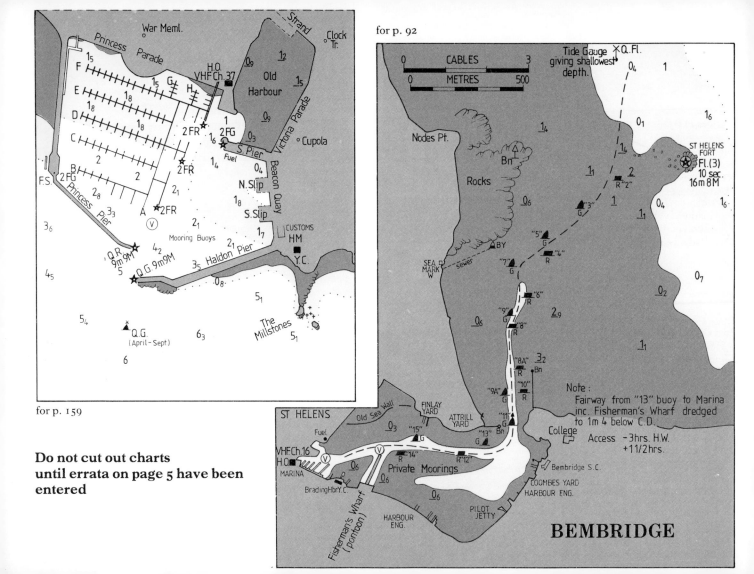

for p. 92

for p. 159

Do not cut out charts
until errata on page 5 have been
entered

BEMBRIDGE

CONTENTS

Harbours which are not accessible at all states of weather or tide. See precautions to be observed at the start of each relevant section. Figures in brackets refer to the most suitable Admiralty chart.

The sixth edition of this book, first published forty-five years ago, has been revised and edited by Captain John Coote, R.N., a retired submariner and newspaper publisher who is also a regular contributor to yachting magazines under the pen-name John Oldham. He is a very experienced cruising and offshore racing navigator. I wish to extend to him my sincere gratitude for the enthusiasm he has brought to bear on what I know has been a comprehensive and difficult task.

The extent of this revision reflects the completion of the new IALA buoyage system all along the South Coast, except in a few creeks and rivers. This book has been written with the owner of a yacht drawing around 2mo in mind, so it does not claim to cover the many shallow reaches which extend inland from some of the harbours reviewed . All the existing harbour plans have had to be redrawn. This work has been carried out with great precision by James Petter of Petersfield.

The opportunity presented by such a major revision has enabled the layout of the book to be changed, so that the harbour plans now appear beside the relevant text for each port—just as they did in the first edition of 1937!

It also seemed logical to lead the book with the section on Passage Data and Principal Headlands, to which have been added Distance Tables between the points mentioned. Also included for the first time are tidal charts for the South Coast and the times and heights of HW Dover for the next three years. These are intended as a guide for planning voyages. In some cases, such as where there is a double tide, it is as well to consult local tables. The back endpaper shows the new IALA buoyage system in colour and the new IALA Port Traffic Control signals which are expected to be introduced soon, replacing those old familiar cones, balls and flags with coded lights by day and night.

Every harbour mentioned in this book has been revisited during the fieldwork period of April to September 1981, and calls made upon thirty-eight harbour masters. Without exception they have readily given their whole-hearted co-operation. For my part I hope that the advice offered by this book to yachtsmen visiting ports for the first time will make life easier for these custodians of our overcrowded harbours and add to every sailor's enjoyment of one of the most interesting cruising-grounds in the world.

I am grateful to those contributors to the fifth edition whose efforts remain up to date. The pictures used, other than my own, have been duly credited. Captain Coote has been greatly helped by Mr Ken Armitstead and officers under training at the Britannia Royal Naval College, Dartmouth, and by Lieutenant-Commander Peter Whelan, Sub-Lieutenant David Griffiths and others from the Royal Naval Engineering College, Manadon. Between them they verified the revisions required to each harbour from the Helford River to Torbay. All the harbours between Portland and Chichester were checked in the agreeable company of Major-General Jim Gavin and his wife Barbara in their Nicholson '36' *Corruna*.

To the best of my knowledge the information contained in this book is correct at the time of going to press, but there remains the possibility that further changes will take place—such as the depths over shifting sands—or that points of detail have been overlooked. Each harbour covered is headed by a reference to the appropriate Admiralty chart where available—the most reliable guide, but due to the process of their publication, not necessarily up to date in every detail. A worthwhile £1 investment is the *Small Craft Edition of Admiralty Notices to Mariners*, published quarterly, summarizing alterations to charts between the Gironde and the Elbe. It is obtainable from any outlet which sells Admiralty charts. An annual subscription is recommended.

I am indebted to the Controller of H.M. Stationery Office, the Institute of Oceanographic Sciences and the Hydrographer of the Navy for access given to Captain Coote to their published data during the compilation of this book. There is also a number of local, privately published guides at some ports, such as those mentioned for Chichester Harbour and the Scilly Isles.

It is wise to acquire a copy of the local bye-laws governing any port to be visited. In all cases it should be assumed that Rule 9(b) of the Regulations for Preventing Collisions at Sea applies:

'A vessel of under 20 metres in length or a sailing vessel shall not impede the passage of a vessel which can safely navigate only within a narrow channel or fairway.'

Readers are invited to contribute any corrections, new information or constructive criticisms to Captain J. O. Coote, c/o Faber and Faber Ltd, 3 Queen Square, London WC1N 3AU.

K. Adlard Coles
January 1982

PREFACE TO THIS EDITION

This partly revised interim edition of the book coincides with the publication of a companion volume covering the north coast of France from Dunkerque to Brest, including the Channel Islands. The two books now form the *Shell Pilot to the English Channel*, Adlard Coles's original work covering South Coast harbours now being Part 1. The times of HW and LW Dover have been revised up to the end of 1987. All significant amendments brought about by the passage of time are listed on pages 3–5.

This new two-part publication recognizes the growing trend among cruising owners to go further afield and enjoy the contrasting features and lifestyles to be found on opposite sides of the Channel—a comparatively rare indulgence when the original *Sailing on the South Coast* was published in 1936.

John Coote
October 1984

Times of High Water The average time differences for each harbour applied to the time of HW Dover have been supplied by the Institute of Oceanographic Sciences, or have been estimated where data are not available. To arrive at the time of HW in a harbour take the time of HW at Dover and add or subtract the difference shown in the introductory notes for each port covered by this book. These constants are only approximate; for greater accuracy, where harbours are a long way from Dover, look up the predicted times of HW for the nearest standard port in Admiralty Tide Tables and then apply the time difference for whichever secondary port you are interested in. Nearly all ports have their own local tide tables, generally available at the harbour office, marinas or local newsagents.

Double High Waters occur at Southampton, in the West Solent ports and are even more evident in Christchurch and Poole. For these harbours the first HW at spring tides is included in the tidal data; in the Solent the second HW occurs about 2 hours later. HW at neap tides is always later than first HW springs, but there are long stands of tide, sometimes existing for several hours. Hence the average times of local HW referred to Dover would at best be approximations. However, predictions for each day of the year can be found in ATT.

Charted Depths and Data The charted depths given in this book are shown in metres; they indicate the depth of water *below chart datum* which is reduced to the level of LAT, or the drying heights (figures underlined) above it. Figures are given in the tidal data for each harbour for extra water at MHWS, MLWS, MHWN and MLWN which may be added to the charted depths or interpolated for intermediate states of tide. It will be noted that in many harbours 0m6 (2 ft) may be added to the charted depths

at MLWS and as much as 1m8 (6 ft) at MLWN; these are of great significance when navigating in shallow channels. Also note that tidal levels may be affected by weather conditions. For example, fresh northerly to easterly winds may bring low runs of tide sometimes lowering the levels of the extent of 0m6 (2 ft).

Heights of conspicuous landmarks other than lighthouses are shown in brackets in metres. Thus 'Chy (99)' indicates a chimney 99 metres above sea-level at its top.

Distances at sea are expressed in nautical miles or cables; on land in statute miles and kilometres.

Bearings and Courses Distances are given in nautical miles, cables and metres. Bearings and courses are True, to which Variation must be added and Deviation applied for ship's magnetic compass readings.

Approach The directions assume that the vessel is approaching from seaward, and objects are described on the port or starboard hand of a ship entering the harbour.

Notation of Charts—Lights Lights outside harbours only are shown, except (1) leading lights placed inside, and (2) important buoys used for proceeding up harbour.

Lights are symbolized, the word 'light' or 'Lt' omitted.

Nature of light is noted, e.g. F fixed, Gp Fl group flashing, etc., and in the case of other than white lights, the colour, e.g. R, G, etc. followed by elevation in metres (m) and range (M) miles. Bearings are generally expressed to the nearest degree true and cardinal or half cardinal points are used only to indicate approximate directions. The limits of sectors and arcs of visibility and the alignment of directional lights and leading lights are given as *seen by an observer from seaward* as true compass bearings.

Buoys are symbolized, and the word 'buoy' omitted. Colour and shape are not always described, but symbol conforms to shape of buoy and, where scale allows, to configuration, i.e. solid black for green buoys, outline or patched shading for white or red, chequers and stripes shown as such. The positions of mooring buoys cannot always be shown on the harbour plans, often being precluded by scale, but visitors' moorings are referred to in the text.

Beacons are either symbolized as Bn or shown as small round 'o'. Point where pole crosses base line indicates exact position.

Coloured Area Heavy stipple indicates parts which dry out at LAT. Green indicates parts where there are less than 2 metres at LAT and is bounded by dotted line. All depths over 2 metres are left white.

Anchorage Symbol (♆) is intended to draw attention to proximity of anchorage, and does not necessarily indicate precise or only spot for letting go. Anchorages are being increasingly occupied by moorings, but are referred to in the text.

Minor posts, withys, dolphins, etc., inside harbours are sometimes precluded by scale.

ABBREVIATIONS TIDAL

ATT	Admiralty Tide Tables
HW	High Water
LW	Low Water
LAT	Lowest Astronomical Tide
MHHW	Mean Higher High Water
MHWS	Mean High Water Springs
MHWN	Mean High Water Neaps
MLWS	Mean Low Water Springs
MLWN	Mean Low Water Neaps

OTHER ABREVIATIONS

Alt	Alternating
B	Black
Bl	Blue
BlW	Blue and White
Bn	Beacon
BW	Black and White
BY	Black and Yellow
Cheq	Chequers
con	conical
Dir	Directional
ev	every
F	Fixed
Fl	Flashing
FS	Flagstaff
G	Green
Gp	Group
H	Horizontal
h.	hour(s)
HM	Harbour Master
Int Qk Fl	Interrupted Quick Flashing
Iso	Isophase
km	kilometres
kt	knot
LFl	Long Flashing
Lt	Light
Lt Ho	Lighthouse
L V	Light-vessel
m	metres
m.	minutes (time)
M	Miles (nautical)
Mag	Magnetic
Mo	Morse Code Signal
NB	Notice Board
Occ	Occulting
Occas	Occasional
Or	Orange

PA	Position approximate
Qk Fl	Quick Flashing
R	Red
Ra Refl	Radar Reflector
Ro Bn	Radiobeacon
RW	Red and White
RY	Red and Yellow
S	Stripes
SC	Sailing Club
sec.	seconds (time)
Sph	Spherical
Tr	Tower
Vert	Vertical
vis	visible
V Qk Fl	Very Quick Flashing
W	White
Y	Yellow
YC	Yacht Club
⊘	Transit
→⊢	Right-hand edge
⊢←	Left-hand edge
Ⓥ	Visitors' berths

VHF VOICE FREQUENCIES

Ch 9	156.450 MHz
10	156.500
11	156.550
12	156.600
13	156.650
14	156.700
16	156.800 (Calling)
37	157.850 (Marina band)
67	156.375 (Coastguards)
74	156.725
88	162.025 (VHF Lt Ho see p. 14)

CONVERSIONS

Cable = 0.1 NM	200 yds
Nautical Mile	1.85 km
Statute Mile	1.69 km
Fathom	1.83 metres

DEPTH CONVERSION SCALE.   Fathoms & Feet —— Metres & Decimetres

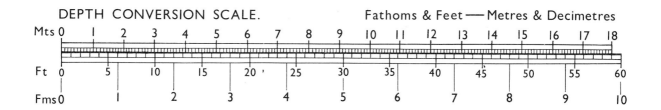

VHF RADIO LIGHTHOUSES: CHANNEL 88 (162.025 MHz)

For boats with VHF radio able to receive Ch 88 (162.025 MHz) there are some recently established VHF shore transmitters which will give their bearing from seaward to an accuracy of 2 degrees, regardless of the motion or compass heading of the receiving boat. Quadrantal errors and the effect of uninsulated guardrails or wrap-around metal construction are also irrelevant.

The operation is simple: on acquiring the signal, which leads off with the Morse call sign, start counting the beats until there is a sudden null. By reference to the tables below the bearing of the VHF lighthouse ashore is thus obtained in degrees (true) from seaward. Its range is governed by line-of-sight propagation, so those shown on the tables below are approximate, depending, *inter alia*, on the height of your own VHF antenna.

Bearing of Lt Ho from seaward in Degrees True

	Beats	0	1	2	3	4	5	6	7	8	9
V3 Anvil Point Lt Ho	0	—	—	—	—	—	—	—	247	249	251
Call sign: Al (·− ·−··)	10	253	255	257	259	261	263	265	267	269	271
Range: 14M	20	273	275	277	279	281	283	285	287	289	291
Alternate with	30	293	295	297	299	301	303	305	307	309	311
Scratchells Bay (V6)	40	313	315	317	319	321	323	325	327	329	331
	50	333	335	337	339	341	343	345	347	349	351
	60	353	355	357	359	001	003	005	007	—	—
V6 Scratchells Bay	0	—	—	—	—	—	—	—	337	339	341
0.4M Needles Lt 280°	10	343	345	347	349	351	353	355	357	359	001
Call sign: HD (···· −··)	20	003	005	007	009	011	013	015	017	019	021
Range: 30M	30	023	025	027	029	031	033	035	037	039	041
Alternate with	40	043	045	047	049	051	053	055	057	059	061
Anvil Point Lt (V3)	50	063	065	067	069	071	073	075	077	079	081
	60	083	085	087	089	091	093	095	097	—	—
V9 North Foreland Lt Ho	0	—	—	—	—	—	—	—	240	242	244
Call sign: ND (−· −··)	10	246	248	250	252	254	256	258	260	262	264
Range: 20M	20	266	268	270	272	274	276	278	280	282	284
Alternate with	30	286	288	290	292	294	296	298	300	302	304
Calais Main Lt (V12)	40	306	308	310	312	314	316	318	320	322	324
	50	326	328	330	332	334	336	338	340	342	344
	60	346	348	350	352	354	356	358	360	—	—

PART ONE

PASSAGE DATA AND PRINCIPAL HEADLANDS

(for tidal charts, see inside front cover)

Distances are given in nautical miles. Courses and bearings are True.

TIDE TABLES

The ensuing pages give the times and heights of High Water DOVER from January 1985 to December 1987 inclusive. The times of High Water (HW) are shown in green throughout. They may be used in conjunction with the South Coast tidal charts inside the front cover and the times and heights given for each harbour in this book.

Times are expressed in four figures as GMT. Add one hour when BST is in force. See the foot of each page for the inclusive dates of British Summer Time (BST) where known at the time of going to press.

Datum of Predictions is also Chart Datum which is 3.67 metres below Ordnance Datum at Newlyn.

Depths and heights are given in metres to one place of decimals. The following conversion table is for use with the Tide Tables:

Metres	Feet/inches	Metres	Feet/inches
0.1	0′4″	1.0	3′3″
0.2	0′8″	2.0	6′7″
0.3	1′0″	3.0	9′10″
0.4	1′4″	4.0	13′1″
0.5	1′8″	5.0	16′5″
0.6	2′0″	6.0	19′8″
0.7	2′4″	7.0	23′0″
0.8	2′8″	8.0	26′3″
0.9	2′11″	9.0	29′6″

JANUARY 1985

D	HW		LW		D	HW		LW	
1	0604	5.5	0028	2.5	16	0614	5.8	0050	2.0
Tu	1856	5.1	1312	2.2	W	1859	5.6	1338	1.7
2	0710	5.5	0128	2.4	17	0724	5.8	0211	2.0
W	2002	5.3	1415	2.1	Th	2011	5.6	1454	1.7
3	0811	5.6	0236	2.3	18	0832	5.9	0325	1.9
Th	2056	5.6	1521	1.9	F	2117	5.8	1603	1.6
4	0903	5.7	0345	2.0	19	0935	6.0	0430	1.7
F	2141	5.8	1619	1.6	Sa	2212	6.1	1702	1.4
5	0946	5.9	0442	1.7	20	1028	6.2	0526	1.4
Sa	2220	6.1	1709	1.4	Su	2257	6.3	1757	1.3
6	1024	6.1	0532	1.4	21	1113	6.3	0617	1.3
Su	2257	6.3	1756	1.2	22	1154	6.3	0704	1.1
7	1101	6.2	0618	1.2	Tu			1930	1.2
M	2332	6.5	1838	1.1	23	0012	6.5	0747	1.1
8	1140	6.3	0700	1.1	W	1231	6.3	2006	1.2
Tu			1917	1.1	24	0048	6.5	0823	1.1
9	0011	6.6	0740	1.0	Th	1306	6.2	2036	1.3
W	1222	6.4	1954	1.1	25	0121	6.5	0856	1.2
10	0053	6.6	0818	1.0	F	1341	6.1	2101	1.5
Th	1309	6.4	2032	1.1	26	0158	6.4	0925	1.4
11	0137	6.6	0857	1.0	Sa	1418	5.9	2127	1.6
F	1357	6.3	2111	1.2	27	0234	6.2	0956	1.6
12	0223	6.5	0939	1.1	Su	1500	5.7	2157	1.8
Sa	1447	6.2	2155	1.4	28	0317	6.0	1031	1.8
13	0312	6.3	1026	1.2	M	1546	5.4	2235	2.0
Su	1542	6.0	2242	1.6	29	0402	5.7	1113	2.0
14	0406	6.1	1119	1.5	Tu	1638	5.1	2325	2.3
M	1642	5.8	2339	1.8	30	0454	5.4		
15	0506	5.9			W	1740	4.9	1207	2.2
Tu	1747	5.6	1224	1.6	31	0557	5.2	0025	2.5
					Th	1900	4.9	1309	2.3

FEBRUARY 1985

D	HW		LW		D	HW		LW	
1	0716	5.1	0137	2.5	16	0832	5.5	0312	2.0
F	2019	5.2	1426	2.2	Sa	2114	5.6	1555	1.8
2	0829	5.3	0304	2.3	17	0941	5.8	0424	1.7
Sa	2114	5.5	1546	1.9	Su	2206	5.9	1701	1.5
3	0922	5.6	0417	1.8	18	1030	6.0	0525	1.4
Su	2156	5.9	1647	1.5	M	2245	6.1	1758	1.2
4	1004	5.9	0512	1.4	19	1108	6.1	0617	1.1
M	2234	6.2	1739	1.3	Tu	2320	6.3	1846	1.1
5	1044	6.2	0603	1.1	20	1140	6.2	0700	1.0
Tu	2312	6.5	1827	1.0	W	2353	6.4	1923	1.0
6	1125	6.4	0649	0.9	21			0735	1.0
7			0731	0.7	Th	1211	6.3	1951	1.0
Th	1208	6.6	1949	0.8	22	0025	6.5	0804	1.0
8	0035	6.8	0809	0.6	F	1242	6.2	2011	1.1
F	1253	6.7	2022	0.6	23	0057	6.5	0829	1.0
9	0120	6.8	0844	0.6	Sa	1313	6.2	2030	1.2
Sa	1340	6.6	2056	0.8	24	0128	6.4	0853	1.1
10	0204	6.7	0922	0.7	Su	1344	6.0	2056	1.3
Su	1426	6.4	2134	1.0	25	0158	6.3	0921	1.3
11	0249	6.5	1002	1.0	M	1415	5.8	2124	1.5
M	1515	6.2	2214	1.3	26	0226	6.0	0952	1.5
12	0338	6.2	1048	1.3	Tu	1447	5.6	2157	1.8
Tu	1609	5.8	2302	1.7	27	0257	5.7	1028	1.8
13	0435	5.9	1146	1.7	W	1527	5.3	2240	2.1
W	1712	5.5			28	0338	5.4	1115	2.1
14	0544	5.6	0010	2.0	Th	1620	5.0	2334	2.4
Th	1831	5.3	1306	2.0					
15	0706	5.4	0142	2.1					
F	1959	5.3	1436	2.0					

MARCH 1985

D	HW		LW		D	HW		LW	
1	0440	5.1			16	0703	5.2	0128	2.1
F	1740	4.8	1215	2.3	Sa	1951	5.2	1423	2.1
2	0611	4.9	0046	2.5	17	0839	5.4	0303	1.9
Sa	1933	4.9	1334	2.3	Su	2103	5.5	1545	1.8
3	0757	5.1	0220	2.3	18	0941	5.7	0416	1.5
Su	2040	5.3	1511	2.0	M	2150	5.8	1649	1.4
4	0857	5.5	0349	1.8	19	1021	5.9	0513	1.2
M	2127	5.8	1621	1.6	Tu	2226	6.1	1743	1.1
5	0941	5.8	0449	1.3	20	1052	6.1	0601	1.0
Tu	2207	6.2	1718	1.2	W	2258	6.3	1825	1.0
6	1021	6.3	0542	0.9	21	1118	6.2	0641	0.9
W	2248	6.6	1810	0.9	Th	2329	6.4	1857	1.0
7	1104	6.6	0629	0.6	22	1146	6.2	0710	0.9
Th	2330	6.8	1856	0.7	F			1920	1.0
8	1147	6.8	0714	0.5	23	0000	6.5	0734	0.9
F			1934	0.6	Sa	1215	6.3	1937	1.0
9	0012	6.9	0751	0.4	24	0029	6.4	0757	0.9
Sa	1232	6.8	2005	0.5	Su	1245	6.2	2001	1.0
10	0057	6.9	0825	0.4	25	0056	6.4	0822	1.0
Su	1317	6.7	2036	0.6	M	1310	6.1	2027	1.1
11	0141	6.8	0901	0.6	26	0117	6.2	0850	1.1
M	1402	6.5	2111	0.8	Tu	1334	5.9	2058	1.3
12	0225	6.5	0939	0.9	27	0138	6.0	0919	1.4
Tu	1449	6.2	2152	1.2	W	1359	5.7	2131	1.6
13	0312	6.2	1024	1.3	28	0206	5.8	0955	1.7
W	1541	5.8	2240	1.6	Th	1434	5.5	2209	1.9
14	0410	5.7	1123	1.8	29	0247	5.5	1038	2.0
Th	1644	5.4	2350	2.0	F	1528	5.2	2302	2.2
15	0525	5.3			30	0352	5.1	1137	2.2
F	1811	5.1	1249	2.1	Sa	1648	4.9		
					31	0533	4.8	0011	2.3
					Su	1849	5.0	1255	2.3

All times GMT. Add 1 hour for BST (31 March–27 October)

16

APRIL 1985

D	HW		LW	D	HW		LW
1	0727	5.1	0144 2.1	16	0915	5.6	0352 1.4
M	2004	5.4	1434 2.0	Tu	2119	5.8	1620 1.4
2	0829	5.6	0315 1.6	17	0953	5.8	0447 1.1
Tu	2056	5.9	1550 1.5	W	2155	6.0	1709 1.2
3	0915	6.0	0419 1.1	18	1021	6.0	0532 1.0
W	2139	6.3	1649 1.1	Th	2227	6.2	1749 1.1
4	0957	6.4	0513 0.7	19	1048	6.1	0607 1.0
Th	2221	6.7	1742 0.8	F	2259	6.3	1817 1.1
5	1040	6.7	0603 0.5	20	1118	6.2	0634 1.0
F	2305	6.9	1828 0.6	Sa	2332	6.4	1839 1.0
6	1125	6.8	0648 0.3	21	1149	6.2	0657 0.9
Sa	2349	7.0	1906 0.5	Su			1904 1.0
7			0726 0.3	22	0000	6.4	0724 0.9
Su	1210	6.8	1940 0.5	M	1218	6.2	1934 1.0
8	0034	6.9	0804 0.3	23	0024	6.3	0755 0.9
M	1256	6.7	2016 0.5	Tu	1242	6.1	2006 1.1
9	0119	6.7	0842 0.5	24	0045	6.1	0825 1.1
Tu	1341	6.5	2054 0.8	W	1306	6.0	2039 1.3
10	0204	6.4	0922 0.9	25	0109	6.0	0857 1.3
W	1427	6.1	2138 1.1	Th	1335	5.8	2112 1.5
11	0253	6.0	1010 1.4	26	0142	5.8	0932 1.5
Th	1519	5.7	2231 1.6	F	1415	5.6	2153 1.7
12	0352	5.6	1113 1.9	27	0230	5.5	1017 1.8
F	1623	5.3	2344 1.9	Sa	1512	5.4	2244 1.9
13	0511	5.2		28	0341	5.2	1113 2.0
Sa	1747	5.1	1234 2.1	Su	1633	5.2	2350 2.0
14	0656	5.1	0114 2.0	29	0522	5.1	
Su	1926	5.2	1401 2.1	M	1814	5.2	1228 2.0
15	0822	5.3	0243 1.7	30	0657	5.3	0114 1.8
M	2033	5.5	1519 1.8	Tu	1928	5.6	1359 1.8

MAY 1985

D	HW		LW	D	HW		LW
1	0758	5.7	0240 1.4	16	0910	5.7	0407 1.4
W	2022	6.0	1514 1.4	Th	2117	6.0	1623 1.5
2	0847	6.1	0345 1.0	17	0943	5.9	0449 1.3
Th	2110	6.4	1613 1.1	F	2155	6.1	1659 1.4
3	0932	6.4	0440 0.7	18	1019	6.0	0523 1.2
F	2155	6.7	1704 0.9	Sa	2230	6.2	1730 1.3
4	1017	6.6	0529 0.5	19	1052	6.1	0553 1.1
Sa	2238	6.9	1751 0.7	Su	2304	6.3	1803 1.2
5	1104	6.7	0615 0.4	20	1127	6.2	0625 1.0
Su	2325	6.9	1834 0.6	M	2334	6.2	1838 1.1
6	1151	6.7	0659 0.4	21	1158	6.2	0659 0.9
M			1916 0.6	Tu			1914 1.1
7	0011	6.8	0742 0.5	22	0001	6.2	0733 1.0
Tu	1239	6.6	1959 0.7	W	1228	6.1	1949 1.1
8	0059	6.6	0826 0.7	23	0027	6.1	0806 1.1
W	1326	6.4	2044 0.9	Th	1257	6.1	2025 1.2
9	0147	6.3	0912 1.0	24	0059	6.0	0840 1.2
Th	1412	6.1	2132 1.2	F	1333	6.0	2101 1.3
10	0237	5.9	1003 1.4	25	0141	5.8	0918 1.4
F	1501	5.5	2227 1.5	Sa	1418	5.8	2142 1.5
11	0335	5.5	1102 1.8	26	0234	5.6	1003 1.6
Sa	1559	5.5	2333 1.8	Su	1514	5.6	2231 1.6
12	0447	5.2		27	0343	5.4	1057 1.8
Su	1711	5.3	1211 2.1	M	1623	5.5	2332 1.6
13	0617	5.1	0048 1.9	28	0505	5.4	
M	1835	5.3	1324 2.1	Tu	1740	5.6	1203 1.8
14	0735	5.2	0205 1.8	29	0622	5.6	0046 1.6
Tu	1944	5.5	1436 1.9	W	1849	5.8	1321 1.7
15	0829	5.5	0312 1.6	30	0724	5.8	0202 1.4
W	2034	5.7	1535 1.7	Th	1948	6.1	1433 1.5
				31	0818	6.1	0307 1.1
				F	2039	6.4	1534 1.3

JUNE 1985

D	HW		LW	D	HW		LW
1	0908	6.3	0404 0.9	16	0952	5.9	0438 1.5
Sa	2128	6.6	1628 1.1	Su	2203	6.0	1652 1.5
2	0957	6.4	0458 0.8	17	1031	6.0	0518 1.3
Su	2217	6.7	1720 1.0	M	2240	6.1	1736 1.3
3	1048	6.5	0550 0.7	18	1108	6.1	0558 1.2
M	2308	6.7	1810 0.9	Tu	2313	6.1	1818 1.2
4	1139	6.5	0639 0.7	19	1142	6.2	0639 1.1
Tu	2358	6.6	1900 0.9	W	2346	6.1	1859 1.1
5			0730 0.8	20			0717 1.1
W	1228	6.5	1949 0.9	Th	1215	6.2	1937 1.1
6	0048	6.4	0818 0.9	21	0021	6.1	0754 1.1
Th	1313	6.3	2037 1.0	F	1252	6.2	2013 1.1
7	0135	6.2	0907 1.2	22	0100	6.1	0829 1.2
F	1355	6.2	2127 1.2	Sa	1331	6.2	2051 1.1
8	0222	5.9	0955 1.5	23	0145	6.0	0907 1.3
Sa	1440	6.0	2217 1.4	Su	1416	6.1	2132 1.2
9	0312	5.6	1042 1.7	24	0237	5.9	0949 1.4
Su	1531	5.8	2309 1.6	M	1507	6.0	2217 1.3
10	0410	5.4	1134 2.0	25	0335	5.8	1037 1.5
M	1628	5.6		Tu	1603	5.9	2309 1.4
11	0518	5.2	0005 1.8	26	0440	5.7	1133 1.7
Tu	1734	5.5	1228 2.1	W	1706	5.9	
12	0629	5.2	0106 1.9	27	0544	5.7	0011 1.5
W	1843	5.6	1324 2.1	Th	1810	5.9	1239 1.7
13	0731	5.3	0209 1.9	28	0648	5.8	0121 1.5
Th	1944	5.6	1423 2.1	F	1913	6.0	1351 1.7
14	0825	5.5	0310 1.8	29	0749	5.9	0230 1.4
F	2036	5.8	1519 1.9	Sa	2012	6.1	1500 1.6
15	0910	5.7	0357 1.7	30	0849	6.0	0336 1.3
Sa	2122	5.9	1607 1.7	Su	2110	6.2	1603 1.5

All times GMT. Add 1 hour for BST (31 March–27 October)

JULY 1985

D	HW	LW	D	HW	LW
1	0948 6.2	0437 1.2	16	1010 5.9	0451 1.6
M	2206 6.3	1704 1.3	Tu	2219 5.9	1713 1.5
2	1042 6.3	0536 1.1	17	1045 6.1	0537 1.3
Tu	2301 6.4	1800 1.2	W	2254 6.0	1801 1.3
3	1132 6.4	0632 1.0	18	1119 6.3	0622 1.2
W	2351 6.4	1853 1.0	Th	2329 6.2	1845 1.1
4		0727 1.0	19	1156 6.4	0706 1.1
Th	1215 6.4	1945 1.0	F		1926 1.0
5	0038 6.3	0815 1.1	20	0007 6.3	0744 1.1
F	1256 6.4	2033 1.0	Sa	1235 6.5	2004 0.9
6	0119 6.2	0858 1.2	21	0049 6.4	0818 1.1
Sa	1334 6.3	2117 1.1	Su	1317 6.5	2039 0.9
7	0159 6.0	0936 1.4	22	0135 6.4	0853 1.1
Su	1415 6.2	2156 1.3	M	1401 6.4	2117 0.9
8	0243 5.8	1010 1.6	23	0223 6.3	0931 1.2
M	1458 6.1	2234 1.5	Tu	1447 6.3	2157 1.1
9	0331 5.6	1044 1.9	24	0314 6.1	1013 1.4
Tu	1546 5.9	2312 1.7	W	1536 6.2	2242 1.3
10	0423 5.4	1120 2.1	25	0409 5.9	1059 1.6
W	1640 5.7	2356 2.0	Th	1633 6.0	2336 1.5
11	0525 5.2		26	0508 5.7	
Th	1742 5.5	1205 2.2	F	1734 5.8	1200 1.8
12	0632 5.2	0045 2.1	27	0615 5.6	0043 1.7
F	1850 5.4	1300 2.3	Sa	1843 5.7	1316 2.0
13	0741 5.2	0144 2.1	28	0730 5.6	0202 1.8
Sa	1957 5.4	1406 2.3	Su	1957 5.7	1439 1.9
14	0840 5.4	0254 2.0	29	0844 5.7	0321 1.7
Su	2054 5.6	1521 2.1	M	2108 5.9	1555 1.7
15	0928 5.7	0357 1.8	30	0949 6.0	0431 1.5
M	2141 5.7	1623 1.8	Tu	2210 6.1	1701 1.5
			31	1038 6.2	0537 1.3
			W	2301 6.3	1800 1.2

AUGUST 1985

D	HW	LW	D	HW	LW
1	1120 6.4	0636 1.2	16	1054 6.4	0607 1.2
Th	2343 6.3	1855 1.0	F	2306 6.4	1829 1.0
2	1158 6.5	0726 1.1	17	1132 6.7	0652 1.0
F		1941 0.9	Sa	2346 6.6	1912 0.8
3	0021 6.3	0806 1.1	18		0731 0.9
Sa	1234 6.5	2022 0.9	Su	1212 6.8	1949 0.7
4	0057 6.3	0840 1.2	19	0029 6.7	0802 0.9
Su	1310 6.5	2056 1.0	M	1255 6.8	2022 0.7
5	0133 6.2	0905 1.3	20	0113 6.6	0832 0.9
M	1345 6.4	2125 1.2	Tu	1337 6.7	2056 0.7
6	0209 6.0	0928 1.5	21	0158 6.5	0907 1.0
Tu	1423 6.3	2152 1.4	W	1420 6.5	2134 0.9
7	0249 5.8	0953 1.7	22	0246 6.3	0946 1.3
W	1503 6.1	2221 1.6	Th	1507 6.3	2216 1.2
8	0332 5.6	1027 1.9	23	0336 6.0	1031 1.6
Th	1546 5.8	2259 1.9	F	1600 6.0	2308 1.6
9	0421 5.3	1109 2.2	24	0435 5.6	1130 1.9
F	1635 5.4	2346 2.2	Sa	1706 5.6	
10	0523 5.0		25	0550 5.4	0021 2.0
Sa	1740 5.1	1204 2.4	Su	1828 5.4	1256 2.2
11	0650 4.9	0043 2.3	26	0724 5.3	0151 2.1
Su	1912 5.0	1312 2.5	M	2005 5.5	1433 2.1
12	0809 5.1	0157 2.3	27	0851 5.6	0319 1.9
M	2026 5.2	1439 2.4	Tu	2124 5.8	1555 1.7
13	0903 5.5	0322 2.1	28	0948 5.9	0434 1.6
Tu	2117 5.5	1556 2.0	W	2216 6.0	1701 1.4
14	0943 5.8	0424 1.7	29	1030 6.2	0537 1.3
W	2155 5.8	1652 1.5	Th	2255 6.2	1758 1.1
15	1019 6.2	0518 1.4	30	1104 6.4	0629 1.1
Th	2230 6.1	1742 1.2	F	2327 6.3	1848 0.9
			31	1137 6.6	0712 1.0
			Sa	2358 6.4	1927 0.9

SEPTEMBER 1985

D	HW	LW	D	HW	LW
1		0744 1.0	16	1146 7.0	0706 0.8
Su	1210 6.6	1958 0.9	M		1924 0.6
2	0029 6.4	0808 1.1	17	0004 6.9	0734 0.7
M	1242 6.6	2023 1.0	Tu	1228 7.0	1957 0.6
3	0100 6.3	0825 1.2	18	0048 6.8	0806 0.8
Tu	1314 6.5	2046 1.1	W	1310 6.9	2032 0.7
4	0133 6.1	0846 1.4	19	0131 6.6	0844 0.9
W	1344 6.4	2110 1.3	Th	1354 6.6	2111 0.9
5	0204 5.9	0914 1.6	20	0218 6.3	0925 1.2
Th	1413 6.1	2141 1.6	F	1442 6.3	2156 1.3
6	0236 5.7	0948 1.9	21	0310 5.9	1012 1.6
F	1443 5.8	2216 1.9	Sa	1536 5.9	2252 1.8
7	0312 5.4	1028 2.2	22	0410 5.5	1119 2.0
Sa	1519 5.4	2301 2.2	Su	1648 5.4	
8	0403 5.0	1120 2.5	23	0533 5.2	0014 2.2
Su	1617 5.0	2357 2.4	M	1831 5.2	1255 2.2
9	0530 4.8		24	0727 5.4	0148 2.2
M	1807 4.8	1227 2.6	Tu	2020 5.4	1432 2.0
10	0727 5.0	0110 2.5	25	0844 5.6	0315 1.9
Tu	1954 5.0	1358 2.5	W	2122 5.8	1549 1.6
11	0827 5.4	0246 2.3	26	0934 6.0	0423 1.5
W	2047 5.4	1527 2.0	Th	2206 6.1	1649 1.2
12	0911 5.8	0357 1.8	27	1010 6.3	0519 1.2
Th	2127 5.9	1626 1.5	F	2237 6.2	1742 1.0
13	0949 6.3	0452 1.4	28	1040 6.5	0605 1.1
F	2203 6.3	1718 1.1	Sa	2302 6.4	1824 0.9
14	1027 6.6	0543 1.1	29	1111 6.6	0642 1.0
Sa	2241 6.6	1805 0.8	Su	2330 6.4	1857 0.9
15	1105 6.9	0628 0.9	30	1142 6.7	0707 1.1
Su	2322 6.8	1848 0.6	M		1921 1.0

All times GMT. Add 1 hour for BST (31 March–27 October)

OCTOBER 1985

D	HW		LW		D	HW		LW	
1	0000	6.4	0724	1.1	16			0704	0.7
Tu	1212	6.7	1942	1.0	W	1203	7.1	1930	0.6
2	0029	6.4	0745	1.2	17	0024	6.9	0744	0.8
W	1241	6.6	2006	1.1	Th	1246	6.9	2011	0.7
3	0057	6.3	0813	1.3	18	0110	6.7	0826	1.0
Th	1304	6.4	2036	1.3	F	1331	6.6	2054	1.1
4	0121	6.1	0844	1.5	19	0158	6.3	0912	1.3
F	1326	6.2	2107	1.5	Sa	1422	6.2	2145	1.5
5	0147	5.9	0918	1.8	20	0250	6.0	1006	1.7
Sa	1351	5.9	2141	1.8	Su	1521	5.8	2248	1.9
6	0218	5.6	0957	2.1	21	0350	5.5	1120	2.0
Su	1426	5.6	2223	2.2	M	1635	5.3		
7	0305	5.3	1047	2.4	22	0509	5.2	0008	2.2
M	1524	5.1	2319	2.4	Tu	1829	5.2	1248	2.1
8	0426	5.0	1151	2.5	23	0700	5.3	0134	2.2
Tu	1709	4.8			W	2004	5.5	1415	1.9
9	0632	5.0	0032	2.5	24	0816	5.6	0253	1.9
W	1914	5.1	1320	2.4	Th	2058	5.8	1527	1.5
10	0745	5.4	0208	2.3	25	0904	6.0	0356	1.5
Th	2012	5.6	1451	1.9	F	2136	6.0	1624	1.2
11	0836	5.9	0322	1.8	26	0939	6.2	0448	1.3
F	2056	6.0	1553	1.4	Sa	2206	6.2	1711	1.1
12	0917	6.4	0420	1.3	27	1010	6.4	0529	1.2
Sa	2135	6.5	1645	1.0	Su	2233	6.3	1750	1.1
13	0957	6.8	0509	1.0	28	1042	6.6	0601	1.2
Su	2216	6.8	1733	0.7	M	2304	6.4	1818	1.1
14	1038	7.0	0553	0.9	29	1115	6.6	0622	1.2
M	2257	7.0	1815	0.6	Tu	2334	6.5	1841	1.1
15	1119	7.1	0631	0.8	30	1146	6.6	0646	1.2
Tu	2340	7.0	1852	0.5	W			1906	1.1
					31	0005	6.4	0716	1.2
					Th	1211	6.5	1935	1.1

NOVEMBER 1985

D	HW		LW		D	HW		LW	
1	0032	6.3	0748	1.3	16	0057	6.6	0818	1.0
F	1232	6.3	2008	1.2	Sa	1319	6.5	2047	1.2
2	0055	6.2	0823	1.5	17	0144	6.4	0910	1.3
Sa	1256	6.2	2040	1.5	Su	1409	6.1	2142	1.6
3	0121	6.0	0857	1.7	18	0233	6.1	1007	1.6
Su	1326	6.0	2115	1.7	M	1505	5.8	2242	1.9
4	0157	5.8	0936	1.9	19	0329	5.7	1113	1.8
M	1408	5.7	2156	2.0	Tu	1613	5.6	2350	2.2
5	0247	5.5	1023	2.1	20	0434	5.5		
Tu	1508	5.3	2248	2.3	W	1742	5.2	1225	1.9
6	0400	5.3	1123	2.2	21	0557	5.4	0102	2.2
W	1644	5.1	2357	2.4	Th	1914	5.4	1340	1.9
7	0539	5.3			22	0719	5.6	0212	2.1
Th	1829	5.2	1245	2.1	F	2012	5.6	1450	1.7
8	0659	5.6	0126	2.2	23	0815	5.8	0315	1.9
F	1933	5.7	1409	1.8	Sa	2054	5.8	1548	1.5
9	0755	6.0	0242	1.8	24	0900	6.1	0406	1.7
Sa	2022	6.1	1515	1.3	Su	2131	6.0	1633	1.4
10	0843	6.4	0341	1.4	25	0953	6.0	0440	1.8
Su	2107	6.4	1609	1.0	M	2206	6.2	1709	1.4
11	0927	6.8	0431	1.2	26	1016	6.4	0516	1.5
M	2150	6.7	1657	0.8	Tu	2241	6.3	1737	1.3
12	1010	7.0	0518	1.0	27	1046	6.4	0546	1.4
Tu	2235	6.9	1742	0.7	W	2316	6.4	1805	1.2
13	1055	7.0	0600	0.9	28	1123	6.4	0619	1.3
W	2322	6.9	1825	0.7	Th	2349	6.4	1839	1.1
14	1142	7.0	0643	0.9	29	1151	6.3	0655	1.2
Th			1909	0.7	F			1913	1.1
15	0010	6.8	0730	0.9	30	0017	6.4	0731	1.3
F	1229	6.8	1957	0.9	Sa	1217	6.2	1948	1.3

DECEMBER 1985

D	HW		LW		D	HW		LW	
1	0045	6.3	0808	1.4	16	0131	6.5	0910	1.2
Su	1245	6.1	2022	1.4	M	1357	6.2	2136	1.5
2	0117	6.2	0843	1.5	17	0215	6.3	1002	1.4
M	1321	6.0	2056	1.6	Tu	1446	5.9	2227	1.8
3	0155	6.0	0921	1.7	18	0303	6.1	1054	1.6
Tu	1406	5.8	2135	1.8	W	1539	5.6	2316	2.0
4	0242	5.9	1004	1.8	19	0357	5.8	1147	1.8
W	1504	5.6	2223	2.0	Th	1642	5.4		
5	0342	5.7	1058	1.9	20	0459	5.7	0008	2.2
Th	1620	5.4	2320	2.1	F	1754	5.3	1245	2.0
6	0455	5.6			21	0610	5.6	0103	2.3
F	1742	5.5	1205	1.9	Sa	1907	5.3	1349	2.0
7	0608	5.8	0035	2.1	22	0720	5.6	0206	2.3
Sa	1849	5.7	1321	1.7	Su	2008	5.5	1454	2.0
8	0712	6.0	0152	1.9	23	0819	5.8	0308	2.2
Su	1945	5.9	1430	1.5	M	2058	5.7	1546	1.8
9	0806	6.3	0257	1.7	24	0910	5.9	0357	2.0
M	2039	6.2	1529	1.2	Tu	2142	5.9	1627	1.7
10	0858	6.5	0355	1.5	25	0953	6.0	0440	1.8
Tu	2129	6.4	1624	1.1	W	2223	6.1	1704	1.5
11	0948	6.7	0448	1.3	26	1033	6.1	0520	1.5
W	2221	6.6	1716	1.0	Th	2259	6.3	1742	1.3
12	1040	6.7	0540	1.2	27	1106	6.1	0601	1.4
Th	2313	6.7	1808	0.9	F	2332	6.4	1821	1.2
13	1130	6.7	0632	1.0	28	1136	6.2	0641	1.3
F			1900	0.9	Sa			1859	1.2
14	0003	6.7	0726	1.0	29	0003	6.4	0720	1.2
Sa	1221	6.6	1954	1.0	Su	1205	6.2	1934	1.2
15	0048	6.6	0818	1.0	30	0035	6.4	0757	1.2
Su	1310	6.4	2046	1.2	M	1241	6.2	2008	1.3
					31	0109	6.4	0830	1.3
					Tu	1319	6.1	2040	1.4

All times GMT. Add 1 hour for BST (31 March–27 October)

JANUARY 1986

D	HW		LW		D	HW		LW	
1	0148	6.3	0907	1.3	16	0234	6.3	1020	1.4
W	1402	6.0	2117	1.5	Th	1504	5.8	2226	1.8
2	0230	6.2	0946	1.4	17	0319	6.1	1055	1.7
Th	1451	5.9	2157	1.6	F	1553	5.6	2257	2.0
3	0319	6.1	1031	1.5	18	0410	5.9	1133	1.9
F	1550	5.8	2245	1.8	Sa	1649	5.3	2337	2.3
4	0417	5.9	1123	1.6	19	0508	5.6		
Sa	1655	5.6	2343	2.0	Su	1800	5.1	1219	2.2
5	0522	5.9			20	0621	5.4	0031	2.5
Su	1803	5.6	1229	1.7	M	1921	5.1	1320	2.3
6	0628	5.9	0056	2.1	21	0740	5.3	0140	2.5
M	1909	5.7	1344	1.7	Tu	2027	5.3	1439	2.3
7	0733	5.9	0213	2.0	22	0843	5.4	0305	2.4
Tu	2015	5.8	1456	1.6	W	2119	5.6	1546	2.0
8	0836	6.1	0327	1.8	23	0934	5.6	0409	2.0
W	2121	6.0	1603	1.4	Th	2203	5.8	1635	1.7
9	0938	6.2	0434	1.6	24	1013	5.8	0458	1.7
Th	2220	6.3	1706	1.3	F	2238	6.1	1722	1.5
10	1035	6.4	0534	1.3	25	1045	5.9	0544	1.4
F	2311	6.5	1807	1.1	Sa	2309	6.3	1805	1.3
11	1129	6.5	0634	1.1	26	1116	6.1	0628	1.2
Sa	2356	6.6	1906	1.0	Su	2342	6.4	1848	1.1
12			0728	1.0	27	1149	6.3	0709	1.1
Su	1215	6.5	1958	1.0	M			1926	1.1
13	0036	6.6	0818	0.9	28	0015	6.5	0745	1.0
M	1257	6.4	2043	1.1	Tu	1227	6.4	1957	1.1
14	0114	6.6	0903	1.0	29	0053	6.6	0818	1.0
Tu	1338	6.2	2122	1.3	W	1306	6.4	2025	1.1
15	0154	6.5	0943	1.1	30	0131	6.6	0849	1.0
W	1419	6.1	2156	1.5	Th	1347	6.3	2057	1.1
					31	0212	6.4	0924	1.0
					F	1430	6.2	2134	1.3

FEBRUARY 1986

D	HW		LW		D	HW		LW	
1	0254	6.3	1003	1.2	16	0322	5.9	1037	1.8
Sa	1519	6.0	2216	1.5	Su	1552	5.3	2242	2.0
2	0343	6.1	1049	1.5	17	0407	5.5	1119	2.1
Su	1616	5.7	2305	1.8	M	1648	5.0	2333	2.4
3	0444	5.8	1147	1.8	18	0508	5.1		
M	1722	5.5			Tu	1819	4.8	1214	2.4
4	0553	5.6	0012	2.1	19	0652	4.8	0038	2.6
Tu	1838	5.3	1307	1.9	W	1951	4.9	1327	2.5
5	0712	5.5	0142	2.2	20	0815	5.0	0209	2.5
W	2006	5.4	1436	1.9	Th	2050	5.2	1503	2.3
6	0834	5.6	0315	2.0	21	0908	5.2	0338	2.1
Th	2125	5.7	1559	1.7	F	2134	5.6	1609	1.9
7	0948	5.9	0433	1.6	22	0946	5.6	0435	1.7
F	2220	6.1	1712	1.4	Sa	2207	5.9	1701	1.5
8	1041	6.2	0539	1.2	23	1017	5.9	0523	1.3
Sa	2304	6.3	1815	1.1	Su	2240	6.2	1749	1.2
9	1125	6.4	0636	0.8	24	1049	6.2	0610	1.0
Su	2342	6.5	1909	0.9	M	2313	6.5	1834	1.0
10			0727	0.8	25	1125	6.4	0652	0.8
M	1204	6.4	1952	0.8	Tu	2350	6.7	1912	0.9
11	0018	6.6	0808	0.7	26			0728	0.7
Tu	1239	6.4	2027	0.9	W	1204	6.6	1940	0.8
12	0053	6.6	0843	0.8	27	0029	6.7	0757	0.7
W	1314	6.3	2056	1.0	Th	1243	6.6	2005	0.8
13	0128	6.6	0912	0.9	28	0109	6.7	0827	0.7
Th	1349	6.2	2115	1.3	F	1326	6.5	2036	0.8
14	0205	6.5	0938	1.2					
F	1427	6.0	2136	1.5					
15	0243	6.2	1003	1.5					
Sa	1507	5.7	2204	1.7					

MARCH 1986

D	HW		LW		D	HW		LW	
1	0148	6.6	0901	0.8	16	0202	6.2	0924	1.3
Sa	1406	6.3	2112	1.0	Su	1422	5.8	2131	1.5
2	0229	6.4	0939	1.0	17	0230	5.9	0957	1.6
Su	1453	6.1	2153	1.3	M	1456	5.4	2209	1.9
3	0318	6.1	1024	1.4	18	0304	5.4	1037	2.0
M	1548	5.7	2242	1.7	Tu	1541	5.1	2255	2.2
4	0417	5.7	1125	1.8	19	0353	5.0	1129	2.3
Tu	1655	5.3	2354	2.0	W	1652	4.7	2356	2.5
5	0533	5.3			20	0533	4.6		
W	1824	5.1	1253	2.1	Th	1856	4.7	1236	2.5
6	0713	5.2	0137	2.1	21	0733	4.7	0120	2.5
Th	2012	5.2	1434	2.0	F	2005	5.0	1413	2.4
7	0854	5.5	0317	1.8	22	0829	5.1	0300	2.1
F	2124	5.6	1603	1.6	Sa	2051	5.5	1534	1.9
8	0955	5.9	0433	1.4	23	0910	5.5	0403	1.6
Sa	2210	6.0	1712	1.2	Su	2129	5.9	1630	1.5
9	1038	6.1	0536	1.0	24	0945	5.9	0455	1.1
Su	2248	6.3	1810	0.9	M	2206	6.3	1720	1.1
10	1112	6.3	0628	0.7	25	1020	6.3	0543	0.8
M	2320	6.5	1855	0.8	Tu	2244	6.6	1805	0.9
11	1143	6.4	0712	0.6	26	1058	6.6	0625	0.7
Tu	2354	6.6	1931	0.7	W	2322	6.8	1843	0.7
12			0745	0.6	27	1139	6.7	0702	0.5
W	1215	6.4	1958	0.8	Th			1912	0.6
13	0028	6.6	0812	0.7	28	0003	6.8	0731	0.5
Th	1248	6.3	2016	0.9	F	1221	6.7	1941	0.6
14	0102	6.6	0834	0.9	29	0043	6.8	0805	0.5
F	1320	6.2	2034	1.1	Sa	1303	6.6	2018	0.7
15	0133	6.4	0857	1.1	30	0126	6.6	0842	0.7
Sa	1351	6.0	2100	1.3	Su	1347	6.4	2057	0.9
					31	0209	6.3	0924	1.0
					M	1436	6.0	2141	1.2

All times GMT. Add 1 hour for BST.

APRIL 1986

D	HW	LW	D	HW	LW
1	0303 5.9	1014 1.4	16	0220 5.5	1006 1.9
Tu	1532 5.7	2237 1.6	W	1458 5.3	2228 2.0
2	0407 5.5	1123 1.9	17	0311 5.1	1054 2.2
W	1642 5.3		Th	1604 5.0	2325 2.2
3	0533 5.2	0000 1.9	18	0442 4.7	1157 2.3
Th	1821 5.1	1256 2.1	F	1750 4.9	
4	0733 5.2	0140 1.9	19	0639 4.8	0041 2.2
F	2005 5.3	1432 1.9	Sa	1912 5.2	1324 2.3
5	0850 5.6	0311 1.5	20	0742 5.2	0212 1.9
Sa	2104 5.7	1550 1.5	Su	2006 5.6	1447 1.9
6	0941 5.9	0420 1.1	21	0829 5.6	0322 1.5
Su	2148 6.0	1652 1.1	M	2050 6.0	1549 1.5
7	1017 6.1	0516 0.8	22	0910 6.1	0417 1.1
M	2221 6.2	1744 0.9	Tu	2132 6.4	1641 1.1
8	1047 6.2	0604 0.7	23	0950 6.4	0506 0.8
Tu	2254 6.4	1825 0.8	W	2213 6.7	1727 0.9
9	1116 6.3	0642 0.7	24	1031 6.6	0550 0.6
W	2327 6.5	1856 0.9	Th	2254 6.8	1807 0.8
10	1149 6.3	0712 0.8	25	1115 6.7	0629 0.5
Th		1917 0.9	F	2337 6.8	1843 0.7
11	0001 6.5	0734 0.8	26		0706 0.5
F	1221 6.3	1937 0.9	Sa	1200 6.7	1923 0.6
12	0034 6.5	0757 0.9	27	0022 6.7	0747 0.5
Sa	1252 6.2	2002 1.0	Su	1248 6.6	2005 0.7
13	0100 6.3	0823 1.0	28	0110 6.5	0830 0.7
Su	1319 6.0	2033 1.2	M	1338 6.3	2051 0.9
14	0123 6.1	0854 1.2	29	0202 6.2	0919 1.1
M	1344 5.8	2107 1.4	Tu	1429 6.0	2143 1.2
15	0147 5.8	0928 1.5	30	0258 5.8	1019 1.5
Tu	1415 5.6	2143 1.7	W	1525 5.7	2248 1.5

MAY 1986

D	HW	LW	D	HW	LW
1	0404 5.5	1130 1.8	16	0258 5.3	1027 1.9
Th	1633 5.4		F	1545 5.3	2259 1.9
2	0532 5.2	0005 1.7	17	0419 5.1	1123 2.1
F	1801 5.2	1250 1.9	Sa	1704 5.3	
3	0716 5.3	0130 1.6	18	0550 5.1	0004 1.9
Sa	1933 5.4	1412 1.7	Su	1819 5.4	1236 2.1
4	0820 5.6	0249 1.4	19	0656 5.4	0124 1.7
Su	2030 5.7	1521 1.4	M	1920 5.7	1355 1.9
5	0907 5.8	0353 1.1	20	0748 5.7	0234 1.4
M	2112 6.0	1620 1.2	Tu	2011 6.1	1500 1.6
6	0942 6.0	0447 0.9	21	0836 6.1	0334 1.1
Tu	2149 6.2	1708 1.1	W	2057 6.4	1556 1.3
7	1014 6.1	0530 0.9	22	0921 6.3	0426 0.9
W	2226 6.3	1746 1.1	Th	2142 6.6	1647 1.1
8	1048 6.2	0605 1.0	23	1007 6.5	0513 0.8
Th	2301 6.4	1812 1.1	F	2228 6.7	1734 0.9
9	1125 6.3	0632 1.0	24	1057 6.6	0601 0.7
F	2336 6.4	1836 1.1	Sa	2318 6.7	1822 0.8
10		0656 1.0	25	1149 6.6	0649 0.7
Sa	1200 6.2	1904 1.0	Su		1912 0.8
11	0008 6.3	0726 1.0	26	0010 6.6	0740 0.7
Su	1231 6.2	1938 1.1	M	1242 6.5	2002 0.8
12	0034 6.1	0758 1.0	27	0104 6.4	0832 0.9
M	1259 6.0	2013 1.2	Tu	1333 6.3	2054 0.9
13	0057 6.0	0832 1.2	28	0159 6.2	0927 1.1
Tu	1326 5.9	2049 1.4	W	1420 6.1	2150 1.1
14	0126 5.8	0905 1.4	29	0253 5.9	1024 1.4
W	1359 5.7	2127 1.6	Th	1512 5.9	2251 1.3
15	0205 5.5	0943 1.7	30	0352 5.6	1125 1.6
Th	1444 5.5	2207 1.8	F	1610 5.7	2354 1.5
			31	0502 5.4	
			Sa	1719 5.5	1228 1.7

JUNE 1986

D	HW	LW	D	HW	LW
1	0625 5.4	0102 1.5	16	0504 5.4	1150 1.9
Su	1836 5.6	1333 1.8	M	1730 5.7	
2	0730 5.5	0212 1.5	17	0608 5.5	0034 1.6
M	1941 5.7	1439 1.7	Tu	1832 5.8	1259 1.9
3	0820 5.6	0315 1.4	18	0707 5.7	0142 1.5
Tu	2032 5.9	1536 1.6	W	1930 6.0	1409 1.7
4	0905 5.8	0409 1.3	19	0802 5.9	0247 1.4
W	2117 6.0	1624 1.5	Th	2025 6.2	1514 1.6
5	0946 5.9	0451 1.3	20	0857 6.1	0348 1.2
Th	2159 6.1	1701 1.5	F	2118 6.3	1614 1.4
6	1026 6.1	0525 1.3	21	0953 6.3	0447 1.1
F	2238 6.2	1733 1.4	Sa	2213 6.4	1715 1.2
7	1105 6.2	0554 1.2	22	1049 6.4	0546 1.0
Sa	2316 6.2	1805 1.3	Su	2309 6.5	1812 1.0
8	1142 6.2	0627 1.1	23	1144 6.5	0645 0.9
Su	2350 6.1	1842 1.2	M		1910 0.9
9		0703 1.1	24	0007 6.5	0742 0.9
M	1214 6.2	1920 1.2	Tu	1235 6.5	2005 0.8
10	0018 6.0	0738 1.1	25	0059 6.4	0836 0.9
Tu	1245 6.1	1958 1.2	W	1320 6.4	2057 0.8
11	0046 6.0	0813 1.2	26	0148 6.3	0927 1.0
W	1316 6.1	2034 1.3	Th	1404 6.3	2148 0.9
12	0120 5.9	0849 1.4	27	0236 6.1	1014 1.2
Th	1351 6.0	2111 1.4	F	1449 6.2	2237 1.1
13	0201 5.7	0925 1.5	28	0325 5.8	1101 1.5
F	1433 5.8	2150 1.5	Sa	1539 6.0	2326 1.3
14	0251 5.6	1004 1.7	29	0419 5.6	1147 1.7
Sa	1524 5.7	2235 1.6	Su	1634 5.8	
15	0355 5.5	1052 1.8	30	0522 5.5	0017 1.6
Su	1626 5.7	2329 1.7	M	1739 5.7	1236 1.9

All times GMT. Add 1 hour for BST.

JULY 1986

D	HW	LW	D	HW	LW
1	0631 5.4	0114 1.8	16	0522 5.6	
Tu	1849 5.6	1333 2.1	W	1747 5.8	1210 1.9
2	0735 5.4	0220 1.9	17	0627 5.6	0055 1.7
W	1954 5.7	1437 2.1	Th	1853 5.8	1324 2.0
3	0832 5.6	0321 1.9	18	0735 5.6	0209 1.7
Th	2049 5.7	1536 2.0	F	2002 5.8	1443 1.9
4	0922 5.7	0409 1.8	19	0847 5.8	0322 1.6
F	2138 5.8	1623 1.8	Sa	2110 6.0	1559 1.6
5	1006 5.9	0449 1.6	20	0953 6.1	0435 1.4
Sa	2221 5.9	1704 1.6	Su	2214 6.2	1709 1.3
6	1045 6.1	0527 1.5	21	1049 6.3	0544 1.2
Su	2259 6.0	1744 1.4	M	2311 6.4	1812 1.1
7	1122 6.2	0607 1.3	22	1136 6.5	0649 1.0
M	2332 6.0	1827 1.3	Tu		1912 0.8
8	1154 6.2	0646 1.2	23	0000 6.5	0745 0.9
Tu		1906 1.2	W	1219 6.6	2004 0.7
9	0001 6.1	0724 1.2	24	0046 6.5	0833 0.8
W	1225 6.3	1945 1.1	Th	1300 6.6	2050 0.6
10	0032 6.1	0801 1.2	25	0127 6.4	0914 0.9
Th	1259 6.3	2020 1.2	F	1340 6.6	2132 0.8
11	0109 6.1	0832 1.3	26	0208 6.2	0949 1.2
F	1335 6.2	2054 1.2	Sa	1420 6.4	2209 1.0
12	0148 6.0	0904 1.3	27	0250 6.0	1020 1.4
Sa	1413 6.2	2129 1.2	Su	1504 6.3	2244 1.3
13	0232 5.9	0941 1.5	28	0336 5.8	1049 1.7
Su	1457 6.1	2209 1.3	M	1552 6.0	2319 1.7
14	0322 5.8	1021 1.6	29	0428 5.5	1123 2.0
M	1548 6.0	2254 1.5	Tu	1647 5.7	
15	0420 5.7	1109 1.8	30	0534 5.3	0000 2.0
Tu	1645 5.9	2347 1.6	W	1757 5.4	1211 2.3
			31	0655 5.2	0056 2.2
			Th	1919 5.3	1316 2.4

AUGUST 1986

D	HW	LW	D	HW	LW
1	0805 5.3	0213 2.3	16	0726 5.4	0149 2.0
F	2026 5.4	1444 2.4	Sa	2002 5.5	1432 2.0
2	0901 5.5	0328 2.2	17	0857 5.7	0319 1.8
Sa	2121 5.5	1552 2.1	Su	2124 5.9	1559 1.7
3	0946 5.8	0420 1.9	18	0956 6.0	0438 1.5
Su	2204 5.7	1642 1.7	M	2220 6.2	1709 1.3
4	1024 6.0	0505 1.6	19	1042 6.4	0549 1.2
M	2238 5.9	1727 1.4	Tu	2306 6.4	1812 0.9
5	1057 6.2	0550 1.4	20	1122 6.6	0648 0.9
Tu	2306 6.0	1811 1.2	W	2346 6.5	1906 0.7
6	1127 6.4	0632 1.2	21	1158 6.7	0735 0.8
W	2336 6.2	1853 1.1	Th		1952 0.6
7		0712 1.2	22	0022 6.6	0815 0.8
Th	1200 6.5	1931 1.0	F	1235 6.8	2030 0.6
8	0010 6.3	0745 1.1	23	0059 6.5	0846 0.9
F	1234 6.5	2004 1.0	Sa	1312 6.7	2103 0.8
9	0046 6.4	0812 1.1	24	0135 6.3	0910 1.2
Sa	1310 6.5	2033 1.0	Su	1348 6.6	2129 1.0
10	0124 6.3	0840 1.2	25	0212 6.1	0929 1.4
Su	1347 6.4	2104 1.0	M	1426 6.4	2155 1.4
11	0204 6.2	0914 1.3	26	0251 5.9	0955 1.7
M	1425 6.3	2141 1.2	Tu	1505 6.0	2224 1.7
12	0247 6.0	0952 1.5	27	0336 5.5	1030 2.0
Tu	1508 6.1	2221 1.4	W	1550 5.6	2302 2.1
13	0339 5.8	1037 1.7	28	0433 5.2	1118 2.4
W	1604 5.9	2313 1.7	Th	1654 5.1	2354 2.4
14	0441 5.6	1134 2.0	29	0605 4.9	
Th	1711 5.6		F	1842 4.9	1219 2.6
15	0556 5.4	0022 1.9	30	0734 5.0	0107 2.6
F	1831 5.4	1257 2.2	Sa	2005 5.0	1351 2.6
			31	0834 5.3	0244 2.4
			Su	2101 5.3	1521 2.3

SEPTEMBER 1986

D	HW	LW	D	HW	LW
1	0919 5.7	0350 2.1	16	0948 6.1	0438 1.3
M	2141 5.6	1617 1.8	Tu	2216 6.3	1705 1.0
2	0955 6.0	0441 1.7	17	1026 6.4	0539 1.0
Tu	2209 5.9	1705 1.4	W	2251 6.5	1801 0.8
3	1026 6.3	0527 1.4	18	1059 6.7	0629 0.8
W	2235 6.2	1750 1.1	Th	2322 6.6	1849 0.6
4	1057 6.5	0612 1.2	19	1133 6.8	0710 0.6
Th	2308 6.4	1832 1.0	F	2354 6.6	1927 0.6
5	1130 6.7	0650 1.1	20		0741 0.9
F	2343 6.6	1909 0.9	Sa	1208 6.8	1958 0.7
6		0721 1.0	21	0028 6.5	0802 1.0
Sa	1205 6.6	1938 0.8	Su	1242 6.8	2022 0.9
7	0019 6.6	0744 1.0	22	0102 6.4	0822 1.2
Su	1242 6.7	2006 0.8	M	1314 6.6	2044 1.1
8	0057 6.6	0813 1.0	23	0134 6.2	0847 1.4
M	1317 6.6	2039 0.9	Tu	1345 6.4	2111 1.4
9	0135 6.4	0850 1.1	24	0206 5.9	0917 1.7
Tu	1354 6.4	2115 1.1	W	1415 6.0	2142 1.7
10	0218 6.2	0929 1.4	25	0242 5.6	0953 2.0
W	1439 6.1	2157 1.4	Th	1450 5.6	2221 2.1
11	0310 5.8	1016 1.7	26	0327 5.2	1040 2.4
Th	1536 5.8	2252 1.8	F	1539 5.1	2312 2.5
12	0416 5.5	1120 2.1	27	0445 4.9	1140 2.6
F	1651 5.4		Sa	1739 4.7	
13	0540 5.2	0012 2.2	28	0643 4.9	0019 2.7
Sa	1834 5.4	1255 2.2	Su	1926 4.8	1304 2.7
14	0742 5.3	0152 2.1	29	0752 5.2	0155 2.6
Su	2027 5.5	1439 2.0	M	2023 5.2	1442 2.3
15	0858 5.7	0325 1.8	30	0839 5.6	0312 2.2
M	2131 5.9	1600 1.5	Tu	2101 5.6	1543 1.8

All times GMT. Add 1 hour for BST

22

OCTOBER 1986

D	HW		LW		D	HW		LW	
1 W	0915	6.0	0407	1.7	16 Th	1000	6.5	0515	1.0
	2132	6.0	1634	1.3		2226	6.4	1737	0.8
2 Th	0949	6.4	0455	1.3	17 F	1033	6.7	0600	0.9
	2203	6.3	1719	1.0		2255	6.5	1819	0.8
3 F	1024	6.7	0540	1.1	18 Sa	1106	6.8	0634	1.0
	2238	6.6	1801	0.9		2327	6.6	1852	0.9
4 Sa	1059	6.9	0618	1.0	19 Su	1140	6.8	0657	1.1
	2315	6.8	1838	0.8				1916	0.9
5 Su	1136	6.9	0648	0.9	20 M	0001	6.5	0719	1.1
	2353	6.8	1907	0.7		1214	6.7	1940	1.0
6 M			0716	0.9	21 Tu	0035	6.4	0745	1.2
	1214	6.9	1938	0.8		1243	6.5	2006	1.2
7 Tu	0034	6.7	0751	0.9	22 W	0104	6.2	0816	1.4
	1252	6.7	2015	0.9		1309	6.3	2037	1.4
8 W	0114	6.5	0830	1.1	23 Th	0133	6.0	0850	1.6
	1333	6.4	2057	1.2		1335	6.0	2111	1.7
9 Th	0201	6.2	0915	1.4	24 F	0204	5.8	0928	1.9
	1423	6.1	2145	1.6		1408	5.6	2149	2.1
10 F	0256	5.8	1009	1.8	25 Sa	0246	5.5	1012	2.1
	1528	5.6	2251	2.0		1456	5.2	2235	2.4
11 Sa	0406	5.4	1126	2.1	26 Su	0349	5.1	1106	2.5
	1652	5.3				1626	4.8	2337	2.6
12 Su	0537	5.2	0019	2.2	27 M	0529	5.0		
	1902	5.3	1303	2.1		1822	4.9	1221	2.5
13 M	0737	5.4	0155	2.1	28 Tu	0650	5.2	0103	2.6
	2023	5.7	1436	1.7		1927	5.2	1351	2.2
14 Tu	0840	5.8	0317	1.6	29 W	0747	5.6	0223	2.2
	2115	6.0	1548	1.3		2013	5.6	1458	1.8
15 W	0925	6.2	0420	1.2	30 Th	0832	6.1	0324	1.8
	2155	6.3	1647	0.9		2053	6.0	1553	1.4
					31 F	0912	6.4	0414	1.4
						2131	6.4	1641	1.1

NOVEMBER 1986

D	HW		LW		D	HW		LW	
1 Sa	0950	6.7	0501	1.2	16 Su	1041	6.6	0553	1.3
	2210	6.6	1725	0.9		2306	6.5	1812	1.1
2 Su	1030	6.9	0542	1.1	17 M	1118	6.6	0617	1.3
	2249	6.8	1803	0.8		2342	6.5	1836	1.1
3 M	1109	6.9	0617	1.0	18 Tu	1151	6.5	0646	1.2
	2333	6.8	1839	0.8				1906	1.2
4 Tu	1151	6.9	0655	0.9	19 W	0015	6.4	0720	1.3
			1917	0.8		1221	6.4	1938	1.2
5 W	0017	6.7	0737	1.0	20 Th	0045	6.3	0755	1.4
	1236	6.7	2001	1.0		1248	6.2	2012	1.4
6 Th	0104	6.5	0823	1.1	21 F	0114	6.2	0832	1.6
	1327	6.4	2050	1.3		1316	6.0	2047	1.6
7 F	0157	6.3	0915	1.4	22 Sa	0147	6.0	0908	1.8
	1423	6.0	2148	1.6		1352	5.7	2124	1.9
8 Sa	0253	5.9	1019	1.7	23 Su	0227	5.8	0949	2.0
	1529	5.7	2258	1.9		1440	5.4	2204	2.2
9 Su	0356	5.6	1133	1.9	24 M	0321	5.6	1038	2.1
	1648	5.4				1550	5.2	2258	2.3
10 M	0516	5.4	0018	2.1	25 Tu	0433	5.4	1140	2.2
	1842	5.4	1256	1.8		1719	5.1		
11 Tu	0657	5.5	0138	1.9	26 W	0549	5.4	0007	2.4
	1952	5.7	1416	1.6		1829	5.3	1256	2.1
12 W	0802	5.8	0250	1.6	27 Th	0652	5.7	0124	2.3
	2043	5.9	1522	1.3		1926	5.6	1406	1.8
13 Th	0850	6.1	0350	1.4	28 F	0744	6.0	0230	2.0
	2122	6.1	1619	1.1		2013	5.9	1505	1.5
14 F	0928	6.3	0441	1.3	29 Sa	0832	6.3	0329	1.7
	2156	6.3	1706	1.0		2100	6.2	1559	1.2
15 Sa	1004	6.5	0522	1.3	30 Su	0918	6.5	0421	1.5
	2230	6.4	1744	1.1		2145	6.5	1648	1.1

DECEMBER 1986

D	HW		LW		D	HW		LW	
1 M	1003	6.7	0511	1.3	16 Tu	1101	6.3	0550	1.4
	2231	6.6	1734	1.0		2326	6.4	1810	1.3
2 Tu	1051	6.7	0558	1.1	17 W	1136	6.3	0625	1.3
	2322	6.7	1821	0.9				1843	1.3
3 W	1140	6.7	0646	1.0	18 Th	0001	6.4	0703	1.3
			1909	0.9		1207	6.2	1920	1.3
4 Th	0012	6.7	0735	1.0	19 F	0031	6.4	0740	1.3
	1234	6.6	2001	1.0		1235	6.1	1955	1.4
5 F	0103	6.6	0829	1.0	20 Sa	0100	6.3	0818	1.4
	1327	6.4	2057	1.2		1306	6.0	2029	1.5
6 Sa	0152	6.4	0924	1.2	21 Su	0134	6.2	0853	1.5
	1422	6.1	2155	1.5		1341	5.9	2101	1.7
7 Su	0242	6.2	1023	1.4	22 M	0211	6.1	0929	1.6
	1518	5.9	2255	1.7		1425	5.7	2138	1.8
8 M	0336	5.9	1125	1.5	23 Tu	0254	6.0	1010	1.7
	1621	5.6	2357	1.9		1517	5.5	2219	2.0
9 Tu	0438	5.8			24 W	0348	5.8	1058	1.8
	1740	5.5	1231	1.6		1623	5.4	2309	2.1
10 W	0553	5.7	0102	1.9	25 Th	0449	5.7	1157	1.9
	1856	5.5	1338	1.6		1729	5.4		
11 Th	0706	5.8	0208	1.9	26 F	0553	5.7	0014	2.2
	1955	5.7	1446	1.6		1832	5.5	1304	1.9
12 F	0805	5.9	0308	1.8	27 Sa	0653	5.8	0128	2.2
	2044	5.8	1542	1.5		1931	5.7	1412	1.7
13 Sa	0856	6.1	0400	1.7	28 Su	0752	6.0	0239	2.0
	2128	6.0	1630	1.5		2030	5.9	1517	1.5
14 Su	0941	6.2	0442	1.7	29 M	0850	6.2	0346	1.8
	2210	6.2	1708	1.4		2129	6.1	1620	1.3
15 M	1021	6.3	0518	1.6	30 Tu	0946	6.3	0451	1.5
	2249	6.3	1739	1.4		2227	6.4	1719	1.2
					31 W	1042	6.5	0550	1.2
						2319	6.6	1818	1.0

All times GMT. Add 1 hour for BST

23

JANUARY 1987

D	HW	LW	D	HW	LW
1	1139 6.6	0646 1.0	16	1150 6.1	0650 1.3
Th		1914 1.0	F		1907 1.2
2	0008 6.7	0741 0.9	17	0011 6.4	0728 1.2
F	1231 6.6	2009 0.9	Sa	1218 6.2	1942 1.3
3	0055 6.7	0833 0.8	18	0042 6.4	0804 1.2
Sa	1319 6.5	2101 1.0	Su	1250 6.2	2013 1.3
4	0138 6.6	0924 0.9	19	0114 6.4	0836 1.2
Su	1406 6.3	2149 1.2	M	1324 6.1	2042 1.4
5	0222 6.5	1012 1.0	20	0149 6.3	0907 1.3
M	1453 6.1	2233 1.4	Tu	1401 6.0	2111 1.5
6	0308 6.3	1059 1.3	21	0225 6.2	0941 1.4
Tu	1543 5.9	2316 1.7	W	1442 5.9	2146 1.6
7	0400 6.1	1147 1.6	22	0304 6.1	1019 1.5
W	1641 5.6		Th	1531 5.7	2227 1.8
8	0459 5.8	0003 2.0	23	0355 5.9	1106 1.7
Th	1750 5.4	1242 1.8	F	1630 5.5	2319 2.1
9	0610 5.6	0057 2.2	24	0457 5.7	
F	1903 5.4	1348 2.0	Sa	1737 5.4	1208 1.9
10	0723 5.6	0208 2.3	25	0605 5.6	0031 2.2
Sa	2009 5.5	1457 2.0	Su	1852 5.4	1324 1.9
11	0827 5.7	0317 2.2	26	0721 5.6	0157 2.2
Su	2105 5.7	1553 1.9	M	2012 5.5	1446 1.8
12	0921 5.8	0409 2.0	27	0837 5.8	0325 1.9
M	2152 5.9	1637 1.8	Tu	2129 5.8	1606 1.6
13	1007 5.9	0452 1.8	28	0948 6.0	0442 1.5
Tu	2234 6.1	1715 1.6	W	2226 6.2	1718 1.3
14	1048 6.0	0532 1.6	29	1045 6.3	0547 1.2
W	2311 6.3	1753 1.4	Th	2313 6.5	1822 1.0
15	1120 6.1	0611 1.4	30	1133 6.5	0648 0.8
Th	2342 6.3	1831 1.3	F	2357 6.7	1920 0.8
			31		0741 0.6
			Sa	1219 6.6	2009 0.7

FEBRUARY 1987

D	HW	LW	D	HW	LW
1	0038 6.8	0829 0.5	16	0018 6.5	0748 1.0
Su	1302 6.6	2051 0.7	M	1227 6.3	1954 1.0
2	0117 6.8	0910 0.6	17	0050 6.5	0815 1.0
M	1342 6.5	2127 0.9	Tu	1300 6.3	2019 1.1
3	0157 6.7	0946 0.8	18	0121 6.5	0842 1.0
Tu	1423 6.3	2156 1.2	W	1334 6.2	2047 1.1
4	0239 6.5	1020 1.1	19	0152 6.4	0912 1.1
W	1507 6.0	2223 1.5	Th	1409 6.1	2121 1.3
5	0324 6.2	1052 1.5	20	0227 6.2	0949 1.3
Th	1555 5.7	2254 1.9	F	1451 5.9	2200 1.6
6	0414 5.9	1132 1.9	21	0315 6.0	1033 1.6
F	1655 5.3	2337 2.2	Sa	1548 5.6	2249 1.9
7	0519 5.4		22	0417 5.6	1133 1.9
Sa	1815 5.1	1225 2.3	Su	1658 5.3	
8	0645 5.2	0042 2.5	23	0534 5.3	0000 2.2
Su	1937 5.1	1348 2.4	M	1828 5.1	1257 2.1
9	0805 5.2	0222 2.5	24	0713 5.3	0138 2.2
M	2042 5.3	1515 2.3	Tu	2018 5.3	1434 2.0
10	0907 5.4	0339 2.2	25	0851 5.6	0321 1.8
Tu	2134 5.6	1612 2.0	W	2129 5.7	1606 1.6
11	0956 5.6	0431 1.9	26	0953 6.0	0440 1.3
W	2214 5.9	1657 1.7	Th	2217 6.2	1718 1.2
12	1031 5.8	0516 1.5	27	1041 6.3	0544 0.9
Th	2248 6.1	1739 1.4	F	2259 6.5	1819 0.8
13	1059 5.9	0558 1.3	28	1122 6.5	0641 0.6
F	2316 6.3	1819 1.2	Sa	2337 6.7	1912 0.6
14	1125 6.1	0638 1.1			
Sa	2346 6.4	1857 1.1			
15	1154 6.3	0716 1.0			
Su		1930 1.1			

MARCH 1987

D	HW	LW	D	HW	LW
1		0730 0.4	16	1126 6.4	0653 0.8
Su	1200 6.6	1952 0.5	M	2347 6.5	1906 0.8
2	0015 6.8	0809 0.4	17		0723 0.8
M	1238 6.6	2026 0.6	Tu	1200 6.5	1930 0.9
3	0053 6.8	0843 0.5	18	0021 6.6	0748 0.8
Tu	1314 6.5	2051 0.8	W	1234 6.5	1955 0.9
4	0130 6.7	0911 0.7	19	0053 6.5	0816 0.8
W	1352 6.3	2112 1.1	Th	1309 6.4	2026 0.9
5	0206 6.5	0936 1.1	20	0126 6.4	0850 0.9
Th	1430 6.0	2136 1.4	F	1345 6.2	2103 1.1
6	0246 6.2	1004 1.5	21	0204 6.2	0928 1.2
F	1511 5.7	2209 1.7	Sa	1429 5.9	2145 1.4
7	0328 5.7	1040 1.9	22	0253 5.8	1016 1.6
Sa	1602 5.3	2251 2.1	Su	1528 5.6	2238 1.8
8	0426 5.2	1127 2.3	23	0402 5.4	1122 1.9
Su	1720 4.9	2350 2.4	M	1644 5.2	2357 2.0
9	0605 4.8		24		0533 5.1
M	1859 4.8	1238 2.6	Tu	1831 5.0	1255 2.1
10	0740 4.8	0120 2.6	25	0735 5.2	0141 2.0
Tu	2012 5.0	1425 2.5	W	2016 5.3	1437 1.9
11	0846 5.1	0304 2.3	26	0854 5.7	0318 1.5
W	2104 5.4	1539 2.1	Th	2115 5.8	1600 1.4
12	0934 5.4	0404 1.8	27	0945 6.1	0430 1.0
Th	2143 5.7	1630 1.7	F	2159 6.2	1706 1.0
13	1002 5.7	0451 1.4	28	1026 6.3	0530 0.7
F	2214 6.0	1715 1.4	Sa	2237 6.5	1801 0.7
14	1026 5.9	0534 1.2	29	1101 6.5	0622 0.5
Sa	2244 6.2	1757 1.1	Su	2313 6.7	1848 0.6
15	1054 6.2	0615 1.0	30	1136 6.5	0706 0.4
Su	2315 6.4	1835 1.0	M	2350 6.8	1923 0.6
			31		0740 0.5
			Tu	1212 6.5	1948 0.7

All times GMT. Add 1 hour for BST

APRIL 1987

D	HW	LW	D	HW	LW
1	0027 6.7	0806 0.6	16		0723 0.7
W	1248 6.4	2011 0.8	Th	1211 6.5	1934 0.8
2	0102 6.6	0832 0.8	17	0029 6.5	0757 0.7
Th	1323 6.2	2034 1.0	F	1252 6.4	2012 0.9
3	0134 6.3	0858 1.1	18	0109 6.3	0834 0.9
F	1357 6.0	2105 1.3	Sa	1335 6.2	2054 1.1
4	0208 6.0	0928 1.4	19	0155 6.0	0921 1.2
Sa	1433 5.7	2139 1.6	Su	1427 5.9	2143 1.4
5	0243 5.6	1004 1.8	20	0256 5.7	1016 1.6
Su	1517 5.3	2221 2.0	M	1531 5.5	2245 1.7
6	0334 5.1	1049 2.2	21	0410 5.4	1130 1.9
M	1623 4.9	2316 2.3	Tu	1647 5.3	
7	0509 4.7	1151 2.5	22	0549 5.2	0008 1.8
Tu	1803 4.8		W	1829 5.2	1300 1.9
8	0656 4.7	0034 2.5	23	0733 5.4	0142 1.6
W	1921 5.0	1323 2.5	Th	1954 5.5	1429 1.6
9	0801 4.9	0212 2.3	24	0834 5.8	0305 1.2
Th	2015 5.3	1449 2.2	F	2049 5.9	1541 1.2
10	0844 5.5	0321 1.8	25	0921 6.0	0410 0.9
F	2057 5.7	1546 1.8	Sa	2131 6.2	1640 1.0
11	0917 5.6	0413 1.4	26	0959 6.2	0506 0.7
Sa	2132 6.0	1635 1.4	Su	2209 6.4	1730 0.8
12	0948 6.0	0459 1.1	27	1034 6.3	0554 0.6
Su	2206 6.3	1719 1.2	M	2247 6.6	1811 0.8
13	1021 6.2	0542 0.9	28	1111 6.4	0632 0.7
M	2241 6.5	1800 1.0	Tu	2325 6.6	1842 0.9
14	1057 6.4	0621 0.8	29	1149 6.4	0702 0.7
Tu	2316 6.6	1834 0.9	W		1907 0.9
15	1133 6.5	0653 0.7	30	0001 6.6	0728 0.8
W	2353 6.6	1903 0.8	Th	1225 6.3	1935 1.0

MAY 1987

D	HW	LW	D	HW	LW
1	0036 6.4	0757 0.9	16	0017 6.4	0745 0.8
F	1300 6.2	2006 1.1	Sa	1248 6.4	2008 0.9
2	0107 6.2	0827 1.1	17	0109 6.3	0833 0.9
Sa	1331 6.0	2042 1.3	Su	1341 6.2	2057 1.0
3	0137 5.9	0901 1.4	18	0206 6.0	0925 1.2
Su	1405 5.8	2118 1.6	M	1434 6.0	2152 1.2
4	0212 5.5	0938 1.7	19	0307 5.8	1026 1.5
M	1447 5.5	2159 1.9	Tu	1531 5.8	2257 1.4
5	0301 5.2	1020 2.1	20	0414 5.6	1136 1.6
Tu	1545 5.2	2249 2.1	W	1637 5.6	
6	0419 4.9	1115 2.3	21	0539 5.5	0010 1.5
W	1701 5.1	2354 2.2	Th	1800 5.5	1250 1.6
7	0550 4.8		22	0659 5.6	0127 1.4
Th	1817 5.1	1227 2.4	F	1914 5.7	1404 1.5
8	0657 5.0	0114 2.1	23	0758 5.8	0239 1.2
F	1917 5.4	1347 2.2	Sa	2011 5.9	1508 1.4
9	0748 5.3	0226 1.8	24	0846 5.9	0342 1.1
Sa	2006 5.7	1450 1.9	Su	2057 6.1	1606 1.2
10	0830 5.6	0324 1.5	25	0928 6.0	0435 1.0
Su	2049 6.0	1545 1.5	M	2141 6.3	1652 1.2
11	0910 6.0	0414 1.2	26	1009 6.1	0520 1.0
M	2128 6.3	1635 1.3	Tu	2221 6.4	1732 1.2
12	0949 6.2	0502 1.0	27	1049 6.2	0557 1.1
Tu	2207 6.5	1722 1.1	W	2302 6.4	1803 1.2
13	1030 6.4	0546 0.8	28	1129 6.3	0627 1.1
W	2248 6.5	1803 1.0	Th	2342 6.3	1835 1.2
14	1112 6.5	0625 0.8	29		0657 1.1
Th	2330 6.5	1842 0.9	F	1207 6.3	1909 1.1
15	1158 6.5	0704 0.7	30	0018 6.2	0730 1.1
F		1923 0.8	Sa	1242 6.2	1945 1.2
			31	0049 6.0	0805 1.2
			Su	1314 6.1	2023 1.3

JUNE 1987

D	HW	LW	D	HW	LW
1	0120 5.8	0840 1.4	16	0208 6.2	0934 1.0
M	1348 5.9	2101 1.5	Tu	1426 6.3	2159 0.9
2	0157 5.6	0915 1.6	17	0300 6.1	1028 1.2
Tu	1427 5.8	2141 1.7	W	1517 6.1	2254 1.1
3	0242 5.4	0955 1.8	18	0356 5.9	1123 1.4
W	1515 5.6	2224 1.8	Th	1612 5.9	2353 1.2
4	0342 5.2	1041 2.0	19	0459 5.7	
Th	1614 5.5	2318 1.9	F	1716 5.8	1221 1.5
5	0452 5.1	1136 2.1	20	0608 5.6	0055 1.4
F	1719 5.4		Sa	1824 5.8	1323 1.7
6	0557 5.2	0021 1.9	21	0712 5.6	0201 1.5
Sa	1819 5.5	1243 2.1	Su	1928 5.8	1426 1.7
7	0653 5.4	0127 1.8	22	0809 5.7	0305 1.5
Su	1914 5.7	1349 2.0	M	2026 5.9	1525 1.7
8	0745 5.6	0229 1.6	23	0901 5.8	0400 1.5
M	2004 6.0	1451 1.8	Tu	2117 6.0	1616 1.6
9	0833 5.8	0327 1.4	24	0948 5.9	0447 1.5
Tu	2051 6.2	1550 1.6	W	2203 6.1	1659 1.6
10	0921 6.1	0423 1.2	25	1031 6.1	0526 1.4
W	2139 6.3	1648 1.4	Th	2248 6.1	1737 1.4
11	1010 6.3	0516 1.1	26	1112 6.2	0601 1.4
Th	2228 6.4	1742 1.2	F	2327 6.1	1814 1.3
12	1101 6.4	0607 1.0	27	1150 6.2	0636 1.3
F	2320 6.4	1832 1.0	Sa		1852 1.3
13	1154 6.5	0656 0.9	28	0003 6.1	0712 1.3
Sa		1921 0.9	Su	1224 6.2	1931 1.2
14	0015 6.4	0748 0.9	29	0034 6.0	0748 1.3
Su	1248 6.5	2012 0.8	M	1256 6.2	2009 1.3
15	0113 6.4	0840 0.9	30	0104 5.9	0823 1.4
M	1337 6.4	2104 0.8	Tu	1328 6.1	2046 1.3

All times GMT. Add 1 hour for BST.

25

JULY 1987

D	HW		LW		D	HW		LW	
1	0138	5.9	0857	1.5	16	0237	6.3	1013	1.0
W	1405	6.1	2121	1.4	Th	1450	6.4	2235	0.9
2	0219	5.7	0929	1.6	17	0324	6.1	1052	1.3
Th	1444	6.0	2159	1.5	F	1539	6.2	2319	1.2
3	0305	5.6	1006	1.8	18	0416	5.9	1134	1.6
F	1531	5.8	2240	1.7	Sa	1633	6.0		
4	0400	5.5	1049	1.9	19	0516	5.6	0008	1.5
Sa	1624	5.7	2329	1.8	Su	1737	5.7	1224	1.9
5	0458	5.4	1143	2.1	20	0627	5.4	0107	1.8
Su	1720	5.7			M	1850	5.6	1328	2.1
6	0557	5.4	0028	1.8	21	0737	5.4	0219	2.0
M	1819	5.7	1248	2.1	Tu	2001	5.6	1443	2.1
7	0657	5.5	0133	1.8	22	0839	5.6	0327	2.0
Tu	1920	5.7	1359	2.1	W	2101	5.6	1546	2.0
8	0759	5.6	0240	1.7	23	0932	5.8	0420	1.8
W	2022	5.9	1512	1.9	Th	2153	5.8	1637	1.8
9	0903	5.9	0349	1.5	24	1017	6.0	0505	1.7
Th	2122	6.0	1626	1.6	F	2237	5.9	1720	1.6
10	1003	6.1	0457	1.3	25	1055	6.2	0544	1.5
F	2221	6.2	1729	1.3	Sa	2313	6.0	1801	1.4
11	1058	6.4	0558	1.1	26	1130	6.3	0622	1.4
Sa	2318	6.4	1827	1.0	Su	2343	6.0	1841	1.3
12	1147	6.6	0657	1.0	27			0700	1.3
Su			1923	0.8	M	1201	6.3	1919	1.2
13	0011	6.5	0752	0.8	28	0011	6.1	0735	1.3
M	1235	6.7	2015	0.6	Tu	1231	6.4	1955	1.2
14	0102	6.5	0844	0.8	29	0041	6.1	0806	1.3
Tu	1320	6.6	2104	0.6	W	1303	6.4	2027	1.2
15	0151	6.5	0931	0.8	30	0113	6.1	0834	1.3
W	1405	6.6	2150	0.7	Th	1335	6.3	2057	1.2
					31	0148	6.0	0903	1.4
					F	1408	6.2	2128	1.3

AUGUST 1987

D	HW		LW		D	HW		LW	
1	0223	5.9	0934	1.6	16	0335	5.9	1040	1.7
Sa	1442	6.1	2202	1.5	Su	1552	6.0	2313	1.7
2	0304	5.7	1010	1.8	17	0431	5.5	1122	2.1
Su	1524	5.9	2244	1.7	M	1654	5.6		
3	0356	5.5	1055	2.0	18	0546	5.2	0005	2.2
M	1620	5.7	2337	1.9	Tu	1819	5.2	1225	2.4
4	0459	5.4	1158	2.2	19	0710	5.2	0126	2.4
Tu	1727	5.5			W	1944	5.2	1359	2.5
5	0612	5.3	0046	2.0	20	0820	5.3	0254	2.4
W	1845	5.4	1319	2.2	Th	2051	5.4	1524	2.2
6	0740	5.4	0206	2.0	21	0917	5.6	0357	2.1
Th	2009	5.6	1449	2.0	F	2145	5.6	1620	1.9
7	0903	5.7	0332	1.7	22	1000	5.9	0447	1.8
F	2124	5.9	1614	1.6	Sa	2224	5.8	1705	1.6
8	1002	6.1	0449	1.4	23	1034	6.2	0529	1.6
Sa	2221	6.2	1722	1.2	Su	2252	6.0	1747	1.3
9	1048	6.5	0554	1.1	24	1104	6.3	0608	1.4
Su	2311	6.5	1821	0.8	M	2315	6.1	1825	1.2
10	1133	6.7	0655	0.9	25	1132	6.4	0645	1.2
M	2357	6.7	1917	0.6	Tu	2342	6.3	1902	1.1
11			0748	0.7	26			0716	1.2
Tu	1215	6.9	2006	0.4	W	1203	6.5	1934	1.0
12	0041	6.7	0832	0.6	27	0012	6.3	0742	1.2
W	1257	6.9	2050	0.4	Th	1232	6.5	2002	1.0
13	0124	6.6	0910	0.7	28	0043	6.3	0806	1.2
Th	1338	6.8	2128	0.6	F	1302	6.5	2029	1.1
14	0205	6.4	0941	0.9	29	0113	6.3	0833	1.3
F	1419	6.6	2203	0.9	Sa	1328	6.4	2057	1.2
15	0249	6.2	1009	1.3	30	0144	6.1	0904	1.5
Sa	1503	6.4	2235	1.3	Su	1358	6.2	2131	1.4
					31	0220	5.9	0941	1.7
					M	1439	6.0	2212	1.7

SEPTEMBER 1987

D	HW		LW		D	HW		LW	
1	0310	5.7	1027	2.0	16	0458	5.1	1137	2.5
Tu	1535	5.7	2305	2.0	W	1744	4.9		
2	0419	5.4	1132	2.2	17	0636	5.0	0029	2.7
W	1652	5.3			Th	1924	4.9	1314	2.7
3	0546	5.1	0021	2.2	18	0755	5.2	0215	2.6
Th	1835	5.2	1300	2.3	F	2037	5.2	1454	2.4
4	0747	5.3	0154	2.1	19	0851	5.5	0328	2.3
F	2023	5.5	1444	2.0	Sa	2127	5.5	1553	1.9
5	0901	5.8	0329	1.7	20	0932	5.9	0419	1.9
Sa	2128	6.0	1607	1.5	Su	2157	5.8	1640	1.6
6	0950	6.2	0442	1.3	21	1003	6.2	0501	1.6
Su	2214	6.4	1712	1.0	M	2219	6.0	1719	1.3
7	1033	6.6	0546	0.9	22	1031	6.4	0539	1.3
M	2255	6.7	1810	0.6	Tu	2242	6.2	1758	1.1
8	1112	6.9	0641	0.7	23	1059	6.6	0615	1.2
Tu	2334	6.8	1902	0.4	W	2311	6.4	1834	1.0
9	1151	7.0	0727	0.6	24	1130	6.6	0646	1.1
W			1945	0.4	Th	2342	6.5	1904	1.0
10	0014	6.8	0804	0.7	25			0713	1.1
Th	1229	7.0	2022	0.5	F	1200	6.7	1933	0.9
11	0053	6.7	0832	0.8	26	0012	6.5	0738	1.1
F	1309	6.9	2053	0.7	Sa	1229	6.6	1959	1.0
12	0133	6.5	0857	1.1	27	0045	6.4	0808	1.2
Sa	1347	6.7	2121	1.0	Su	1257	6.5	2030	1.1
13	0211	6.2	0924	1.4	28	0117	6.3	0843	1.4
Su	1425	6.3	2150	1.5	M	1331	6.3	2107	1.4
14	0253	5.8	0956	1.8	29	0157	6.0	0924	1.6
M	1510	5.9	2227	1.9	Tu	1415	6.0	2152	1.7
15	0343	5.4	1038	2.2	30	0250	5.7	1014	1.9
Tu	1607	5.3	2315	2.4	W	1518	5.6	2252	2.0

All times GMT. Add 1 hour for BST

OCTOBER 1987

D	HW		LW		D	HW		LW	
1	0403	5.3	1126	2.2	16	0537	5.0		
Th	1648	5.2			F	1839	4.8	1225	2.6
2	0544	5.1	0017	2.2	17	0703	5.1	0114	2.7
F	1900	5.2	1300	2.2	Sa	1954	5.0	1402	2.4
3	0744	5.4	0157	2.1	18	0804	5.4	0236	2.4
Sa	2023	5.7	1442	1.8	Su	2042	5.4	1508	2.0
4	0846	5.9	0322	1.6	19	0846	5.8	0331	2.0
Su	2115	6.1	1555	1.2	M	2111	5.7	1557	1.6
5	0932	6.4	0428	1.2	20	0921	6.1	0416	1.6
M	2157	6.5	1655	0.8	Tu	2139	6.1	1640	1.3
6	1010	6.7	0525	0.9	21	0953	6.4	0458	1.4
Tu	2234	6.7	1749	0.6	W	2209	6.3	1720	1.1
7	1047	6.9	0614	0.8	22	1026	6.6	0537	1.2
W	2309	6.8	1836	0.5	Th	2240	6.5	1758	1.0
8	1125	7.0	0653	0.8	23	1058	6.7	0612	1.1
Th	2347	6.8	1914	0.6	F	2313	6.6	1832	0.9
9			0723	0.8	24	1130	6.7	0645	1.1
F	1203	7.0	1945	0.7	Sa	2349	6.6	1903	0.9
10	0025	6.6	0748	1.0	25			0716	1.1
Sa	1239	6.8	2013	0.9	Su	1204	6.6	1935	1.0
11	0102	6.5	0818	1.2	26	0025	6.5	0751	1.2
Su	1314	6.6	2042	1.2	M	1241	6.5	2012	1.1
12	0138	6.2	0849	1.4	27	0106	6.3	0832	1.3
M	1349	6.2	2112	1.6	Tu	1323	6.2	2056	1.4
13	0215	5.9	0925	1.8	28	0154	6.1	0918	1.6
Tu	1427	5.8	2149	2.0	W	1416	5.9	2148	1.7
14	0300	5.5	1007	2.2	29	0253	5.8	1016	1.8
W	1519	5.3	2234	2.4	Th	1528	5.5	2254	2.0
15	0404	5.2	1104	2.5	30	0406	5.5	1130	2.0
Th	1651	4.8	2340	2.7	F	1659	5.3		
					31	0539	5.3	0018	2.1
					Sa	1853	5.5	1302	1.9

NOVEMBER 1987

D	HW		LW		D	HW		LW	
1	0716	5.6	0148	1.9	16	0656	5.4	0126	2.5
Su	2001	5.8	1427	1.5	M	1935	5.3	1405	2.1
2	0816	6.0	0303	1.5	17	0749	5.7	0229	2.2
M	2051	6.2	1535	1.2	Tu	2019	5.6	1503	1.8
3	0903	6.3	0403	1.2	18	0834	6.0	0324	1.9
Tu	2132	6.4	1631	0.9	W	2058	5.9	1553	1.5
4	0943	6.6	0455	1.1	19	0914	6.3	0414	1.6
W	2209	6.5	1722	0.8	Th	2136	6.2	1641	1.2
5	1021	6.8	0539	1.0	20	0952	6.5	0501	1.4
Th	2247	6.6	1803	0.8	F	2214	6.4	1725	1.1
6	1101	6.8	0614	1.1	21	1028	6.6	0546	1.3
F	2325	6.6	1836	0.9	Sa	2254	6.6	1805	1.0
7	1139	6.8	0643	1.1	22	1108	6.6	0625	1.2
Sa			1907	1.0	Su	2336	6.6	1843	1.0
8	0004	6.6	0714	1.1	23	1151	6.5	0703	1.1
Su	1215	6.6	1937	1.1	M			1921	1.0
9	0041	6.4	0748	1.3	24	0021	6.6	0745	1.1
M	1250	6.4	2009	1.3	Tu	1238	6.4	2005	1.2
10	0114	6.2	0825	1.5	25	0109	6.4	0832	1.2
Tu	1323	6.1	2043	1.6	W	1331	6.2	2054	1.4
11	0149	6.0	0903	1.7	26	0201	6.3	0922	1.3
W	1359	5.7	2119	2.0	Th	1429	6.0	2149	1.6
12	0230	5.8	0943	2.0	27	0256	6.0	1020	1.5
Th	1447	5.4	2202	2.3	F	1534	5.8	2254	1.8
13	0324	5.5	1034	2.3	28	0356	5.8	1129	1.6
F	1557	5.0	2257	2.5	Sa	1647	5.6		
14	0434	5.3	1140	2.4	29	0509	5.7	0008	1.9
Sa	1726	4.9			Su	1811	5.6	1245	1.6
15	0551	5.2	0010	2.6	30	0628	5.7	0123	1.8
Su	1839	5.0	1256	2.4	M	1920	5.8	1359	1.5

DECEMBER 1987

D	HW		LW		D	HW		LW	
1	0734	5.9	0230	1.7	16	0648	5.6	0120	2.4
Tu	2015	5.9	1505	1.3	W	1926	5.4	1402	2.0
2	0827	6.1	0331	1.5	17	0742	5.8	0225	2.2
W	2103	6.1	1603	1.2	Th	2018	5.7	1503	1.7
3	0914	6.3	0423	1.5	18	0832	6.0	0329	2.0
Th	2146	6.2	1651	1.2	F	2107	5.9	1602	1.5
4	0959	6.4	0505	1.4	19	0921	6.1	0431	1.7
F	2228	6.4	1732	1.2	Sa	2155	6.2	1657	1.3
5	1041	6.5	0542	1.4	20	1009	6.3	0525	1.4
Sa	2311	6.5	1807	1.2	Su	2244	6.4	1747	1.2
6	1122	6.5	0617	1.3	21	1058	6.4	0614	1.2
Su	2349	6.5	1839	1.2	M	2332	6.6	1835	1.1
7			0652	1.3	22	1149	6.5	0700	1.1
M	1200	6.4	1913	1.3	Tu			1921	1.0
8	0025	6.4	0730	1.3	23	0019	6.7	0748	1.0
Tu	1235	6.2	1948	1.4	W	1239	6.5	2009	1.1
9	0059	6.3	0808	1.4	24	0107	6.6	0836	0.9
W	1307	6.0	2023	1.6	Th	1331	6.4	2058	1.1
10	0133	6.2	0846	1.6	25	0154	6.5	0927	1.0
Th	1342	5.8	2057	1.8	F	1423	6.3	2150	1.3
11	0209	6.1	0925	1.8	26	0243	6.4	1019	1.1
F	1425	5.6	2134	2.0	Sa	1517	6.1	2242	1.5
12	0254	5.9	1007	1.9	27	0335	6.2	1113	1.3
Sa	1518	5.4	2217	2.2	Su	1614	5.9	2337	1.7
13	0348	5.7	1057	2.1	28	0433	6.0		
Su	1623	5.2	2309	2.4	M	1719	5.7	1212	1.5
14	0448	5.6	1156	2.1	29	0537	5.9	0038	1.9
M	1729	5.1			Tu	1828	5.6	1319	1.7
15	0550	5.5	0012	2.4	30	0648	5.8	0144	2.0
Tu	1829	5.2	1259	2.1	W	1935	5.6	1427	1.7
					31	0754	5.8	0251	2.0
					Th	2036	5.7	1531	1.7

All times GMT. Add 1 hour for BST.

DISTANCE TABLES BETWEEN PRINCIPAL HEADLANDS ALONG SOUTH COAST
(in nautical miles)

The shortest navigable distances on the rhumb-line between safe distances off each headland

	DUNGENESS	OWERS	ANVIL POINT	BERRY HEAD	BOLT HEAD	DODMAN	RUNNEL STONE
N. FORELAND							
DUNGENESS							
BEACHY HEAD	30						
OWERS	65						
ST CATHERINES	89	24					
ANVIL POINT	114	49					
PORTLAND BILL	134	69	20				
BERRY HEAD	174	109	60				
START POINT	182	117	68	13			
BOLT HEAD	188	123	74	19			
RAME HEAD	206	141	92	36	17		
DODMAN	227	162	113	57	39		
LIZARD	246	181	132	75	56	22	
RUNNEL STONE	265	200	151	94	75	42	
LONGSHIPS	294	229	180	123	105	71	32

DISTANCE TABLES FOR PASSAGES BETWEEN HARBOURS ON SOUTH COAST
(in nautical miles)

The shortest navigable distances on the rhumb-line between harbour entrances or bars

	BRIGHTON	PORTSMOUTH	LYMINGTON	WEYMOUTH	SALCOMBE	FOWEY	PENZANCE
BRIGHTON							
CHICHESTER	34						
PORTSMOUTH	41						
COWES	47	8					
LYMINGTON	56	17					
POOLE	74	35	19				
WEYMOUTH	97	57	40				
DARTMOUTH	135	100	84	52			
SALCOMBE	144	110	95	64			
PLYMOUTH	165	132	115	82	17		
FOWEY	178	144	129	96	36		
FALMOUTH	194	160	143	113	50	20	
PENZANCE	219	183	168	135	74	48	
SCILLY	246	211	195	163	102	76	37

1. *South Foreland and lighthouse. (Photo : Aerofilms Ltd.)*

The following information will help the recognition of principal headlands, and includes brief notes on the tidal streams to be found off them. Tidal charts of the South Coast are inside the front cover. Local tidal charts can be found in Reed's Nautical Almanac. These notes are arranged from east to west.

Admiralty Chart No. 1828

North Foreland   Conspicuous white 8-sided light tower 57m elevation on bold, nearly perpendicular chalk cliffs. At position 3.2 miles 141° from headland: north stream—0120 Dover; south-going stream +0440 Dover. Springs 2¾ knots.

VHF Lt Ho call sign "ND" (see p. 14).

South Foreland   Bold irregular chalk cliff over 90m high. Two lighthouses on the summit, eastern and lower one disused. Western white square castellated tower elevation 114m; tidal streams between South Foreland and Deal. North about −0145 Dover: south about +0415 Dover, spring rate 2¼ knots.

Admiralty Chart No. 2451

Dungeness   A low promontory with steep beach at its south-east end. Prominent lighthouse black round tower, white bands, 40m elevation. Old lighthouse and nuclear power station adjacent to west. Anchorage in roads on either side of Dungeness according to direction of wind. At position 2.4M 140° from Dungeness High lighthouse the east stream begins −0200 Dover. West stream +0430 Dover. Spring rate of about 2 knots.

Beachy Head   This is a very prominent chalk headland. About a mile west of the head is a disused lighthouse, but the operative lighthouse is situated off the rocks below Beachy Head which extend seaward; to the south-east of Beachy Head there are the rocks known as the Head Ledge extending some ½ mile from the cliffs. The lighthouse tower has a broad red band and an elevation of 31m. Seven miles east of Beachy Head are the Royal Sovereign shoals with 3m8 least water over which there are overfalls. They are marked on the southward by a prominent light tower.

Beachy Head should be given a berth of 2 miles in heavy weather as there are overfalls and rough water to the southward of it. Two miles south of the lighthouse the streams are east −0520 Dover, spring rate 2.6 knots; west +0015 Dover, spring rate 2 knots.

Admiralty Chart No. 2450

Selsey Bill and the Owers Selsey Bill is a low sharp point which is difficult to locate if the visibility is poor. There is a conspicuous hotel on the west side of the point. Southward of the Bill there are groups of rocks and ledges between which lie Looe channel and 7 miles south-east of Selsey Bill the Owers light buoy is moored. By keeping south of the light buoy danger is avoided, but in clear weather and moderate winds the Looe channel, which is marked by buoys, affords a short cut, with the aid of a large-scale chart. Tidal streams in the Looe channel: east +0445 Dover; west −0120 Dover. Rate at springs 2.6 knots but faster between the Malt Owers and the Boulder bank. There are local variations in the directions of the streams. Three miles south of the Owers light buoy the tidal streams are west-south-west −0050 Dover; east-north-east +0540 Dover; 2½ to 3 knots at springs.

St Catherine's Point This point is at the southern extremity of the Isle of Wight and lies comparatively low at the foot of the hill which forms the highest part of the island. The lighthouse is an octagonal castellated tower standing at the back of the cliffs; it has an elevation of 41m.

There is a tide race off St Catherine's owing to the uneven bottom in strong streams. This can be very rough under wind against tide conditions and should be avoided; it is dangerous in

2. *Beachy Head and lighthouse from south-west. (Photo: Aerofilms Ltd.)*

3. *St Catherine's Point.*

31

bad weather. The turbulence of the race varies according to wind, tide and swell and is sometimes rougher or calmer than may be anticipated from the conditions. There are also overfalls to the eastward of St Catherine's off Dunnose and a number of isolated tide rips which locally may be almost as rough as St Catherine's race. Tidal streams between St Catherine's Point and Dunnose: east +0515 Dover; west −0015 Dover; maximum spring rate about 5 knots, weaker seaward.

Admiralty Chart No. 2454

The Needles Rocks The sharp Needles rocks with the lighthouse (elevation 24m) at their seaward end are notable landmarks, but they are by no means conspicuous from a distance in hazy weather. From the west or south-west it is the high white cliffs above Scratchell's Bay just south-east of the Needles which

4. *Needles lighthouse and Scratchell's Bay—VHF Lt Ho call sign "HD" (see p. 14).*

will first be seen, and the high down 3 miles east on which stands Tennyson's Cross. Tidal stream atlases should be referred to in the approaches to the Solent from the west as the streams are strong. The main flood stream from Durlston Head runs east-north-east towards the Needles, west of which the stream divides. The stronger flood stream runs north-east into the Needles Channel while farther south the stream runs east to south-east off the Isle of Wight coast. Conversely on the ebb the local streams join west of the Needles and set west-south-west towards Durlston Head.

In the Needles Channel streams in both directions set strongly across the Shingles. Off Hurst Point the north-east stream begins +0505 Dover and the south-west stream at −0055 Dover and attain 4 to 5 knots at springs. Off the Needles the streams tend to be earlier.

In heavy weather the western end of the Isle of Wight should be avoided if possible, especially in south-west winds when it will be worse still if late on the tide after the ebb stream has started. Entry to the Solent under such conditions is safer through the North Channel which lies north of the Shingles, but in gales it is safer still to make Poole or remain in harbour.

Hengistbury Head This headland, 5 miles east of Bournemouth pier and 1 mile south-west of the entrance of Christchurch harbour, is of local importance as it is the only headland between the Needles and Handfast Point south of Poole and is conspicuous from seaward. It is composed of dark reddish ironstone, but often appears of a yellowish colour from seaward; the shape is shown in the photograph. There are ledges off the headland and comparatively shoal water as far as Christchurch Ledge south cardinal buoy, 2½ miles south-east of it. Tidal streams are fairly strong at springs in the vicinity of the buoy, and there are overfalls on the ebb tide near the buoy and over the ledges. The streams within Christchurch Bay itself are weak.

5. *Hengistbury Head and breakwater from the south-east.*

6. *Anvil Point lighthouse to Durlston Point.*

7. *St Alban's Head from the east.*

33

Peveril Point to St Alban's Head There are two recognized tidal races within this area, a small but vicious one off Peveril Point and the larger race off St Alban's Head. There are also local tide rips and under certain conditions patches of rough water may be found practically the whole way from Handfast Point and Old Harry Rocks to St Alban's.

Peveril ledges extend about 3 cables from the low Peveril Point on the south side of Swanage Bay. The depths on the ledges gradually deepen seaward and the end of the reefs is marked by a R can buoy. The tidal streams set straight across the ledges which constitute a danger if a yacht is becalmed. Three cables eastward of Peveril Point the streams are north-north-east +0500 Dover 1½ knots; south-south-west −0215 Dover, 3 knots. In bad weather Peveril Race extends from the Point to seaward of the buoy and especially to the south-east of it during the west-going stream. On a spring ebb tide the rate probably considerably exceeds the rates given.

Durlston Head is a rough headland of a characteristic shape shown in plate 6, and is easily identified by the castellated building on its summit. About a mile east-south-east of the headland the north-east-going stream begins +0530 Dover; south-west −0030 Dover; 3 knots springs.

Inshore Eddy Between Durlston Head and extending along the Dorset coast westward beyond Lulworth there is an early eddy close inshore contrary to the main English Channel stream farther seaward. The easterly eddy starts about +0400 Dover quickly becoming strong and the westerly about −0200 Dover.

Anvil Head, nearly ½ mile to the south-west of Durlston, is easily located by the conspicuous white lighthouse and white wall round its enclosure which stands above the headland.

St Alban's Head is the most southerly on this part of the coast and its shape with cliffs at the summit falling into rocks at the base is easily recognized from plate 7. Off St Alban's Head there is a considerable tidal race which lies eastward of the head on the flood tide and westward on the ebb. The race varies considerably in its position and its severity. It extends some 3 miles seaward except during southerly winds when it lies closer inshore. It may be avoided by giving the land a berth of 3 miles. 1½ M off the Head the easterly stream begins about +0545 Dover; west −0015 Dover, attaining a rate of between 4 and 5 knots at springs. There is a passage of nearly ½ mile between St Alban's Head and the race but it varies and may be less during onshore winds and is not entirely immune from tidal disturbance. Thus in reasonable weather vessels can avoid the worst of the overfalls by keeping inshore at St Alban's where deep water is found close to the headland. The inshore passage has the advantage of the early fair eddy but a local eddy runs down the west side of St Alban's Head to the south-east nearly continuously.

Portland Bill and Race From well seaward Portland has a characteristic shape, appearing like an island, high and broad on its northern end against the low Chesil Beach and sloping down towards the southern end. Here is situated the round tower with a red band lighthouse with an elevation of 43m.

Portland Race lies south of Portland Bill, a little to the westward during the ebb and to the eastward during the flood, where in bad weather there is confused and dangerous water so far as and over the whole of the Shambles. The worst part of the Race extends nearly 2 miles from the Bill and it is well defined by the area of overfalls. At spring tides the Race sometimes attains a rate exceeding 7 knots, but the rate is not uniform and reference is best made to the Admiralty tidal stream atlas for Approaches to Portland which shows hourly details. It may be added that south-west of Portland, during the west-going stream there is a northerly set into West Bay, which at times is strong. When rounding Portland Bill the navigator has two principal options to choose between. The easier one is to pass outside the Race about 3 miles off the Bill in calm or 5 miles in bad weather, especially at spring tides if the wind is against streams.

8. *Portland from the east.*

9. *Portland Bill and beacon from the south-west.*

10. Berry Head from the south.

The alternative is to use the inner passage which is a channel about ¼ mile wide (varying with direction of wind) which lies between the Bill and the Race. This channel should not be used at night, and even by day only under suitable conditions, for although the water is comparatively smooth, the streams are strong and the overfalls are not entirely avoided off Grove Point and west of the Bill, according to wind direction. The correct timing of the passage is a matter of the utmost importance.

When bound *westward*, round the Bill between ½ hour before and 2½ hours after HW Dover. When bound *eastward*, round the Bill between 4½ hours after and 5 hours before HW Dover. Whether bound west or east through the inner passage close with Portland at least a mile to the northward of the Bill and work southward with a fair tide to arrive off the Bill at the correct time.

Golden Cape A useful landmark 3½ miles east of Lyme Regis and 3 miles west of Bridport. The cape rises to a Golden Cap, 186m high, which has pronounced yellow cliffs at its summit which, with sun on them, may be conspicuous from a long distance even in hazy weather. Inshore streams weak.

Beer Head A conspicuous chalk cliff westward of which lie the red sandstone cliffs of Devon. Inshore streams weak, approximately east +0600 Dover; west HW Dover.

Berry Head Bold limestone headland flat topped, with steep end falling at about 45° to the sea. White lighthouse on summit with an elevation of 58m. Coastal streams: north +0540 Dover; south −0100 Dover. 1½ knots maximum.

36

11. Start Point from the east-north-east.

12. Prawle Point and old signal station from the west-south-west.

37

13. Bolt Tail from the south-west.

Start Point A long sharp-ridged headland, with round white lighthouse, elevation 62m, which is unmistakable. There are rocks off the Start which are awash at HW and extend nearly 3 cables south of the Point. The Start race extends nearly a mile seaward of the Point, and its severity depends much on the conditions of wind, tide and swell. The overfalls can be avoided in daylight by passing close to the rocks but there is an outlying one to the south, so care is needed. It is simpler to give the Point a berth of at least a mile. Three miles southward of the Point the streams are: east-north-east +0455 Dover; west-south-west −0120 Dover, about 2 knots springs. Off Start rocks the streams are about an hour earlier and attain about 4 knots at springs but are irregular at neaps.

Prawle Point This Point lies 3½ miles west of Start Point to the south-east of Salcombe Bar, and has a prominent white Coastguard Station at its summit.

Bolt Head and Bolt Tail Bolt Head stands on the west side of the entrance to Salcombe. The ridge of dark rugged cliffs extending to Bolt Tail is conspicuous.

Rame Head is conspicuous when one is approaching Plymouth Sound.

Dodman Point is a most conspicuous headland standing about halfway between Fowey and Falmouth. It is precipitous, 110m high, with a stone cross near south-west extremity. Irregular bottom and tide rips 1½ miles seaward.

14. Bolt Head from the south-east with Starehole Bay on the right.

15. Rame Head from the south-east.

16. *Dodman Head from the south-east. Note stone cross at summit.*

17. *St Anthony's Head at the entrance to Falmouth.*

18. Lizard Point and lighthouse. (Photo : Aerofilms Ltd.)

Lizard Point The Lizard is a bold headland with conspicuous white buildings and a white wall round their enclosure which stand near its summit. The octagonal tower of the white lighthouse (elevation 70m) is situated at the eastern end of the buildings. Six cables to eastward there is a coastguard station and Lloyd's signal station, which is in almost continuous use with passing ships making their landfalls and departures.

The group of rocks known as Stag Rocks, some of which are above water and others dry 4 to 5m, extends over ½ mile south of the Lizard. These can be seen at most states of the tide and avoided, but a mile east of Lizard Point lie the Vrogue Rocks off Bass Point which have less than 2m over them at LW. The Craggan Rocks, with 1m5 over them, lie north-east of Bass Point, but these dangers will be avoided by vessels proceeding east or west to the southward of the Stag Rocks. The Lizard Race extends 2 to 3 miles seaward of the Stag Rocks, and at times there is a race south-east of the head. The state of the seas varies considerably according to tide and wind direction, and the seas may be very rough with strong westerly winds against the down channel stream. Under suitable conditions pass outside the Stag Rocks where the streams start east +0415 Dover; west −0345 Dover. Spring rates are 2 and 3 knots respectively and at times stronger. In rough weather or when a swell is running, especially with wind against a spring tide vessels should keep 3 or more miles off Lizard Point.

Note that the Lizard is the most westerly of the conspicuous headlands on the south coast of England. It is a dividing line in the sense that west of it there is only a limited shelter in Penzance Bay but eastward there are many harbours available in bad weather.

Land's End is 20 miles WNW of the Lizard. Although it is higher it is not so conspicuous, due to having no lighthouse on it. The unlit Gwennap Head is its southernmost point, with the dangerous Runnel Stone Rocks running a mile offshore and marked by a YB south cardinal buoy (Qk Fl(6)+LFl 15 sec.) which has been known to drag off its station in severe weather. In calm weather and with local knowledge it is possible to cut inside, but the distance saved is not worth the ulcers.

The ebb tide sets NW off the point for 9½ hours, starting at HW Dover −0300, and runs up to 2½ knots. The east-going flood turns 6 hours before HW Dover and only runs for three hours.

From the vicinity of the Runnel Stone the Wolf Rock (Alt Fl WR 30 sec.) stands out on its own seven miles to the SW, while the Longships Lighthouse 4 miles to the NW (Iso WR 10 sec.) marks the westernmost point of England, excepting the Scilly Isles 20 miles farther west. There are always confused seas around the menacing group of rocks marked by the Longships, and yachts on passage should keep at least a mile to seaward.

PART TWO

HARBOURS AND ANCHORAGES

Distances are given in nautical miles, cables and metres. Bearings and courses are True, to which Variation must be added and Deviation applied for ship's magnetic compass.

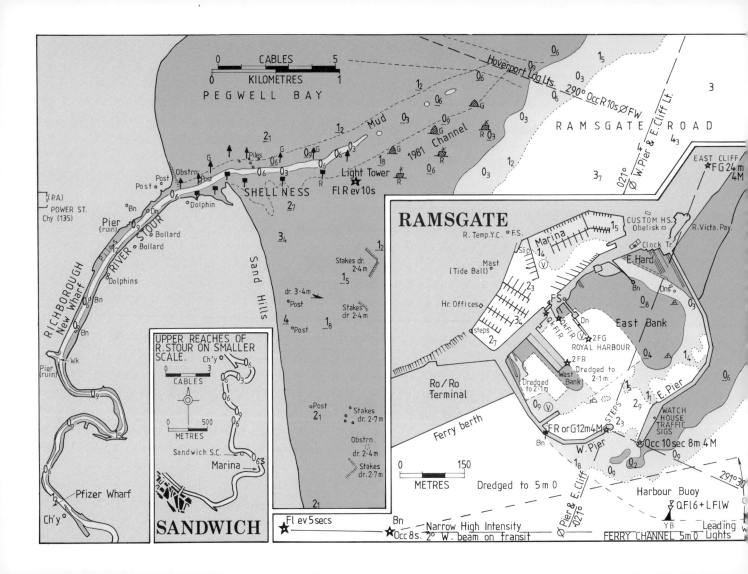

PEGWELL BAY

CABLES
0 _____ 5
KILOMETRES
0 _____ 1

Hoverport Ldg Lts.
290° Occ R 10s Ø FW

Mud

1981 Channel

RAMSGATE ROAD

SHELL NESS

Light Tower
Fl R ev 10s

021°

Ø W. Pier & E. Cliff Lt.

EAST CLIFF
★ FG 24 m
4 M

(P.A.)
POWER ST.
Chy (135)

Pier
(ruin)

Post
Post
Post
Obstrn.
Dolphin
Bn
Dn
Bollard
Bollard
Dolphins
Bn
Bn

RIVER STOUR

Sand Hills

Stakes dr.
2·4 m
1·5

dr. 3·4 m
Post

Stakes
dr. 2·4 m
1·8

Post

RAMSGATE

R. Temp. Y.C. ● F.S.
Marina

CUSTOM HS.
Obelisk
R. Victa. Pav.
Clock Tr.

Mast
(Tide Ball)

Slip
(V)

E. Hard
Bn
Dns

Hr. Offices

FS
QkFl R
QkFl R
Dn
(V) 2 FG
ROYAL HARBOUR

East Bank

steps

2 FR
West
Bank
Dredged to
2·1 m

(Dredged
to 2·1m)
(V)

RICHBOROUGH
New Wharf

Bn

Pier
(ruin)
Wk

UPPER REACHES OF R. STOUR ON SMALLER SCALE.

Ch'y

CABLES
0 _____ 3

METRES
0 _____ 500

Sandwich S.C.

Marina

Pfizer Wharf

Ch'y

Post
Stakes
dr. 2·7 m

Obstrn.
dr. 2·4 m

Stakes
dr. 2·7 m

SANDWICH

Ro/Ro
Terminal

Ferry berth

Ø Pier & E. Cliff
021°

Bn
FR or G 12 m 4 M
W. Pier

E. Pier

WATCH
HOUSE
TRAFFIC
SIGS

STEPS

☆ Occ 10 sec 8m 4 M

METRES
0 _____ 150

Dredged to 5 m 0

FERRY CHANNEL 5m 0

Harbour Buoy
▽ Q Fl 6 + L Fl W
YB

291° 30'

Leading
Lights

★ Fl ev 5 secs   Bn   Narrow High Intensity
★ Occ 8s. 2° W. beam on transit

RAMSGATE

Admiralty Chart No. 1827

High Water   *+oo h. 20 m. Dover.*
Heights above Datum   *MHWS 5m0. MLWS 0m4.*
MHWN 3m9. MLWN 1m2.
Depths   *Off the entrance the depths are variable except in the new East-West Channel to the RO/RO ferry terminal which passes one cable south of the entrance and is dredged to 5m0. Best water, usually about 1m4, lies on the west side of entrance deepening to 2m2 on this side between the pier ends. On the east side a bar often forms which dries out at LAT. For depths within harbours see Plan, but water is much influenced by wind direction. In the Inner Harbour depths are maintained at a fairly constant level of 3m0.*

RAMSGATE is the most easterly of the harbours south of the Thames. It is conveniently situated for yachts making passage between the English Channel and the North Sea. The town is adjacent to the harbour and all facilities are available. A breakwater to protect the new RO/RO terminal is planned.

Approach and Entrance   Approaching from the south either the Ramsgate Channel or the Gull Stream can be used. The Ramsgate Channel lies between Sandwich flats on the west and the Brake sand on the east. It is buoyed. After leaving to starboard the green unlit B2 buoy, steer for the entrance on a transit 021° of the light at the end of the West Pier and the conspicuous tower of the Granville Hotel on the skyline. The floodtide sets strongly east across the entrance and allowance must be made to avoid being swept against the east pierhead or over the shoal lying off it.

From the eastward or northward from the Gull Stream use the Old Cudd Channel. This is entered by bringing the light pillar on the east pierhead in line with the lighthouse on the west pierhead at 291½°. This passes between the BY north cardinal Quern buoy and the south cardinal buoy marking the end of Dike Sand. Three cables to the west leave to starboard the south cardinal Harbour buoy, which is one cable SSE of the East Breakwater light, and thus give the shoals off the east pierhead a wide berth. Enter the harbour on the west side of the entrance. This will avoid the strong tidal set close to the east pier and also the shoal off it.

Note that the shoals outside the harbour are constantly shifting and the buoys and marks are moved from time to time.

19.   Ramsgate harbour entrance from the south on course 021°.

Berthing directions are given from the watch-house on the east pier or by radio on Ch 16 or 17.

Tidal Signals There are no tidal signals displayed in the daytime. At night the tidal light on west pier is F R when the depth is 3m0 or over; G when less than 3m0. During fog a bell at east pier ringing 10 strokes every quarter hour indicates 3m0 or over; 5 strokes slowly, less than 3m0.

Traffic Signals from east pier flagstaff: black flag indicates vessel(s) about to enter harbour and outward vessel(s) to keep clear. At night a white revolving light is exhibited. Two black balls (or red revolving light at night) indicate vessel(s) about to leave harbour; inward vessel(s) may not enter or approach harbour.

Lights East pierhead Lt Occ W 10 sec. 8m 4M. This is also front light for the Old Cudd Channel, the rear light being west pier F R or G (see Tidal Signals), 4M, and these lights in line are 291½°. West pier is front Lt F R or G for south leading line and in line with F G Lt 4M high up on east cliff. These in line bear 021°. *Fog Signal :* Bell from east pier.

If proceeding to the Inner Basin steer to pass between the two Qk Fl R Lts which are exhibited near HW time when the gates are open. Leave the two F R Vert Lts at the south-east corner of the West Bank quay to port and two similar F G Vert Lts at the extremity of the reception pontoon to starboard.

Anchorage Outside, south of harbour on Pegwell Bay under favourable conditions well clear of the new RO/RO terminal and turning area. No anchoring in the harbour.

Visiting yachts are usually directed from the watch-house to lie by the wall of the west pier in 1m7 or alongside the east pier in 2m0. The moorings in the south-west of the harbour are reserved for local yachts.

Inner Harbour The dock gates to the 500-berth marina open about 2 hours before HW and close 1 hour after HW. Lights Qk Fl R on east and west sides of dock gates.

Traffic Signals Daytime: same as outer harbour. Night: two G Lts Vert on mast, vessels may enter. One R over two G Lts, vessels may leave. One R Lt only indicates dock gates will not open at all.

Berthing Directions These will be given as the yacht enters by the Dock Master, from his office on the eastern side of the lock gates. It is better to call the Harbour Authority on Thanet (0843) 52277 before planning a visit. The level is kept at about 3m0.

Facilities Water at all piers on application. Petrol and oil, etc., available. Shops adjacent. EC Thurs. Boat-builders and repairers. Patent slip and scrubbing. Launching site slipways in outer harbour—see HM. Yacht club: R. Temple YC.

20. Ramsgate harbour entrance shaping too close to East Pierhead.

21. Ramsgate showing Marina and new ferry terminal with link-span outside the harbour. (Photo : Sealand Aerial Photography)

22. Ramsgate West Pierhead. This is the correct side for entry or departure. (Photo : Rozelle Raynes)

47

SANDWICH

Admiralty Chart No. 1827

High Water *at bar* +*oo h. 15 m. Dover.*
Heights above Datum *Richborough: MHWS 3m7. MHWN 2m6. Bar dries at LW.*
Tides *The ebb runs for 7 hours and the flood for 5 hours at Sandwich Town.*
Depths *On the bar dries om3 to om9 at chart datum. Entrance channel and river shallow. At HW Springs navigable with a maximum draught of about 4m5 or about 3m0 at Neaps as far as Sandwich.*

23. *Sandwich Town Quay.*

SANDWICH lies 4½ miles from the mouth of the River Stour. It is a town of considerable historic interest. Visiting yachts lie at the town quay.

Approach The River Stour lies at the south-west corner of Pegwell Bay, about 2 miles SW of Ramsgate; the cooling towers of the power station are very conspicuous. Pegwell Bay dries out except for a narrow channel carrying the river water. The channel across the bay tends to shift but is well marked by R and G buoys at its seaward end, and by posts with topmarks at the landward end. A Lt. tower Fl R ev 10 sec. marks the intersection. Approach only in good weather by day. From Ramsgate steer SW to the buoyed entrance channel. Keep an eye open for hovercraft (their flight path is marked by orange spherical buoys) from the Hoverport at the NW of Pegwell Bay.

Once inside the river keep to the middle. The town bridge may be opened at 24 hours' notice; there is then 12 miles of navigable water for boats up to 1m2 draught. The entrance channel and lower reaches are navigable from about 1½ hours before until 2½

hours after HW for a boat with 1m2 draught. Note that just inside the river on the starboard hand is a dolphin which is surmounted by a pole with diamond topmark.

Anchorage and Quay Inside the river there is a marina about 1 mile below the town of Sandwich on the north bank. Here there is about 2m4 MHWS and 1m8 MHWN, but the berths dry at LW. The river becomes narrower and very congested in this reach owing to numerous moorings. Further downstream Richborough Wharf is private and is used by the tankers feeding the power station. There is another small commercial wharf a short distance upstream. At Sandwich the bottom is hard chalk covered by a very thin layer of mud. For deep draught yachts it is wise to make preparations for drying out by the wall.

Facilities Sandwich Sailing and Motor Boat Club, Bayside Marine yard and most facilities at marina. Water at Sandwich Town Quay on application to the Quaymaster (tel 613283). Petrol at garage near quay. Shops. EC Wed. Hotels. Yacht yard above bridge. Sandwich MBC near marina have a slip.

DOVER

Heights above Datum *MHWS 6m9. MLWS 0m8. MHWN 5m3. MLWN 2m0; but irregular, depending on wind conditions.*

Depths *Dover is a large artificial harbour divided into two parts. The big expanse of the outer harbour is a deep-water port. The inner western part between the Admiralty pier and the Prince of Wales pier has about 5m in the entrance, but the depths gradually reduce towards the inner tidal harbour, which dries out at LW except for a narrow channel 0m3 to 0m6 deep. Beyond this are the inner basins. The Wellington Dock, which is used by yachts, has 4m5 Springs, 3m3 Neaps. The Eastern Dock is deep.*

DOVER is a busy port on the south-east corner of England, but owing to its heavy commercial traffic yachtsmen are not encouraged to use the harbour unless they obey the traffic control signals implicitly. They are only welcome to stay for a maximum of two weeks in the Wellington Dock during the period 1 April–30 September. These are the only alongside berths in the harbour available to yachtsmen. Boats which anchor off may not be left untended.

Approach and Entrance Dover harbour is some 2 miles south-west of the South Foreland, and by day the long breakwaters make the harbour easy to identify and at night the breakwater lights will be seen at long range.

Yachts are required to use the western entrance, whenever feasible, owing to the much heavier commercial traffic using the eastern one nowadays. *A careful look out should be kept for the entry signals*, and permission to enter should also be requested by Aldis lamp or International Code signals (SV:I wish to enter; SW:I wish to leave), or yachts fitted with VHF should call up Dover Port Control on Ch 74 or on Ch 16 to establish a working frequency (usually Ch 12). A series of short flashes from Port Control on Admiralty Pier indicates: 'STOP—WAIT'.

All yachts should keep well clear of the actual entrances until the moment they receive their entry or exit signals, in order to leave room for bigger ships to manœuvre or swing round just inside the entrances. Local tidal streams vary considerably and attain their maximum spring rate of 4 knots or more south of the Southern Breakwater.

Traffic Signals covering both entrances are exhibited at the ends of the Eastern Arm, Admiralty Pier and Camber. All traffic is regulated by day or night by IALA port signals using directional high-intensity lights beamed to seaward or inshore, depending to whom they apply. Signals are vertically displayed, as follows:

RRR Flashing	Emergency. Entrance closed.
RRR fixed	Entry or exit prohibited from the direction indicated.
GWG	Ships may proceed to or from direction indicated.

Navigation in Outer Harbour The Harbour Patrol Launch will be found in the outer harbour. When it shows a flashing blue light by night it will act as a radio relay. Any instructions given from it must be observed. Yachts should beware of hovercraft channels across harbour, marked by a line of orange spherical buoys. They should also keep well clear of Channel ferries and cargo ships manœuvring in the fairway.

Inner Harbour Anchorage is not permitted between Admiralty and Prince of Wales Piers. The Granville Dock is not available to yachts. Permission should be asked of Dock Master to lie alongside cross wall until lock gates open when waiting to enter Wellington Dock.

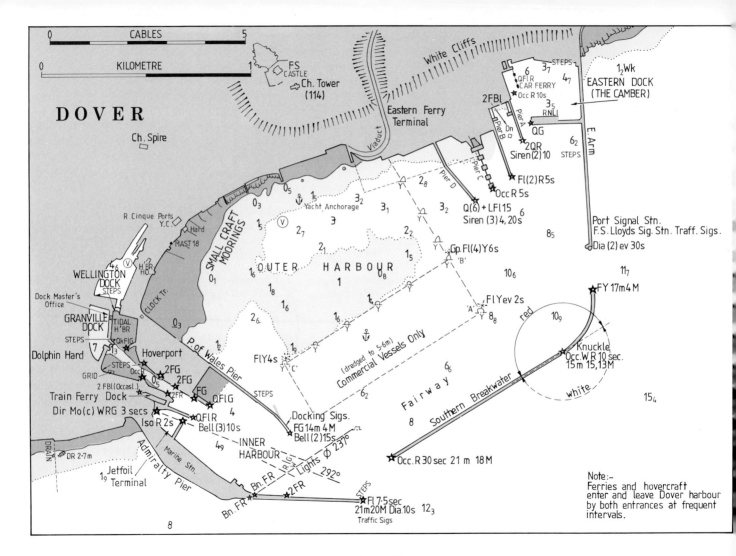

DOVER

CABLES 0 ————— 5

KILOMETRE 0 ————— 1

FS CASTLE
Ch. Tower (114)

White Cliffs

Ch. Spire

Eastern Ferry Terminal

6 3₇ STEPS
QFlR 4₇
CAR FERRY
Occ R 10s
2FBL
3₅
RNLI
QG
2QR
Siren(2)10
6₂ STEPS

½Wk
EASTERN DOCK
(THE CAMBER)
E. Arm

R.Cinque Ports Y.C.
Hard
MAST 18

Viaduct

Pier E
Pier A
Dn
Pier B

0₅ anchor
0₃
Yacht Anchorage
3₂
3₁
Pier C

Fl(2)R5s
OccR 5s
Q(6)+LFl15
Siren (3) 4, 20s
6

Port Signal Stn.
F.S. Lloyds Sig. Stn. Traff. Sigs.
Dia (2) ev 30s

WELLINGTON DOCK
STEPS
4₈ Ⓥ
H'BR HO.

SMALL CRAFT MOORINGS

1₅
Ⓥ
2₇
3
0₈
1₆

OUTER HARBOUR
1

8₅
10₆
11₇

Dock Master's Office
GRANVILLE DOCK
TIDAL H'BR
STEPS
Dolphin Hard
CLOCK Tr.
QkFlG
0₃
7
13

Hoverport
OccR
2FG
2FG
FG
QFlG

Gp.Fl(4)Y6s
'B'
'A' 8₈
FlY ev 2s

★FY 17m4M

red
10₉
white

P. of Wales Pier

FlY4s
'C'

STEPS

Knuckle
Occ.W R 10 sec.
15m 15,13M

GRID
2 FBL(Occasl.)
0₅
2FR
Train Ferry Dock
Dir Mo(c) WRG 3 secs
Iso R 2s

4
QFlR
Bell(3)10s

Docking Sigs.
FG 14m 4M
Bell (2)15s
6₂
Fairway 6₆

8
Southern Breakwater
★Occ.R 30 sec 21 m 18M

15₄

DRAIN
DR 2.7m
Jetfoil Terminal
1₉

Admiralty Pier
Marine Stn.

(dredged to 5·6m)
Commercial Vessels Only

INNER HARBOUR
4₉
Lights Φ 237°
292°

Bn.FR
2FR
Bn. FR
STEPS
★Fl 7·5sec
21m20M Dia.10s 12₃
Traffic Sigs

Note:-
Ferries and hovercraft
enter and leave Dover harbour
by both entrances at frequent
intervals.

8

24. Dover. Anti-clockwise from the top : Camber, Eastern Docks, Wellington Dock, Granville Dock, Hoverport, Admiralty Pier. (Photo : Dover Harbour Board)

Signals for tidal harbour and inner docks   Red neon letters are displayed at height of 5m5, close to fixed green light at seaward end of Prince of Wales Pier. They operate in conjuction with dock signals (for commercial vessels or very big yachts only). Small craft need not usually pay attention to these unless there is something big blocking the channel.

Fairway Signals by Day and Night—Letter 'W' Illuminated: Vessels are permitted to pass *inward* through fairway from Outer Harbour to Tidal Harbour or Wellington Dock only, and no vessel may pass outward while this signal is shown. Letter 'G' Illuminated: Vessels are permitted to pass *inward* to Granville Dock, and no vessel may pass outward, etc. No Signal Letter Illuminated: Vessels are permitted to pass *outward* through fairway from Tidal Harbour to Outer Harbour, and *no vessel may pass inward unless letters are illuminated.*

Wellington Dock Signals exhibited from top of 9m0 tower on west side of dock entrance. *By Day and Night*—Yellow Panel Illuminated (visible to seaward): Vessels are permitted to enter Wellington Dock, and none may leave dock or tidal Harbour while this signal is shown. Red Panel Illuminated (visible to dock): Departure permitted from Wellington Dock and no vessel may enter dock or Tidal Harbour while this signal is shown.

Note: (a) At night a fixed all-round R Lt will be exhibited simultaneously on each of the north and south pierheads during tide times; (b) A single G Lt is displayed at cope level on each side of the Granville or Wellington Dock entrances when a vessel is about to enter or leave the dock.

Craft intending to leave Wellington Dock should inform the Dock Master's office beforehand (tel. 206560) or by visiting him near the swingbridge at the entrance.

Jetfoil Terminal is inshore of the new breakwater running NNE of the Marine station. Its entrance is on a directional light 292° Mo (C) WRG 3 sec.

Anchorage   East of Prince of Wales Pier, as near to the shore as soundings permit. The Royal Cinque Ports YC has one visitors' mooring which may be used by yachts. Private moorings off the club may not be picked up without prior permission from the club. Yachts are not permitted to use the Camber or Eastern

25.   Dover—outer harbour and yacht anchorage.

26. *Dover—entrance to Wellington Dock with swingbridge open.*

Docks. In bad weather or by prior arrangement pass into inner Wellington Dock, which is open from approx. 1 hour before HW until just after HW.

Lights   At western entrance Lt Fl W 7½ sec. 21m 20M is exhibited on the west side from a white tower on the end of the Admiralty Pier. On the east side there is a Lt R Occ 30 sec. 21 m 18M at the south-west end of the Southern Breakwater, and at the knuckle near its NE end a Lt Occ W seaward R, shoreward 10 sec. 15m, 15–13M. At the eastern entrance there is an Or Lt traffic signal 4M at the northern end of the Southern Breakwater and traffic signals are exhibited at the south end of the Eastern Arm. Within the harbour there is a F G all-round Lt 4M at end of Prince of Wales Pier, and there are lights at the Eastern Docks and elsewhere.

Fog Signals   Diaphone 10 sec. at end of Admiralty Pier. Diaphone (2) ev 30 sec. at south end of Eastern Arm. Within the harbour, bell (2) 15 sec. at Prince of Wales Pier. At the Eastern Dock siren (2) 10 sec. at Camber 'A' Pier when required by ferries and siren 5 sec. at end of 'B' Pier.

Facilities   Water at Wellington Dock or by courtesy at yacht club. Chandlery, fuel and stores available. EC Wed. Scrubbing and minor repairs at Dolphin Hard by arrangement at Dock Master's office. Yacht club: R. Cinque Ports YC. Launching site: from beach below centre promenade, boats up to 4m8 long. Car park. Two stations. Buses to all parts.

Admiralty Chart No. 1991

High Water — *oo h. 12 m. Dover.*
Heights above Datum *MHWS 7m1. MLWS om7.
MHWN 5m7. MLWN 2mo.*
Depths *The outer harbour is dredged to a least depth of 4m5
and is formed by the breakwater which extends into deep water. In
the entrance to the inner harbour there is 5m5 at MHWS and from
3m3 to 4m2 MHWS within the harbour, and at Neaps 1mo less. At
LW it dries out everywhere.*

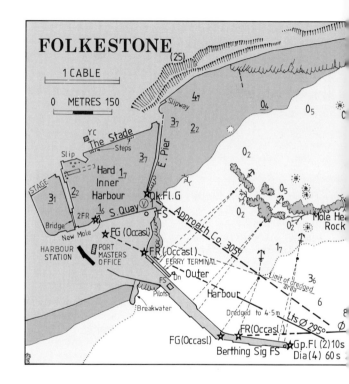

FOLKESTONE is mainly a commercial port with its roll-on roll-off
ferry terminal. The inner harbour is only suitable for yachts with
legs or those prepared to dry out by the rough wall at the east pier.
It is not a good refuge in bad weather and yachts are only welcome
for occasional overnight moorings, as the whole inner harbour is
full up. The inner harbour faces east but the entrance itself
receives extra protection from the west by a long breakwater built
for British Rail ferries and which forms the outer harbour. The
inner harbour is mostly used by fishing boats equipped with legs.
The town itself has all the facilities of a summer holiday resort.

Approach and Entrance Folkestone is about $5\frac{1}{2}$ miles
westward of Dover and is the largest town on the coast between
Dungeness and the Foreland. The town is thus easy to recognize
and the harbour lies nearer it eastern end, behind a conspicuous
outer breakwater. There are rocky ledges to the west of the
breakwater and east of the inner harbour entrance. Of these the
Mole Head Rocks, less than 2 cables east of the inner end of the
outer breakwater, and the ledges off Copt Point are the more
dangerous. To clear these when approaching from the east keep

the South Foreland well open of the Dover cliffs. By night, the
South Foreland light is masked northward of 58° true, so that the
vessel should not go northward of the arc of the light. Eddy on
east stream. Then when the south end of the east pier (Qk Fl G) of
the inner harbour bears 305° alter course leaving the outer
breakwater close to port. Sufficient rise of tide is required as the

27. Folkestone—inner harbour at low water.

water shoals about 2 cables off the inner harbour and shelves gradually to −1m0 at the entrance. For depths within the harbour see *Anchorage and Harbour*.

Signals at the outer end of the new ferry pier are shown for car ferries by means of a black flag or 1, 2 or 3 spherical shapes.

Lights, etc. Outer breakwater Gp Fl W (2) 10 sec. 14m 22M. Occasional leading lights F R and F G on a transit of 267° exhibited at the knuckle of outer breakwater and near the ferry pier leading on 295° when a car ferry is expected. East pierhead Qk Fl G Occas. Two F R on mole at south quay when commercial vessel about to enter. Fog diaphone (4) 60 sec. at breakwater head.

Anchorage and Harbour (1) Anchorage outside the inner harbour is inadvisable owing to the ferry traffic and risk of fouling the ground moorings and long chains used for winching off the ferries. It is also exposed and has indifferent holding ground. No yacht may *ever* moor alongside the ferry pier except in dire medical emergency. (2) Yachts may lie in the inner harbour if there is room inside the east pier on legs or alongside the pier. At LAT the harbour dries 1m0 at the entrance, about 2m2 in the centre and up to 3m7 at the northern end of the east pier. Yachtsmen must calculate the tide level by reference to the heights above datum at the head of the chapter, but boats up to 1m5 draught can enter 3 hours either side of HW. The swing bridge at western end of inner harbour is permanently fixed and the shallow inner basin (controlled by Folkestone Corporation) can be entered only by boats able to pass below it.

Facilities Water at quay. Good shopping centre, EC Wed. Station. Buses to all parts. Yacht club: Folkestone SC near slipway in inner harbour.

RYE

Admiralty Chart No. 1991

High Water *at entrance* −*00 h. 05 m. Dover.*

Heights above Datum *near approach*: *MHWS 7m7. MHWN 6m0. Dries LW. Harbour MHWS 5m3. MHWN 3m6.*

Depths *In the channel there is only a fresh-water trickle at MLWS. At MHWS there is about 3m4 to 4m5 in the harbour alongside the catwalk staging and 1m6 to 2m8 at MHWN.*

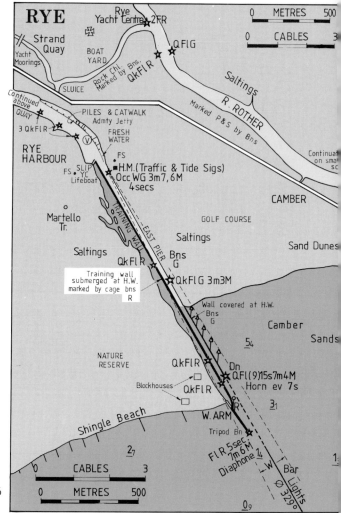

RYE HARBOUR is ¾ mile within the entrance, and is a small village. The town itself is another 2 miles up the river which is navigable at high water and is increasingly used by cargo vessels; it is one of the Cinque Ports and so charming that it attracts many visitors. There are good hotels.

Rye Harbour entrance once had a somewhat bad reputation owing to the loss of the lifeboat crew west of the entrance in 1928. Since then, however, the entrance has been improved and it is clearly marked. Given an offshore wind and fair weather and the right state of tide, strangers should not find the entrance unduly difficult. A south-west wind Force 5 is definitely uncomfortable and probably too much for a first attempt. Power is desirable, as the tide runs very hard in the narrow channel—the flood is stronger than the ebb, which is unusual in rivers.

Approach and Entrance The entrance lies at the apex of Rye Bay. From the eastward follow the low coast from Dungeness for some 7 miles keeping about a mile offshore until reaching the RW Rye Fairway safe-water buoy (Fl 10 sec.) 1.8 miles SE of the conspicuous west pier and the tripod beacon. Westward of the entrance the shore is also low (but hills behind) for a distance of 5 miles to Fairlight, which is high and can be

28.   Entrance to Rye from the south-east at low water.

recognized by the square tower of the church, and its coastguard station.

The entrance and channel to Rye Harbour, from 30 to 45m wide, lie between the east and west piers. On the west side a long training wall has a groyne which extends to seaward of the entrance. This training wall is covered between half tide and HW (depths above 2m4), and is marked by a series of pole beacons with cage topmarks some on top of dolphins; three Qk Fl R Lts at night placed at irregular intervals along the wall as far as Rye Harbour and three Fl R Lts at the bend beyond it. At its seaward extremity there stands a tripod light dolphin Fl R 5 sec. 7m 6M. The east pier is also long, though it does not extend as far seaward; at its end there is a light post Qk Fl (9) 15 sec. 7m 5M with a Qk Fl G three cables NW where the east bank begins. At MHWS the tops of this east pier are just showing, but it is marked by two posts with conical topmarks.

Vessels making for Rye should head up towards the Rye Fairway buoy, then alter course to 329° to enter the harbour. There is always an easterly set across the harbour entrance, especially on the flood tide. Within the entrance a course mid-channel is possibly the best to take, although the deeper water is on the west side. However, care must be taken on the flood when side currents flowing across the training wall may affect steering. The cage beacons are fixed to the *inside* edge of the training wall except for one off the HM's office—a prominent solitary house on the east bank of the Rother opposite the lifeboat slip.

The entrance should not be approached by vessels with a draught of 2m earlier than 3 hours before HW; the best time to enter is from 1 hour before HW; the best time to leave is not later than 1 hour after HW (but for yachts of moderate draught $2\frac{1}{2}$ hours either side is possible with care at springs). A tide gauge is fitted to the end of the eastern breakwater.

Tidal Signals are shown by day from a mast just behind the Harbour Office, about $\frac{3}{4}$ mile within the entrance on the east side, and by night from the roof of the Office when any merchant ship (irrespective of size) is expected, but the signals are hard to see in poor visibility. *By day :* 2m4 on bar, one ball on yard; 2m9 on bar, one ball on each yard; 3m0 on bar, one ball at masthead only; 3m3 on bar, one ball at masthead, one ball on yard; 3m6 on bar, one ball at masthead, one ball on each yard. *By night :* 2m4 to 3m0, a green light; over 3m0, a red light.

Traffic Signals When a cargo vessel is moving in the harbour a black ball is hoisted by day or an amber Qk Fl Lt is exhibited on Harbour Office at night; all vessels must give way.

Lights, etc. From beacon on western arm extension Fl R 5 sec. 7m 6M; on eastern pier end Qk Fl (9) ev 15 sec. 7m 5M. Lights on east side of channel leading up the channel at 329°: front, Qk Fl G; rear, Occ W G with W sector 326.5°—331.5°. Qk Fl R on beacons or dolphins on west side of channel as previously referred to. Fog diaphone on western arm extension.

29. *Rye. Port hand cages mark submerged training wall on the west bank.*

Anchorage and Berths In fair weather yachts awaiting the tide for Rye should anchor close to Rye Fairway buoy (where there is a least depth of 5m9). In west or south-west winds yachts should anchor behind Dungeness, close to the Coastguard's House. With sufficient rise of tide all visiting yachts should moor at special berths provided alongside the piles at Rye Harbour village, about a mile from the entrance on the east side of the river, just beyond the HM's Office. This is about 2 miles from Rye town. The berths are lighted at night. Double mooring is not allowed. Care should be taken when turning at Rye Harbour village at springs.

The large range of tide calls for careful mooring, as winds blowing on to the staging have been the cause of many broken masts or damaged spreaders. Yachts will lie afloat for about 4 hours, then take the bottom, which is hard muddy shingle. A vacant berth may indicate wreckage below water—always consult the HM, who can be contacted VHF Ch 16.

The river is navigable for craft drawing up to 2m7 at MHWS as far as Strand Quay in the heart of the historic old town of Rye, where drying-alongside berths or moorings may be found by prior arrangement. Consult the HM before heading upstream.

Facilities Water is available from a hose-pipe at the south end of catwalk staging—apply to HM (tel. Camber 225). Petrol and oil at Strand Quay. Hose-pipe at corner of catwalk above visitor's berth. Stores at Rye town 2 miles away (3.2 km) or (limited) in Rye Harbour where there is a chandlery or at a caravan site south of village by the Martello tower. EC Tues. PO at harbour and town. Small boat-builders. Launching site: slip

30. Looking downstream at low water. Harbour Master's office at the end of the staging.

with road access at Rye Harbour village, but is only usable for a few hours either side of HW (a power cable marked by beacons runs across near here to the lighthouse). Yacht club: Rye Harbour SC opposite Harbour Office. Station at Rye town. Bus service from Harbour to town, whence buses to all parts.

NEWHAVEN

Admiralty Chart No. 2154

High Water — *oo h. 13 m. Dover.*
Heights above Datum *MHWS 6m6. MLWS om6.*
MHWN 5m2. MLWN 1m9.
Depths *Dredged to 5m5 in the entrance, to 3mo along East
Wharf to Sleeper's Hole, 2m4 up to west side Ballast Wharf and not
less than 1m2 to bridge. Silting and dredging continually occurring.*

NEWHAVEN is primarily a commercial port but it also offers good
facilities for yachts in the marina dredged out of the west bank.
The town itself is not interesting, but the distance by bus to
Seaford or Eastbourne is short, and there are pleasant walks if
weather-bound. There is a regular ferry service to Dieppe.

Approach and Entrance   Newhaven harbour lies just over
7 miles west of Beachy Head, and 3 miles west of Seaford Head.
The town of Seaford is 5 miles westward of Beachy Head and for
some 2 miles west of Seaford the shore is low and shingly. At the
western end of Seaford Bay is Burrow Head, and just eastward at
the foot of this is Newhaven. The big breakwater at the entrance
is conspicuous and makes an easily recognizable landmark.

From the eastward stand well away from Seaford Head and
steer for position off Burrow Head. Alter course when the
entrance bears north, and leave to the westward the outer
breakwater, steering in towards the east pier, which is some 3
cables away. In bad weather, with an onshore wind, there is an
awkward sea off the entrance south of the breakwater. Steer up
mid-channel observing signals shown at southern end of west
pier. Within ½ mile of shore, the west-going stream starts about
1½ to 2 hours before HW.

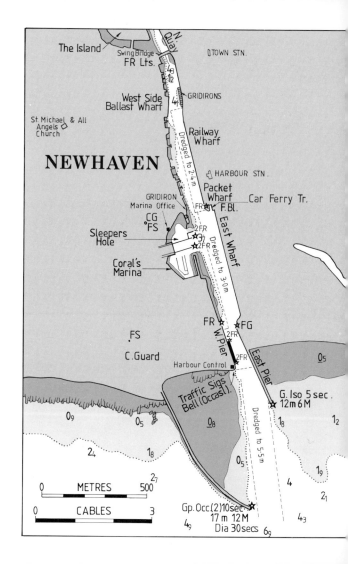

31. Newhaven, showing Marina on west side. (Photo : Aerofilms Ltd.)

32. *Newhaven breakwaters. Seaford Head in the distance.*

Signals Harbour control is located inside the breakwater at the western entrance to the harbour itself. Traffic is controlled by signals as follows:

	By day	*By night*
Entry permitted	R triangle over R ball	G all-round
Departure permitted	R ball over R triangle	R all-round
Free to move in or out	R ball	G Lt over R
No movement permitted	R ball over R triangle over R ball	Lts RGR (Vert)

Lights, etc. At end of outer (western) breakwater Lt Gp Occ (2) W 10 sec. 17m 12M; at end of east pier, Iso G Lt 5 sec. 12m 6M. Small F R Lt on west pier and F G on east pier, a cable inside entrance. Diaphone outer breakwater head ev 30 sec. Tide-gauge near base of lighthouse on west pier. When entering at night keep R Lt on Packet Wharf open between F R and F G Lts on west and east piers.

Anchorage and Berths (1) *Outside off Seaford* in settled weather, dangerous if wind shifts onshore. (2) All yachts should seek instructions from Harbour Watch-house on west side of harbour (call on VHF Ch 16). Space is limited. (3) Berthing and hauling out facilities are available in the *350-berth marina in Sleeper's Hole*, 3 cables within entrance on porthand side. Marina watch-house at head of southern marina jetty, or call on Ch 37 (Marina band).

Facilities Fuel and water from marina fuelling pontoon. Ship chandlers, and all stores obtainable. EC Wed. Yacht yard, yacht marina, gridirons and scrubbing hard. Launching site at Sleeper's Hole on application at Coral Marine. Yacht club: Newhaven & Seaford SC. Station and numerous buses to all parts.

BRIGHTON MARINA

Admiralty Chart No. 1991

High Water *at entrance as for Dover.*
Heights above Datum *MHWS 6m5. MLWS 0m7. MHWN 5m1. MLWN 1m9.*
Depths *Dredged to 2m5 at the entrance and along the middle of the fairway inside, shelving to 2m5 off the lock-gates. The inner (non-tidal) basin is maintained at 2m4.*

THIS IMPRESSIVE artificial harbour, which has been built out into the Channel from Black Rock 1 mile east of the Palace Pier, Brighton, is the biggest marina development in Europe. At present it provides berths for over 1,850 boats, with room for more. It is an accessible port of refuge for yachts making the passage from the Straits of Dover to the Solent.

Approach and Entrance The marina is enclosed by a $\frac{3}{4}$ mile long eastern breakwater and a western one which extends farther to seaward to protect the entrance from W to SSW. In strong winds from the SE the outer entrance can be very rough, but the double entrance, spending beach and wave screen ensure that it is always calm inside. The recommended all-weather approach is to line up the Lt at the head of the W breakwater with the broad white stripe on the high-rise hospital building on the skyline on a course of 300° (see plate 33). In westerly winds do not shape to cut close round the west pierhead, since waves tend to bounce back there.

Lights At the end of the west breakwater there is a Lt Qk Fl R 9½m 7M. At the end of the east breakwater there is the principal lighthouse Gp Fl (4) WR 20 sec. 16m 18M, with its red sector between 260° and 295°, white 295° through north to 100° and obscured elsewhere. In fog there is a diaphone (2) ev 30 sec. At the same point is a Qk Fl G 8m 7M and a Ro Bn call-sign BT on 303.4 kHz, range 10M.

The entrance channel is marked by four R can buoys to port. Nos 2 and 6 have Fl R 3 sec., while the second of the three G conical buoys to starboard has Fl G 3 sec. The inner pierheads are marked by 2 F R and 2 F G (vert) to port and starboard respectively. A bottle-shaped fairway buoy is moored 1 mile SSE of the entrance.

Harbour and Facilities The layout of the berths is shown

33. Brighton Marina. Best approach from south-east. Note prominent vertical stripe on seaward end of high-rise building.

on the plan opposite. In the tidal basin there are pontoon berths for boats up to 30m long with draughts ranging from 3m0 to 1m5. The HM will allocate berths on VHF Ch 37 or after the visitor has secured alongside the first pontoon on the porthand after entry. The fuelling pontoon is at the NE corner near the lock-gates to the non-tidal basin, boatyard and Travel-hoist. Inside the locked basin are berths for about 850 boats up to 18m long drawing 2m4. Between the two harbours there are car parks, chandlery, stores and most facilities. The Brighton Marina YC welcomes visitors. There is a brokerage service and space for winter lay-up. In Brighton there are all the amenities of a large seaside town, with regular fast trains to London and others along the South Coast.

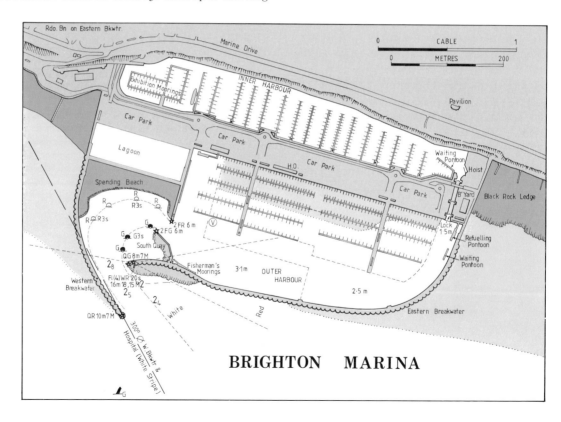

BRIGHTON   MARINA

SHOREHAM

Admiralty Chart No. 2044

High Water   − *oo h. o3 m. Dover.*
Heights above Datum *at entrance MHWS 6m2. MLWS om7. MHWN 5mo. MLWN 1m9.*
Depths   *The lowest charted depth in the approach is 1m7 LAT and 2m1 in the entrance. The dredged depths within the harbour are shown on the plan opposite, but these are liable to silting.*

SHOREHAM HARBOUR consists of a western arm which is the mouth of the River Adur, and a short eastern arm leading through lock gates to the Southwick Canal.

Superficially Shoreham is a good yachting harbour because, once through the locks into Southwick Canal, there are complete shelter and good facilities, and it is in easy reach of London. However, Shoreham is increasingly a very busy commercial port with little room left for casual visitors, so it is advisable that prior berthing arrangements are made by calling the HM on Ch 16 or by telephone (Brighton 592613). Arrival should be reported within 24 hours and there are strict speed limits and other regulations.

Approach and Entrance   Shoreham harbour entrance is about 4 miles west of Brighton Palace Pier. The most conspicuous landmarks are the twin chimneys (marked at night by red lights) of the power station about a mile east-north-east of the entrance. The entrance itself lies between two conspicuous concrete breakwaters. An unlit YB south cardinal buoy nearly 3 cables east-south-east of the entrance marks the outer end of a sewer outfall.

The shallowing water in the approach off the entrance can be very rough in strong winds if at all onshore, particularly on the ebb tide. Newhaven or Brighton are better ports of refuge.

The entrance lies between the two concrete breakwaters and within are east and west piers. Farther north there is a third pier (the middle pier) on the fork of the western and eastern arms.

The leading lights consist of a low light on the duty officer's hut at the end of the middle pier and a high light at rear from a grey circular tower. The structures are conspicuous leading marks by day and approach to the harbour is best made on their transit at 355°. A radio mast (49) is just to the left of the transit.

Off the entrance the west-going stream starts about 2 hours before HW and the east-going 6 hours later. During the west-going stream there is a south-west set across the entrance from the east breakwater towards the west breakwater, where part of it is deflected into the entrance and then north-east towards the end of the east pier. The eddy is strongest 1 hour before HW to ebb 1 hour after HW.

The maximum rate of the main stream at the harbour entrance is about 3 knots, but the flood sets into the western arm, where it can attain 4 knots, and the ebb 5 knots in some parts at springs. In the eastern arm there is practically no stream, but a yacht should be piloted with caution in the vicinity of the division off the middle pier.

The channel in the eastern arm is dredged and leads to the locks into the Southwick Canal. The western arm is only suitable for visiting yachts if able to take the ground. Traffic signals, given below, *must* be observed.

Controlling Signals   *Middle Pier Control Station*—Amber Lt Occ 3 sec. (day and night): entry is prohibited. Ships leaving harbour have priority. *Lifeboat House directed over Eastern Arm*—R Lt Occ 3 sec. (day and night): no movement permitted in the eastern arm. *Lifeboat House directed over Western Arm*—R Lt Occ 3 sec. (day and night): no movement permitted in the western arm.

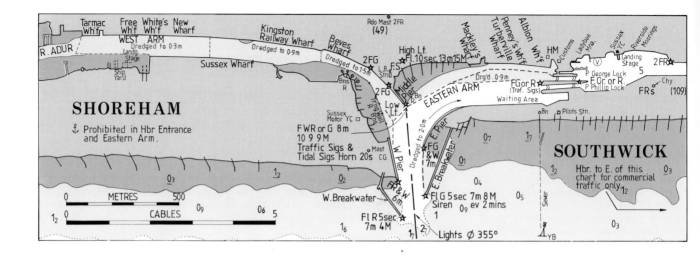

Signals at Locks No vessel may approach to enter the lock until a green pennant by day or a green light by night is exhibited at its outer end. Similarly no vessel may approach to leave until a yellow pennant by day or an amber light by night is exhibited near the inner end of the lock. If a black ball by day or a red light at night is exhibited no vessel may approach for the purpose of entering the lock or mooring at the lead-in. Instructions must be taken from the duty officer on the middle pier, who gives permission for yachts to anchor close to the eastward side of the middle pier, and await lock movements.

Tidal Signals Low light (middle pier) shows red when the tide level does not exceed 2m47 above chart datum; green when 2m47–3m69 of water above chart datum; white when more than 3m69 above chart datum.

Lights, etc. East breakwater Lt Fl G 5 sec. 7m 4M. West breakwater Lt Fl R 5 sec. 7m 4M. These breakwater lights are not always easy to pick up against the background of bright lights. Leading lights (in transit 355° true). High Lt (rear) Fl W 10 sec. 13m 15M. Low Lt (front) F W R or G (according to the height of the tide) 8m. 10, 9, 9M. *Fog Signals*. East breakwater: siren ev 2m. Middle pier: horn ev 20 sec. The latter is only sounded when ships are approaching.

Anchorages and Berths (1) *Outside* clear of fairway with offshore winds and settled weather in suitable depth of water, bottom mostly sand over clay or chalk. (2) Directions for berthing inside the harbour may be obtained from the duty officer on the middle pier at all times, but the Harbour Authority is virtually without berthing facilities of its own for yachts. As stated, prior

34. *Shoreham. West pierhead and middle pier.*

35. *Middle pier watch house, with lighthouse open to the right.*

berthing arrangements must be made with the local yards or clubs. *Western arm (all drying berths) :* James Taylor, Watercraft, Sussex Motor YC, Lighthouse Club. *Eastern arm :* Truslers. *Southwick Canal :* Riverside Yard, Ladybee, Sussex Yacht Club are all on the north side immediately inside the lock gates. Between them they have about 300 berths, most of them permanently occupied. Yachts should not proceed east of this point.

Facilities Water at yards or by courtesy at Sussex Yacht Club. Petrol and oil at local garage adjacent to Southwick Canal moorings as also yacht club, yards, gridiron and scrubbing. Launching sites from beach, adjacent to high lighthouse and middle pier, and from muddy public hards throughout the harbour. Yacht clubs: The Sussex YC, Sussex Motor YC, Lighthouse Club. Trains and frequent buses to Brighton and elsewhere.

LITTLEHAMPTON

Admiralty Chart No. 1991

High Water *at entrance* +*00 h. 04 m. Dover.*
Heights above Datum *MHWS 5m7. MLWS 0m5.*
MHWN 4m6. MLWN 1m7.
Depths *About 0m2 on bar, deepening between piers to about*
1m2 to 2m4, which depths are maintained almost as far as the
swingbridge.

LITTLEHAMPTON is a convenient harbour for yachts except for
the bar (0m2 but subject to change) which can only be crossed
with sufficient tide. Allowance has to be made for the strong
streams in the entrance, and it is dangerous to approach in strong
onshore winds. There are commercial shipping in the harbour
and good facilities for yachts, with the town close by. Half a mile
above the swingbridge a new bridge has been built, which has
about 3m6 headroom at MHWS, and the fixed railway bridge at
Ford has a clearance of 3m3 at HW. At Arundel a new road
bridge has been built ¼ mile downstream of the old bridge with a
clearance of 3m0 at MHWS. Craft which can pass under the
bridges can navigate as far as Arundel, with a least depth of 1m3
MLWS the whole way.

Approach and Entrance   The harbour is situated 10 miles
east of Selsey Bill. The entrance lies between two piers easily
recognizable from seaward and 2½ miles south-west is the Winter
Knoll YB south cardinal buoy (Qk Fl (6) + LFl 10 sec.). The
western pier is the longer, and at its seaward end is a red barrel
beacon. The eastern pier stops short at the esplanade, but there is
a low dickerwork continuation built in the sands for about ¼ mile
seaward. This is submerged from half tide to HW, but is marked

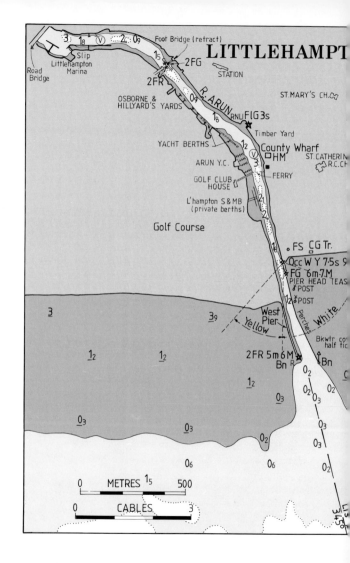

36. *Littlehampton entrance showing starboard hand beacon and posts marking submerged dickerwork.*

37. *Peppermill lighthouse at the root of east pier.*

by perches with small top crosses and at its extremity by a green unlit beacon with white triangular topmark. The leading marks for the entrance are the white peppermill-shaped lighthouse at the inshore end of the short east breakwater and the black steel column for the light at its outer end in transit at 345°. The iron column may be visible only when in line and against the white background of the lighthouse. Keep nearer the eastern side when entering, if the tide is setting on to the western pier. The tide is very fierce up the narrow harbour entrance. It turns to west along the shore nearly 2 hours before HW. Approach should not be

38. Littlehampton harbour office in line with chimney. Visiting yachts secure alongside it for instructions.

attempted in strong onshore winds and on the ebb tide the entrance can be very rough. Newhaven or Brighton are better ports of refuge.

Signals   When black-hulled pilot boat with large white 'P' at bow flies a R W flag by day or shows W over R Lts by night, all boats keep clear as a ship is about to enter or leave harbour. If ship signals one long and two short blasts, keep clear, particularly of narrows at entrance.

Lights   East pier front F G 6m 7M. Rear Occ W Or 7½ sec. 9m 10M. W 287° to 000° Y then to 042°. Lts in line 345°. West pier 2 F R 5m 6M.

Anchorage   (1) *Outside*, south of entrance at distance according to vessel's draught: This is slightly sheltered from the west by Selsey Bill and the Owers but is completely open from the south-west, through south to east-north-east. (2) Visiting yachts may secure temporarily *alongside County Wharf* on the east bank immediately above the ferry (which has right of way at all times). The HM whose office is on this wharf will then direct visitors to a berth, if one is available. Do NOT anchor in the fairway or secure to a pontoon berth on the west bank—they are privately owned, 100 of them by the Arun YC. The HM can be contacted by telephone on Littlehampton 21215/6. (3) There are visitors' berths kept clear at the *Littlehampton Marina* on the left bank beyond the retractable footbridge. Contact on Ch 37 (Marina band) or by telephone on Littlehampton 3553.

Facilities   Water, petrol or diesel from yards or the marina. All stores. EC Wed. Several yacht yards. Launching sites: light boats from hard sand foreshore on west side down river of the Arun YC. Yacht clubs: Arun YC, Littlehampton S & MB. Station. Good service of buses.

CHICHESTER HARBOUR

Admiralty Chart No. 3418

High Water *at entrance* $+oo$ *h. 11 m. Dover.*
Heights above Datum *MHWS 4m9. MLWS 0m7.
MHWN 4m0. MLWN 1m8.*
Depths *The water starts to shoal nearly a mile south of the
Chichester Bar Bn. On the correct approach the least water on the
bar is dredged to 1m0, but may vary from time to time. The entrance
itself is very deep and the main fairway not less than 2m4 as far as
Itchenor, except for a 1m2 patch just NE of the N Winner buoy.*

CHICHESTER HARBOUR is an ideal small boat centre, with over 17
miles of navigable water within its sheltered limits. There is
racing for all small classes, so it is hardly surprising that there are
more sailing clubs here than in any other South Coast harbour.
No less than 6,500 boats are based here, 1,750 of them alongside
in four marinas. Bosham, Emsworth, Itchenor and Birdham are
all attractive villages well worth visiting. There is an 8 kt speed
limit throughout the harbour.

The whole area is controlled by the Chichester Harbour
Conservancy through the Manager/Harbour Master at Itchenor.

Approach and Entrance The entrance to Chichester
harbour lies some 8 miles west of Selsey Bill. There are extensive
sands extending seaward on both sides of the approach and
entrance, named the West Pole, the Middle Pole and the East
Pole. With strong onshore winds there can be a very ugly sea on
the bar, especially on the ebb running $6\frac{1}{2}$ kts at springs when the
approach can be dangerous.

When approaching from east or west keep well offshore until
one or both of the conspicuous marks have been identified. The

39. *New Chichester Bar beacon with tide gauge.*

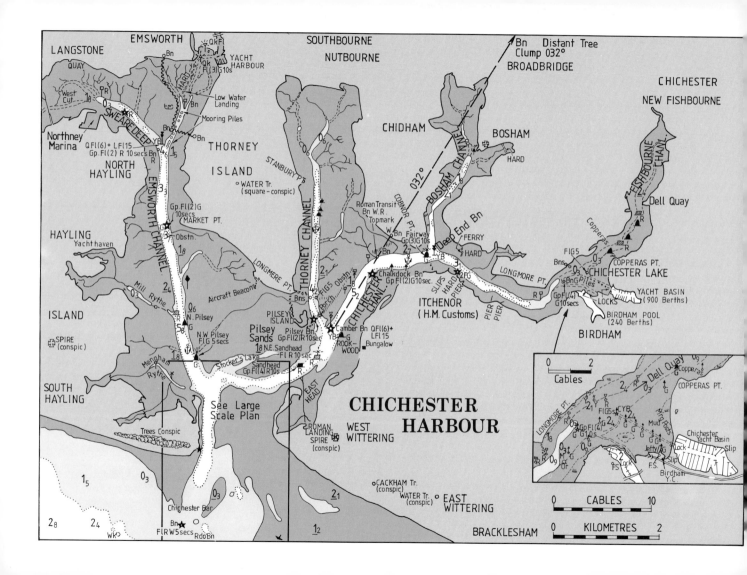

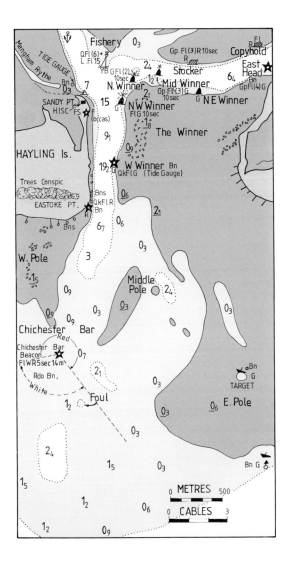

Nab Tower bearing 184° or Chichester Bar Beacon (Fl W R 5 sec. 14m) bearing 004°. It has a Ro Bn call-sign CH range 10M with coded wind information. Long dashes (1–8 clockwise starting at 1 for NE) and one short dot for each Beaufort wind Force. Then alter course for the beacon, which should be left close to port. In the approach the water shoals rapidly from 1 mile south of the beacon gradually falling to 1m5 at the beacon, where there is a tide-gauge which gives the level at chart datum. If the approach is made in thick weather the principal dangers are the East Pole sands, which extend over a mile south-east of the beacon, especially so when the stream is setting eastward.

When Chichester Bar Beacon is abeam, the entrance to Chichester harbour lies immediately east of Eastoke Point, just clear of the right-hand edge of the trees on the sandy point. The distance from $\frac{1}{2}$ cable east of the Chichester Bar Beacon to the entrance is about a mile making good a course of 013° on the West Winner Beacon (Qk Fl G). This course carries 1m0 and lies between the West Pole and the Middle Pole sands. The square tower on Thorney Island looking like a Norman church (actually a water-tower) should be right ahead. As Eastoke Point is approached the water becomes much deeper. Eastoke beacon (Qk Fl R) and small unlit beacons at the ends of groynes will be left to port and course may soon be altered to follow up the entrance channel between the steep shingle shore on the port hand and the wide expanse of the Winner sands on the starboard hand. These dry at LW and are marked by the West Winner beacon and the North-west Winner buoy (Fl 10 sec.). In the entrance channel the tidal streams are fierce and may attain 2.8 knots on the flood or 6.4 knots on a big spring ebb about 2 hours after HW.

Within the entrance the channel divides into two arms. One leads in a northerly direction to Emsworth and is entered between Sandy Point and the Fishery buoy. It is wide and deep nearly as far as the junction with Sweare Deep, where there is the YB south cardinal Emsworth beacon (Qk Fl (6) + L Fl 15 sec.) Beyond this

40. *Hayling Island SC and Sandy Point.*

the channel is shallow and dried out at LW about ½ mile below the town. The other arm bears round the north side of the Winner to the eastward and leads via the Chichester Channel to Itchenor, the Bosham Channel and to Dell Quay.

To enter the Chichester Channel (after passing Hayling Island Sailing Club and Sandy Point on the west side) bear to starboard to the eastward to leave to starboard the North-west Winner (Fl G ev 10 sec.), the G conical North Winner (Fl (6) G 10 sec.), the Mid Winner (Gp Fl (3) G 10 sec.) conical buoys and the East Head beacon (Fl (4) G 10 sec.) with tide-gauge. There is a shoal patch 1m5 close north-north-east of the North Winner buoy but otherwise the channel is from 2m4 to 7m deep. Leave to port the following red can buoys: Stocker (Gp Fl (3) R 10 sec.), Copyhold (unlit) and Sandhead (Fl (4) R 10 sec.).

The next pair of buoys are the North-east Sandhead (Fl R 10 sec.) to port and the G Rookwood buoy to starboard. East of the NE Sandhead buoy the channel bears to the north-east, where

identify and bring Roman Transit beacon (R port hand daymark) in transit with the main channel beacon (white rectangular daymark) on the shore on 032° with Stoke Clump, a conspicuous clump of trees on the distant downs. If it is too misty to see these landmarks it does not matter, for the channel is clearly marked on the port hand by the YB south cardinal Camber beacon (Qk Fl (6) + LFl 15 sec.) at the entrance of the Thorney Channel and on the starboard hand by the Chalkdock beacon (Fl (2) G 10 sec.) and by occasional perches, though these are situated high up on the mud and should be given a wide berth near low water.

After passing the Chalkdock beacon alter course to round the G conical starboard hand Fairway buoy (Gp Fl (3) G 10 sec.) at the junction of the Bosham and Chichester Channels. The former buoy moored at the entrance to Bosham Lake has been replaced by the YB south cardinal junction beacon which is a starboard hand mark for the Bosham Channel and a port hand one for the Itchenor Reach. This channel is deep almost as far as

74

41. East Head beacon.

42. Itchenor landing pontoon. Harbour Master's office in white building. His launch in foreground.

Longmore Point about a mile east of Itchenor, where it then shallows but is marked by buoys.

The Bosham Channel carries 1m8 to within 2 cables of the quay at the village and is marked by R and G perches.

The Thorney Channel is entered by leaving the Camber beacon to starboard, and then leaving Pilsey Island R beacon (Fl (2) R 10 sec.) to port and a G perch to starboard; neither should be passed close to. Then pass between a pair of beacons beyond which the channel is straight and marked by R and G perches. Depths range from 3m7 down to 1m8 to north-east of Stanbury Point.

Lights Chichester Bar beacon carries at Lt Fl W R 5 sec. 14m 8M showing W from 322° to 080° and R elsewhere. Approach in the white sector and leave the beacon ½ cable to port. Then steer 013° for the West Winner beacon (Qk Fl G). After passing the Eastoke beacon porthand light (Qk Fl R) alter course up the entrance channel and proceed referring to the lights already stated in the text and shown in the harbour plans.

Anchorages and Berthing (1) In westerly winds just within the entrance north of *Sandy Point* outside local moorings. (2) *Off East Head*, beyond the beacon. Pleasant anchorage on sandy bottom in settled weather, but very crowded in summer and rather exposed except from south and east. A shallow creek marked by perches leads to the Roman Landing and West Wittering SC. (3) *In Chichester Channel* on the south of the channel leading to the Fairway buoy. (4) At *Itchenor* visiting yachts up to 10 tons should moor temporarily at the visitor's buoy (white with red band) opposite the HM's office. Contact on VHF Ch 16 or telephone Birdham 512301. The HM or his deputy will then allocate a vacant mooring of which some are usually available. (5) *In the marinas at Birdham Pool or the Chichester Yacht Basin*. Allow for sufficient tide as the main channel dries out at MLWS soon after passing Longmore Point. The 250-berth Birdham Pool is normally accessible at half tide. To reach

43. Bosham Creek and church.

it, leave the G Birdham Bn (Gp Fl (4) G 10 sec.) to port and the line of unlit perches leading to the lock-gates close to starboard, disregarding another line farther off the retaining wall, since they point the way to the Birdham YC slip. To reach the 950-berth Chichester Yacht Basin, continue up channel from the Birdham Bn for a further 2 cables to the G Yacht Basin Bn (Fl G 5 sec.), then leave close to starboard the six G piles leading to the lock. This channel is dredged to 1m1. Depths inside both these marinas may vary from time to time, so yachts drawing 2m0 or more must seek directions for berthing at the lock-gates. Both marinas have all the facilities expected of a major yacht harbour. (6) *Bosham Lake.* This historic village is charming, but the creek is full of private moorings and it dries out within 2 cables of the quay. Apply locally or to the HM at Itchenor for temporary facilities or to dry out alongside. There is a public slip on which to leave a dinghy. (7) *Thorney Channel* provides a well-protected

44. *Birdham Pool. Approach to lock close alongside sea wall. (Photo: Sealand Aerial Photography)*

45. *Chichester Yacht Harbour showing piles along approach channel. (Photo: Sealand Aerial Photography)*

46. *Old Bosham at high water. Quay on the left on north shore. (Photo : Sealand Aerial Photography)*

anchorage where space can be found. Facilities ashore are limited to those provided by the Thorney Island SC. The island is under Ministry of Defence control, so that permission must be obtained at the guardroom for access by road. (8) *The Emsworth Channel* is suitable for anchoring almost anywhere on the east side as far as its junction with Sweare Deep, but keep clear of the west side due to private moorings and Fishery Orders. Beyond the YB south cardinal Emsworth Bn (Qk Fl (6) + LFl ev 15 sec.) there are pile moorings in trots on the portland for shoal draught boats. At the NE end of the channel is the Emsworth Yacht Harbour (220 berths). It is advisable to call Emsworth 5211 to check availability and depths at the entrance, which vary between 2m7 at springs and 2m5 at neaps. (9) *The Northney Marina* at the northern end of Hayling Island just short of the Langstone Bridge has 200 berths for boats drawing 1m2. Tel. Hayling Island 5269.

Port Operation   Port Operation and Information Service on VHF Ch 16, HM launch call-sign REGNUM. Details from the HM's Office, Itchenor. Tel. Birdham 512301, or from the useful Chichester Harbour Guide (50p).

Facilities   At Itchenor there are yacht yards and marine engineers. Landing and water by hose at the floating jetty, where there is a tide-gauge. H. C. Darnley & Sons supply chandlery and will fill petrol cans. No shops. The Ship Inn has six bedrooms and a restaurant; some provisions for visitors are available in summer. All facilities from both marinas at Birdham. Occasional buses to Chichester. At Bosham yacht yards and sailmaker, PO and shops. EC Thurs. Buses to Chichester and Portsmouth. In the Emsworth Channel yacht yards at Mengham Rythe and Mill Rythe. Emsworth itself is a small town where there is the yacht harbour and all facilities. EC Wed. Station and buses.

Launching sites: (1) from public hards at end of roads at Itchenor, Bosham, Dell Quay and Emsworth, with car parks near by. (2). Near HW at the north-east side of Hayling Bridge at the slipway administered by the Langstone SC and also at Birdham YC and Dell Quay. (3) at Sandy Point by permission from the Hayling Island SC. (4) At Emsworth from public hard or Emsworth Yacht Harbour. Yacht clubs: Birdham YC, Bosham SC, Chichester Cruising Club (Itchenor), Chichester YC (Birdham), Dell Quay SC, Emsworth SC, Hayling Island SC, Itchenor SC, Langstone SC, Mengham Rythe SC, West Wittering SC, Thorney Island SC.

LANGSTONE HARBOUR

Admiralty Charts Nos 3418 and 2050

High Water *+oo h. 14 m. Dover.*
Heights above Datum *at entrance approx: MHWS 4m8.
MLWS om6. MHWN 3m9. MLWN 1m8.*
Depths *The entrance varies, but there is not less than 2mo
except over the bar between the East and West Winner sands. Within
the harbour over 2m in main channels.*

LANGSTONE HARBOUR is a fine area especially for centreboard
boats. There is also plenty of water for cruising yachts in the main
channels, though there are no deep anchorages immediately off
villages with facilities.

Approach and Entrance The entrance to Langstone
Harbour may be located by the high chimney on its west side, but
the channel leading to it lies between the extensive West and East
Winner sands. The RW Fairway buoy (Fl 10 sec.) is situated
about a mile offshore on Langstone Bar with a depth of 1m7 on a
shoal close north-east of the buoy. The shoals and sands are liable
to change. Approach from the west may be made either from the
direction of the Horse Sand Fort or through the gap in the
submerged barrier a mile north of the fort. In either case bring
the Horse Sand Fort into line with the No Man's Land Fort on a
stern transit of 235° which leads to the isolated danger BRB
beacon SW of the entrance. Least water on this course is 1m8
between the BRB Bn and the Langstone Fairway buoy.

If taking the short cut from the Portsmouth direction pass
through the gap in the submerged barrier. The gap lies nearly a
mile south of Lumps Fort on the Eastney shore and is marked by
a dolphin Qk Fl R on the south side. Keep close to the dolphin in

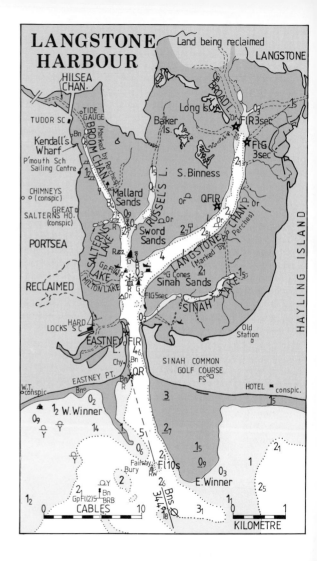

47. *Langstone Harbour west side of entrance including old ferry pontoon.*

1m2 as there is an obstruction on the north-north-west side. Then make good a course of 090° until picking up the back transit of the big forts on 235°.

If approaching from the eastward the danger lies in the East Winner sand, which dries out nearly ½ mile south-east of the Fairway buoy, and has an extension of shoal water with only 0m4 even a mile south-east of the Fairway buoy. The YB south cardinal East Winner buoy is about 4 cables south of the shoal. The buoy should be left to northward and the course should not be altered until the Fairway buoy bears north true which just clears the edge of the East Winner shoal (1m8). Under reasonable conditions Langstone is an easy harbour to enter but the approaches can be dangerous in strong onshore winds, especially near LW on the ebb; the roughest part of all in southerly winds lies about a cable north-north-east of the Fairway buoy, 2 hours after HW when the ebb is at its maximum rate.

On arrival off the Fairway buoy two dolphins will be seen on the west side of the harbour entrance. The beacons on these dolphins in transit at 344° lead clear to the east of the bar, but usually a course can be shaped for a position midway between the dolphins and the Hayling Island shore. The edge of the channel to the entrance is steep-to in places on the east side and thus constitutes a danger when the sands are covered at high water. When in the entrance with land on either hand there is plenty of water, but the streams run very hard in this bottleneck. Once within the harbour alter course to the desired anchorage. With the tide right small craft without masts can pass under Hayling road bridge (2m1 clearance MHWS) to Chichester harbour.

Lights Fairway buoy Fl ev 10 sec. Qk Fl R on outer beacon in entrance and Fl R near Ferry House at north end of the west

81

48. *East side of entrance.*

side of entrance. Three cables within the harbour there are the port hand East Milton buoy Gp Fl (4) R 10 sec. and the starboard hand north-west Sinah buoy Fl G 5 sec. One mile up the Langstone Channel there is a Qk Fl R and a further mile on a Fl R ev 3 sec. and Fl G ev 3 sec. marking the point where the channel splits.

Anchorage and Facilities (1) There are four round white visitors' buoys for temporary use *on the east side of the entrance* near the northern end and just south of the cable beacons. These are adjacent to the HM's office on Hayling Island. Seek his advice for vacant moorings (tel. Hayling Island 3419). Close by there is a water point for filling cans. There is a boatyard where petrol or diesel fuel can be obtained or direct by dinghy about 1½ hours either side of HW. Other facilities are the Ferry Boat Inn, a café and general store. Launching site at slip. Bus service to Hayling

village (EC Wed.) and Havant. Frequent ferries to Eastney in summer, thence bus to Portsmouth. (2) *The Eastney Cruising Association* on east side of entrance (see harbour plan) has two fair-weather visitors' moorings (fierce tide for about an hour about 2 hours after HW); riding light necessary at night. The club is a do-it-yourself concern and hospitable; bar and meals in sailing season. Public launching site at end of road near ferry pontoon. Buses to Portsmouth in summer. (3) *Anywhere* that can be found on the edges of the main channel out of the fairway (which is used by ballast dredgers) and clear of moorings. (4) *Langstone Channel*, although far from facilities, provides plenty of room to anchor in depths ranging from 5mo to 2mo east of South Binness Island. (5) *Eastney Lake* dries out and is full of moorings for craft which can take the mud at LW. The Locks SC has a club house and concrete slip, and there is a general store up

49. Eastney Cruising Association clubhouse. Has two visitors' moorings.

the road. Plans have been approved for a marina in Eastney Lake and the development is under consideration.

Launching sites from the foreshore at the end of the roads leading to the ferry on either side of the entrance, preferably at slack water as the tides run very hard. Car parks adjacent. Other yacht club: Tudor SC on west of Broom Channel.

PORTSMOUTH HARBOUR

Admiralty Charts Nos 2625 and 2631

High Water   + *oo h. 14 m. Dover.*
Heights above Datum *MHWS 4m7. MLWS om6. MHWN 3m8. MLWN 1m8. Flood 7 hours. Ebb 5 hours.*
Depths   *The entrance and main harbour are a deep ship channel. The Fareham Channel has 7 to 9m at the entrance, gradually shallows, and there is little water off Fareham ; Portchester Channel is also deep as far as junction with Tipner Lake but variable in the Portchester reach.*

PRIMARILY a naval port, Portsmouth is not without interest. It is a safe and convenient port with a 250-berth marina on the Gosport side, backed by top boat-building and repair facilities.

The upper reaches and channels provide good small boat sailing. There is a speed limit of 10 kts within 900m of the shore in any part of the dockyard port. Water ski-ing is not permitted within the harbour. Boats with engines must use them from the Southsea War Memorial until clear inside the harbour.

Approach and Entrance   From the eastward the approach is simple, being buoyed for big ships from the YB south cardinal Outer Spit buoy inward, as shown on the chart. From the westward leave Gilkicker Pt a cable to port, then pass 2 cables south of Spit Sand Fort, where course can be altered direct to the deep channel inshore of the Outer Spit buoy. A short cut across the Spit Sand giving 1m8 at MLWS ½ mile west of the Spit Sand Fort is by bringing into transit on 048° the War Memorial on Southsea front with the spire of St Jude's Church. Another swashway available (with sufficient tide above om3 at LAT) lies across the Hamilton Bank by keeping the western edge of the Round Tower on the Portsmouth side of the harbour entrance in line with the left-hand edge of a conspicuous tank at 029½°.

50.   Southsea War Memorial and St Jude's church spire open to the right.

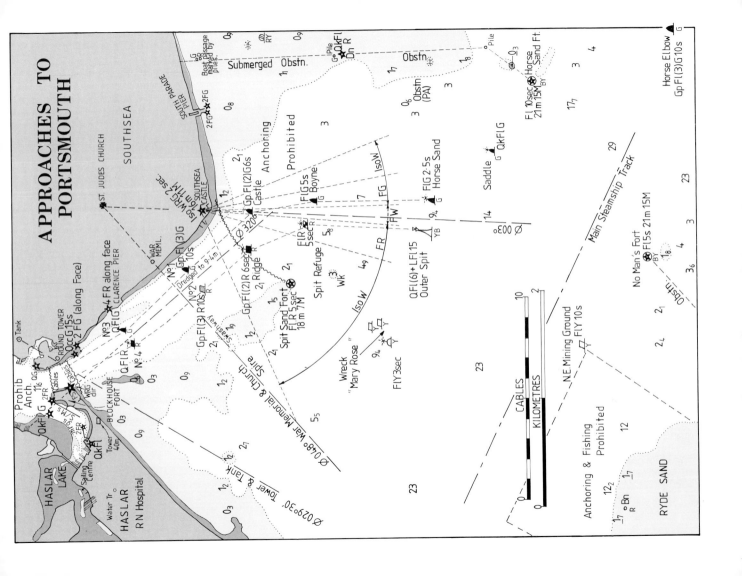

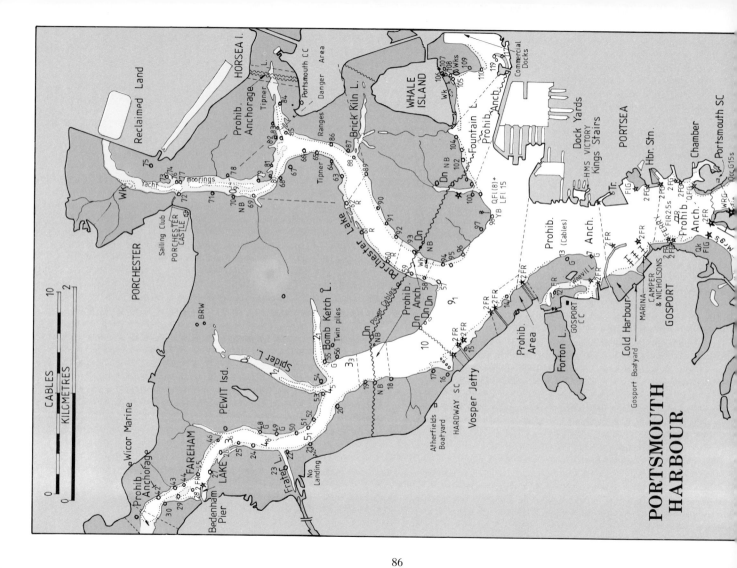

PORTSMOUTH HARBOUR

51. Old Portsmouth at the eastern side of harbour entrance.

In the entrance itself the tides are very strong. The flood runs easy for 3 hours, strong for 4 hours; the ebb easy 1 hour, strong for from 2 to 3 hours, and then easy.

Vessels approaching inshore from the eastward may pass through the gap in the submerged barrier. The gap is about a mile south of Lumps Fort and is marked by a dolphin (Qk Fl R) on the south. Many of the piles on the barrier have been removed, but the remains and many submerged concrete blocks still constitute a danger.

Haslar Creek running SW from Fort Blockhouse near the harbour entrance is full of private moorings and pontoon berths at the Joint Services Sail Training Centre just upstream from the Submarine Memorial (HMS *Alliance*).

Fareham Lake   About 1½ miles from the entrance, Portsmouth harbour divides into two channels. The westward of the two is Fareham Lake. On the eastern side of the entrance to this creek there are three large big-ship mooring dolphins. A number of mooring buoys are placed on either side in the first reach, and above this the channel is marked by posts on the mud on either bank; red posts to port, green to starboard. Where the

Portchester Channel joins the Fareham Channel, there is the red No. 57 port hand beacon. At the end of the NNW channel—over 3 miles up—is the town of Fareham, but for a mile below this there is little water at low tide. This part of the channel between the R piles Nos 18 and 19 is a prohibited anchorage, until the Reach bends to the north-west for over ½ mile before turning northward towards Fareham. The channel continues to be marked by piles. Yachts up to 1m8 draught can proceed to Fareham Quay 2 hours either side of HW after passing under power cables with 19m clearance below them.

Portchester Lake   This is the eastern arm referred to above. It is a wide channel, running near the entrance in a north-easterly direction, but there are several bends to be negotiated before it leads to the village and the ruins of the castle at Portchester. The navigation marks are the same as in Fareham creek, by posts (red posts port, green starboard) but do not approach these closely. Strangers may find as little as 0m4 LAT in parts of the Portchester reach, particularly near Nos 80 and 79 posts. The danger area in Portchester Lake from Tipner Ranges is shown on the harbour plan. Red flags are flown at the butts when firing is in progress and yachts are requested to pass through the area as quickly as possible.

Fountain Lake to the north and east of the Royal Dockyard is in constant use by continental ferries and should be used only by yachts with berths at the Whale Island naval sailing centre.

Lights The approach and entrance to Portsmouth harbour are, of course, clearly marked by lights, which are shown on the chart.

Signals Signals are displayed at Central Signal Station, Fort Blockhouse, or Gilkicker Signal Station or in HM ships as appropriate.

1. *Day.* Red flag with white diagonal bar. *Night.* R Lt over two G Lts Vert. No vessel is to leave the harbour or any of its creeks or lakes or approach north of Outer Spit buoy.

2. *Day.* Red flag with white diagonal bar over one black ball. No vessel is to enter the harbour channel or approach channel from seaward. Outgoing vessels may proceed.

3. *Day.* One black ball over red flag with white diagonal bar. No vessel shall leave the harbour. Ingoing traffic may use the harbour channel and enter Portsmouth harbour.

4. *Day.* Large black pendant. *Night.* W Lt over two R Lts Vert. No vessel to anchor in the Man-of-War anchorages at Spithead.

5. *Day.* International Code Pendant superior to Pendant zero. Keep clear of HM ships under way.

6. *Day.* International Code Pendant superior to Pendant 9. *Night.* Three G Lts Vert. HM ship under way. Give wide berth.

7. *Day.* International Code Pendant superior to Flags NE. *Night.* G over R Lt. Proceed with great caution. Ships (other than car ferries) leaving Camber.

8. *Day.* Flag E. *Night.* R over amber Lt. Submarine entering or leaving Haslar lake. Keep clear.

9. *Day.* International Code Pendant superior to Flag A. *Night.*

Two R Lts H. Have divers down.

Anchorages, etc. Portsmouth harbour and its approaches are under the jurisdiction of the Queen's Harbour Master, tel. Portsmouth 22351, ext. 2008. Boats over 20m may not move without his permission on Ch 11 or 13. (1) *Haslar lake.* No room to anchor, bottom foul. Private moorings mostly for services personnel. Apply to RNSA, or Joint Services Sailing Centre adjacent Haslar Bridge, to ask whether a mooring may be temporarily vacant. Small power boats and shoal draught yachts with lowering masts can proceed under the bridge into Alverstoke Lake where there is room to anchor. (2) *Camper & Nicholson's Marina.* Enquire on VHF Ch 37 or at fuel barge or visitors' berths at end of No. 3 pontoon. All facilities including building and repairs. Also moorings for very large yachts. (3) Just above C. & N. Marina there are the Gosport Borough yacht moorings in *the Cold Harbour* with sets of double moorings let annually. Enquire at Gosport boatyard premises on the quay whether a set is temporarily vacant. (4) *Gosport Cruising Club, Weevil Lake* – apply at Club H.Q. boat for possible temporary mooring. (5) *Hardway.* All available space occupied by moorings. Hardway Sailing Club is hospitable and welcomes visitors from other clubs; it maintains a trot of five fore and aft visitors' moorings off the pontoon and can advise whether any other moorings are temporarily available. The public hard and pontoon landing stage are the only landing places in the vicinity. Club scrubbing piles and launching site, fuels, chandlery and inn are adjacent with short walk to boatyard, shops, restaurant and buses. (6) On east side of harbour entrance is *the Camber*, a small commercial harbour not too suitable for visiting yachts. Permission to berth must first be obtained from the Dock Master at the entrance. Facilities within include yacht yards, sailmaker and chandlery. (7) *Fareham Lake.* Anchorage now full of private moorings. Temporary moorings off Wicor Marine (and launching site near HW); enquire at yard (tel. Fareham 237112)

52.   *The entrance to Camper & Nicholson's marina lies between the fuel jetty and the dolphin. The Cold Harbour and Gosport Borough marinas lie just beyond Camper & Nicholson's.*

whether any mooring vacant. Near Fareham Quay, yacht builder, chandler, launching site at public slipway. Shops, banks, hotel, restaurants, etc. at Fareham. EC Wed. Station and buses. (8) With reduction of danger area from Tipner Ranges, *Spider Lake and Bomb Ketch Lake* are now full of moorings but have no facilities—the nearest being at Hardway or Wicor. (9) *Portchester.* Anchorage difficult as fairway must be kept clear for hovercraft and all available space near Portchester SC is occupied by moorings. Apply to duty officer at club for possibility of temporary use of a mooring. If one is available, the historic castle will be found interesting and facilities are quite good. Club, inn, small shops, club scrubbing and launching site at Portchester hard but often fully booked up and hardly approachable at summer weekends. EC Tues, some Wed. (10) *Portsmouth Cruising Club* has drying moorings and the usual facilities, but no shops near and ½ mile (0.8 km) walk to buses.

Facilities   At Gosport and Portsmouth there are first-rate facilities and shops of every kind. EC Wed at both towns, Southsea Sat. Express rail service from Portsmouth Town or Harbour stations. Ferries and hovercraft to Ryde, I.W. Car ferries to Wooton, I.W., from Camber. Good bus services. Launching sites: (1) Portsmouth from car ferry slip provided ferries are not obstructed; the position is congested during the summer months. (2) From hard in Gosport Borough marina adjacent to Gosport boatyard office, with very limited public car parking near. (3) At hard of Gosport Cruising Club in Weevil Lake 3 hours either side of HW. New public dinghy landing on reclaimed section between C. & N. and Gosport Ferry pontoon. Yacht clubs: R. Albert YC. *Ports 25924,* RNSA, *Ports 23524,* Portsmouth SC, *Ports 20596,* Hardway SC, *Gosport 81875,* Portsmouth Harbour CC, *Ports 64337,* Portchester SC, *Cosham 76375,* Fareham S. & MBC, *Fareham 80738,* Gosport CC.

53. *Upper reaches of Portsmouth harbour. Fountain Lake and Whale Island to the right. Portchester and Fareham Creeks in the distance. (Photo: Aerofilms Ltd.)*

54. *Camper & Nicholson's Marina at Gosport. (Photo: Sealand Aerial Photography)*

BEMBRIDGE HARBOUR

Admiralty Charts Nos 394 or 2050

High Water + *00 h. 14 m. Dover.*
Heights above Datum *in Harbour MHWS 3m1. MHWN 2m3. MLWS 0m3. MLWN 0m4.*
Depths *There are extensive sands which dry at LW but there is always some water (0m2 to 0m6) left flowing out of the actual channels. Within the harbour there are depths of 1m3 at the entrance down to 0m3 in the main channel, but the water is impounded by the bar from about 1 hour before to 2 hours after LWS. Dredged area at St Helen's Marina.*

BEMBRIDGE is a charming harbour at the east end of the Island. The marked channel is approached from the north and lies to the west of St Helen's Fort. The entrance itself is protected from westerly and southerly winds. However there is little room for visiting yachts in its shallow harbour, but there is a small marina at St Helen's.

Approach and Entrance The approach to Bembridge harbour is made from a north-east direction to a yellow beacon with an X topmark 1¾ cables west of St Helen's Fort. The beacon has a tide-gauge which indicates the least depth in the channel between Nos 8 and 9 buoys. It should be left close to port before picking up the channel between the buoys, small G Con to starboard and R cans to port, but do not pass too close to the buoys, especially No. 8. The channel between this buoy and No. 9 is narrow, but deeper at No. 11 starboard hand buoy. Within the harbour gradually bear to starboard to pass between No. 13 G buoy and No. 10 R can buoy and then follow the shallow buoyed channel to St Helen's.

55. *Bembridge light beacon with tide gauge—to be left to port.*
(Photo : George Denny)

Lights St Helen's Fort Gp Fl (3) 10 sec., 16m 8M. The tide gauge beacon west of St Helen's Fort (Qk Fl. Y). Entry at night should not be attempted without local knowledge as there are no lights on the buoys.

Berths, Moorings and Anchorages Anchoring within the harbour is prohibited. Proceed up the buoyed fairway to St Helen's quay and marina, with alongside pontoon berths drawing 1m2 to 1m8 at springs, or lie alongside the quay by arrangement and dry out where there is soft mud in parts.

Twin-keel shoal draught boats can dry out on the port hand of the entrance, on the beach near Bembridge Pt, but the beach is soon filled up at weekends during the season.

Moorings for visiting vessels are very limited and are all privately owned. Applications should be made before arrival to book one on VHF Ch 37 or by telephone on Bembridge 2423 or through the HM on 2828. Vessels should never pick up vacant moorings without prior arrangement.

Anchorage is prohibited within 1 cable of St Helen's Fort but can be found to the north of the fort while waiting sufficient tide to enter the channel, or elsewhere according to weather and depths. In winds between west and south there is good anchorage eastward of Bembridge off Under Tyne outside local moorings, but the landing is rough and it is $\frac{1}{2}$ mile walk to the harbour.

Facilities   There are several good yacht yards and marine engineers. Water by hose and diesel oil, etc., at marina, with Brading Harbour YC adjacent (which welcomes temporary members); shops and PO $\frac{1}{4}$ mile distant at St Helen's. Diesel oil is also supplied by Harbour Engineering at the sheds $\frac{1}{4}$ mile east of BHYC and both diesel and petrol at their embankment premises next to Coombes yard. There are hotels and restaurants, small shops. EC Thurs. Buses to all parts of the Island. Launching sites at concrete ramp near St Helen's seamark, or by arrangement with yards or clubs. Yacht clubs: Bembridge SC, Brading Harbour YC.

56.   *St Helen's Fort.*

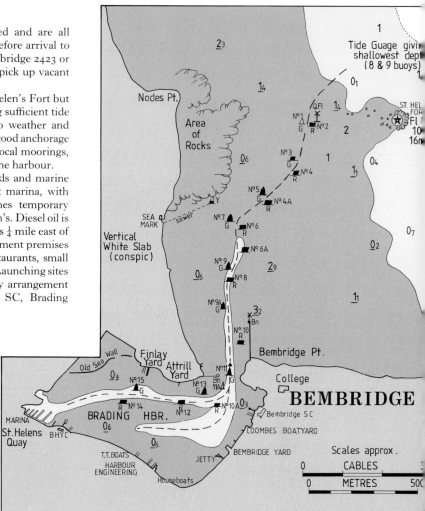

WOOTTON CREEK

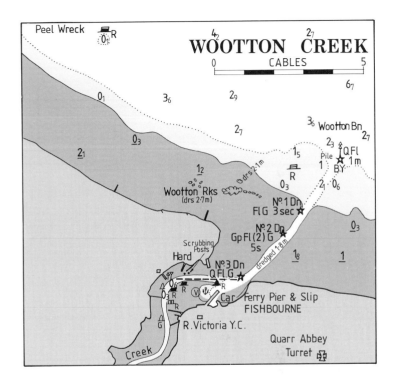

Admiralty Chart No. 394

High Water *+00 h. 14 m. Dover.*
Heights above Datum *MHWS 4m5. MLWS 0m7.*
MHWN 3m6. MLWN 1m7.
  Depths *The channel is dredged to 1m8 up to the ferry slipway.*
Basin dries LAT on soft mud. In the river there is only 0m6 to 0m3.

WOOTTON CREEK is a pretty but overcrowded harbour shared by yachts and the Fishbourne car ferries. The entrance is normally easy to identify and navigate.

Approach and Entrance The entrance to the Creek is clearly marked by a BY north cardinal outer pile and three G dolphins. Make for the outer pile, leaving this and the other three dolphins to starboard. The dredged channel is very narrow and very busy in summer months. Ferries have absolute priority in the dredged channel. When the yacht comes to the third dolphin she may stand on for the end of the ferry pier, leaving this very close to port and with sufficient rise of tide enter the bight situated north-west of the ferry pier. Here she will find anchorage and moorings belonging to the Royal Victoria YC with Berthing Master in attendance. Visiting yachtsmen are welcome. To sail up the river proceed from No. 3 dolphin, turning slowly to starboard on to the 270° transit of leading marks, which consist of two white triangles on the west foreshore near a boathouse. The channel is marked by G buoys to starboard and R buoys to port round the next bend. The channel is narrow, and strangers should be careful not to run on to or cross the finger of mud shown on the harbour plan on the port side of the channel between the Creek channel and the bight moorings. A R buoy sits

on this spit. There are a slip and dinghy park on the starboard side of the Creek just south of the boatyards.

Lights The north cardinal Wootton Bn has a Qk Fl. No. 1 Bn is Fl G 3 sec.; No. 2 is Gp Fl (2) G 5 sec.; No. 3 is Qk Fl G.

Anchorage There is reasonable anchorage in settled weather and offshore winds outside the Creek to north-west of

57. *Wootton beacon at the seaward end of the approach to channel. (Photo : George Denny)*

the pile beacon at the entrance. Within the Creek the only anchorage for boats up to say 1m5 lies in the bight beyond the ferry pier, well clear of the ferries' approach and turning area. Here it dries out at LAT, but yachts sit upright in very soft mud. Anchors should be buoyed. There are also many moorings but it is best to obtain advice from the Berthing Master, who usually meets incoming yachts and directs them to a berth. He can be contacted by phone at Wootton Bridge (0983) 882325.

Shallow draught vessels, which can take the mud, will find room to anchor up river, but there are many moorings in the best parts.

Facilities   At Fishbourne there are an inn and garage, and the R. Victoria YC club house. This club has good facilities with hard, car park, changing rooms, bar and club boatman. Visiting yachts are welcome and temporary membership is available to members of recognized yacht clubs. At Wootton, $\frac{3}{4}$ mile up the river or a mile's walk from Fishbourne, there are three boatyards, garage (water and petrol), PO, shops, inn. EC Thurs. Launching sites: from ferry hard or yacht club by arrangement. Frequent buses from Wootton Bridge to Ryde and Newport.

COWES

Admiralty Chart No. 2793

High Water + *oo h. 14 m. Dover.*

Heights above Datum *MHWS 4m2. MLWS om6. MHWN 3m5. MLWN 1m7.*

Depths *The River Medina has a least depth of 2m1 in the fairway from the entrance as far up as Medham beacon, ½ mile short of the Folly Inn, when depths reduce to om6, getting steadily shallower thereafter. The river dries out on the last 1¼ miles to Newport.*

Cowes is famous as the principal yacht racing centre in the world, and is the headquarters of the Royal Yacht Squadron. It is a town of tradition and character that time has little changed and is the most conveniently placed harbour in the Solent. There is always room to bring up, and the harbour is well protected except from the north and north-east.

Approach and Entrance The entrance is a particularly simple one and well marked. The fairway lies on the west side of the entrance, and is marked by the port hand R (No. 4) light buoy (Fl R 5 sec.) and the unlit starboard hand G Con (No. 3) buoy; in the harbour there are two R port hand buoys of which No. 8 is Qk Fl R.

Approaching from the east, to clear the Shrape Mud near LW steer to the Trinity House buoy (Fl Y ev 2 sec.) and then keep on

58. *The Castle at Cowes, home of the Royal Yacht Squadron.*

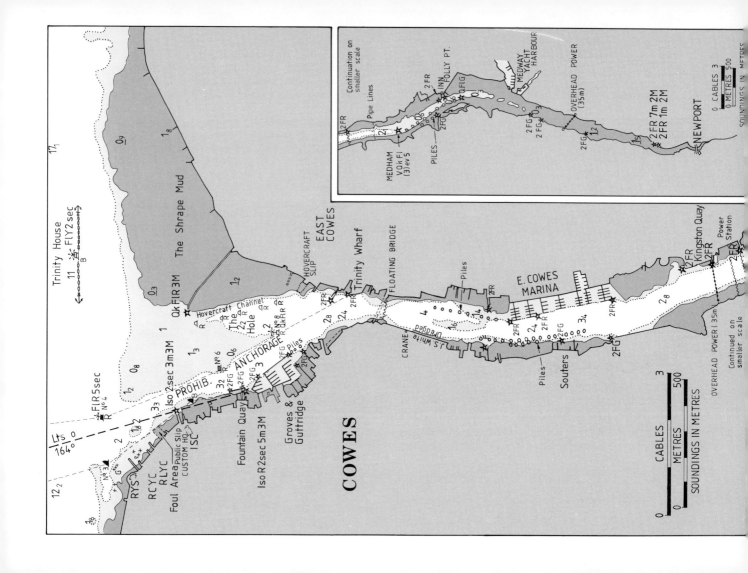

COWES

Trinity House
11 ☼ FIY2sec
B

17₁

0₉

1₈

10

The Shrape Mud

0₃

1₂

QkFlR3M

FlR5sec
R   N°4

Hovercraft Channel
or The
Hole

2₂
R
Qk
R

2
R

N°8
QkFlR R

EAST
COWES

HOVERCRAFT
SLIP

Trinity Wharf

2FR

2FR

FLOATING BRIDGE

Piles

2FR

E. COWES
MARINA

2FR

2FR

2₈

Kingston Quay
2FR

2FR
Power
Station
2FR
2FR

Lts 0
164°

12₂

1₈

N°3
G

2

2₂

3₃

Iso 2·sec 3m3M

1₃
N°6
1

1₂
0₈

0₆

PROHIB.
ANCHORAGE

2FG

3₂
N°6

2
R

2₈

2₄

2FR

1₆

4

2FG

Dredged

4

2FR
2₄

3₄

2FG

2FG

2FR

RYS
RCYC
RLYC
Foul Area Public Slip
CUSTOM HQ
ISC

Fountain Quay
Iso R2sec 5m3M

Groves &
Guttridge

2FG
2FG
Piles

2FG

L.S White

CRANE

Piles

Souters

2FG

OVERHEAD POWER (35m)

Continued on
smaller scale

CABLES   3
METRES   500
SOUNDINGS IN METRES

Inset (upper right)

Continuation on
smaller scale

MEDWAY
YACHT
HARBOUR

OVERHEAD POWER
(35m)

2FR

Pipe Lines

2FR

INN

FOLLY PT.

2FIG

2FR

2FG

PILES

MEDHAM
VQkFl
(3)ev5

2FR

2FG

2FG

1₂

1₅

2FR 7m 2M
2FR 1m 2M

NEWPORT

0 CABLES   3
0 METRES   500
SOUNDINGS IN METRES

59. *The Island Sailing Club and pontoon on left with the Customs Office just to the right.*

the line from the buoy to the north side of the conspicuous Royal Yacht Squadron castle until the fairway is entered. A long breakwater extends across the Shrape bank, affording some shelter from the NE. There is little water to the north of this breakwater, and the temptation to cut across towards W Cowes must be resisted unless the tide permits. A hovercraft fairway on the east side of the harbour and close round the end of the breakwater is marked by orange buoys. It is seldom used nowadays.

Coming from the west, there is deep water a cable offshore but there are ledges of rock east of Egypt Point and off the shore along Cowes Green to the Royal Yacht Squadron. Leave No. 3 outer G buoy to starboard. Note that an early flood or ebb which runs contrary to the main tide will be found between Egypt Point and the Royal Yacht Squadron.

There is a speed limit of 6 kts.

Lights The BY north cardinal Prince Consort buoy, northeast of the entrance, exhibits a Qk Fl W Lt, and there is a Lt (Fl R ev 5 sec.) on the outer (No. 4) port hand buoy. A R Qk Fl Lt is at the end of the eastern breakwater. Leading lights on 164° are: Front Iso 2 sec., Rear Iso R 2 sec. The rear R Lt is visible 120° to 240°. The principal lights in the River Medina are shown on the harbour plan.

Anchorage, Moorings and Marinas Large yachts anchor

60. *Cowes Yacht Haven Marina is close south of the Fountain Pier. Enter at south end near buoy.*

or moor on buoys provided in the roads north of the Shrape bank, or on moorings off Cowes esplanade. Smaller yachts anchor on the Shrape well to the north-west of the breakwater and local moorings in positions depending upon their draught, remembering that at MLWS there is om6 and at MLWN 1m7 more water than shown at chart datum. Anchor should be buoyed to avoid fouling mooring chains.

Four large visitors' moorings are laid off Cowes esplanade for temporary use. There are many private moorings in The Hole on the east side of the harbour and north-west of it. Additional moorings are laid for the various classes of competitors in Cowes Week and the many other regattas regularly held there. None should be picked up without permission of the HM, on Ch 16 or by telephone at 293952.

In strong northerly winds, it is better to enter one of the marinas or proceed up the river beyond the floating bridge where there are visitors' pile moorings for any size of yacht.

The Cowes Yacht Haven Marina (depths om9 to 2m3) at Groves & Guttridge's yard has 130 berths on the starboard hand just beyond the Fountain Pier and the Red Funnel pontoon in the main channel. Outside this there are mooring buoys and two trots of pile moorings where yachts lie abreast in over 2m. *The E Cowes Marina* is situated about 3 cables above the floating bridge on the port hand. It is dredged to provide 220 berths from 2m0 to 3m0 at its outer end.

The depths in the river above the floating bridge vary as shown on the harbour plan and in greater detail on Admiralty Chart 2793, but there is 2m1 as far as Medham beacon situated some 4 cables beyond Kingston Quay. There are many pile moorings on either side of the river; all, including those for visitors, are suitably labelled.

A pleasant stop is on *pile moorings off the Folly Inn* in om6,

61. *The Folly Inn on the east bank of the River Medina. There are pile moorings opposite it.*

which gives 1m4 at MLWS or 2m3 at MLWN. There are a landing pontoon and a restaurant and small shop at the inn. Half a mile farther on there is *the Medina Marina* in which there are berths for yachts up to 2m0 maximum draught. The river dries out but with sufficient rise of tide the lock can be reached. At HW the river is navigable to Newport with the aid of the Admiralty chart.

Facilities Every yachtsman's requirement is catered for. There are yacht yards of world-wide repute with slips and hoists capable of handling boats below maxi-rater size, sailmakers, brokers, yacht chandlers, hotels and restaurants, Customs, bonded stores and many shops of all kinds including yachting outfitters. EC Wed. Bus connections to all parts. Ferry and hydrofoil services to Southampton. Yacht clubs: Royal Yacht Squadron, R. London YC, R. Corinthian YC, Island SC, East Cowes SC, Cowes Corinthian YC. Launching sites: (1) From the slipway off the esplanade near Island SC, with car park adjacent. (2) From the slipway on town quay adjacent to the ferry pontoon, but car parking restricted. (3) Heavy boats can be craned into the water from Thetis jetty by arrangement.

HAMBLE RIVER

Admiralty Chart No. 1905

Double High Water   *First HW Springs approx.* −00 h. 20
m. *Dover.*

Heights above Datum *at Calshot Castle MHWS 4m4.
MLWS 0m6. MHWN 3m6. MLWN 1m8.*

Depths   *3m6 in entrance, and upwards of 2m1 in the channel as
far as Mercury Yacht Harbour. Above this 1m5 will be found to
Bursledon bridge, and in parts this depth is exceeded.*

THE HAMBLE RIVER owes its popularity as a yachting centre to
its excellent facilities, including over 1,200 alongside berths at
four marinas, and being well sheltered. Situated at the entrance of
Southampton Water, it is a good harbour from which cruises may
be made to the Solent or cross-Channel ports, and it is a base for
many offshore and racing yachts. The river is navigable at all
states of the tide, but it is packed solid with moorings as far as
Bursledon bridge and beyond.

Approach and Entrance   Coming abreast of Calshot Castle
from the SE alter course to 351°. Leave to starboard the Hook
pillar bell buoy (Qk Fl G) on to the YB south cardinal Hamble
Point buoy (Qk Fl (6) + LFl 15 sec.).

When approaching from the eastward keep well offshore,
leaving the Coronation buoy a cable to starboard and steering
nothing east of Hamble Point buoy until this is close at hand.

Hamble Point buoy marks the southern extremity of a sand
and mud spit on the west side of the Hamble River. It dries out
for a considerable distance at LW on both sides.

Leaving Hamble Point buoy close to port bring the R port
hand No. 6. beacon in transit with a conspicuous red roof in the

trees at $344\frac{1}{2}°$. Then with the G beacon No. 5 abeam alter course
to 026° transit of Warsash Shore beacon (on the starboard hand
beyond the Navigation School jetty) in line with a beacon at the
Warsash SC on the east bank. However, the channel is well
marked by four red piles with can topmarks on the port hand and
to the starboard by five G piles with cone topmarks. Keep on the
starboard hand under power or with a free wind and do not pass
too close to the piles, some of which dry out.

In the river above Warsash the fairway is as shown on the
harbour chart and clearly defined by the lines of yachts on
moorings and piles.

Lights   First transit: front, No. 6 Pile beacon Gp Occ (2) W
12 sec. in line with rear, Hamble beacon Qk Fl R. A cable before
reaching No. 6 Pile beacon come on to next transit: front,
Warsash Shore beacon Qk Fl G and rear, Warsash SC Bn (Iso, G
6 sec.) at 026°. Above Warsash the river is marked by lights on
piles as shown on the harbour plan: Qk Fl R to port and Qk Fl G
to starboard, with the outboard ends of jetties and pontoons
marked 2 F R to port and 2 F G to starboard.

Anchorage and Berths   To all intents and purposes there is
no room left in the river for anchoring, except by shoal-draught
boats off the fairway. Application can be made to the HM at
Warsash on Ch 16 or by telephone to Locks Heath (04895) 6387.
Visitors can also land at his pontoon in front of the Rising Sun
pub for advice. He may direct boats as follows:

1. *Warsash.* Piles in mid-stream off the Hamble Point Marina.
2. *Off Port Hamble.* Pile moorings on the east side of the fairway.
   In each case some piles are clearly designated for other users
   than visiting yachts.
3. *Hamble Point, Port Hamble, Mercury and Swanwick Marinas*
   usually have vacant berths for short-stay visitors. They can be
   called on VHF Ch 37. Their touch-down berths for visitors
   seeking further instructions are clearly indicated.

Facilities   Customs Office at Hamble, where bonded stores

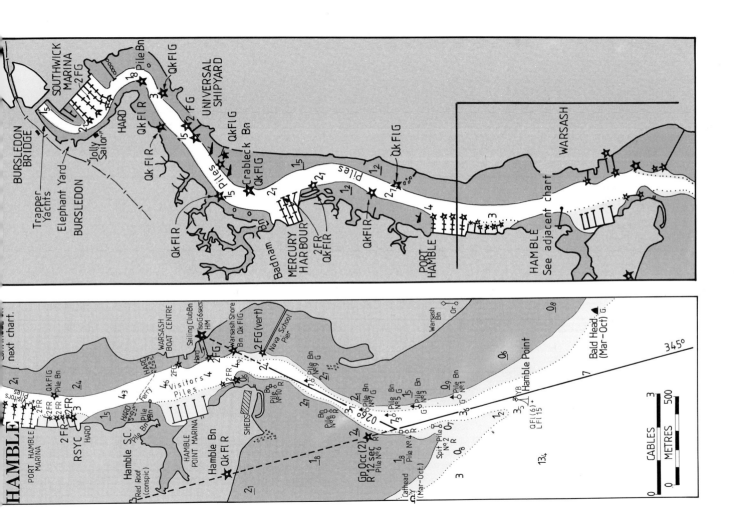

HAMBLE

BURSLEDON BRIDGE
SOUTHWICK MARINA
2 FG
Pile Bn
QkFlG
QkFlG
UNIVERSAL SHIPYARD
2 FG
QkFlR
HARD
Jolly Sailor
Trapper Yachts
Elephant Yard
BURSLEDON
QkFlR
QkFlR
QkFlG
Crableck Bn
QkFlG
Piles
Badnam
MERCURY HARBOUR
2FR
QkFlR
QkFlR
QkFlG
QkFlG
Piles
sailes
PORT HAMBLE
WARSASH
HAMBLE
See adjacent chart

next chart.
PORT HAMBLE MARINA
Visitors Piles
QkFlG
Pile Bn
2 FR
2 FR
2FR
RSYC
HARD
Pile Bn
2 FR
HARD
Red Roof (conspic)
Hamble Bn
QkFlR
SHEDS
HAMBLE POINT MARINA
Visitors Piles
Ferry
WARSASH
WARSASH BOAT CENTRE
Sailing Club Bn IsoG 6 secs
HM
HARD
Warsash Shore
Bn QkFlG
2 FG
2 FG
2 FG (vert)
Nava School Pier
Pile N°9 G
Pile Bn G
Pile Bn N°7 G
Pile N°5 G
Pile N°3 G
Pile Bn N°1 G
Warsash Bn
Hamble Point
Bald Head (Mar–Oct)
345°
020°
Pile N°10 R
Bn N°8 R
Pile N°6 R
Gp Occ(2) R 12 sec Pile N°6
Cathead Pile N°4 R (Mar–Oct)
Spit Pile N°2 R
QFl(6)+ LFl 15
13₄

CABLES   3
0
METRES   500
0

62. *Hamble River with four major marinas. (Photo : Aerofilms Ltd.)*

can be arranged. Water and fuel at all marinas or yacht yards and supply boat in river. Yacht builders and repair yards, marine engineers and chandlers at Warsash, Hamble, Swanwick and Bursledon and at marinas can handle repairs for all types of boats. Three hards available for scrubbing against piles: Warsash, Mercury and at the hard opposite Swanwick Marina. Sailmakers at Sarisbury (Bruce Banks Ltd) and J. R. Williams at Hamble. Proctors Metal Masts at Swanwick. Banks at Hamble and Warsash. Restaurants, shops and POs at Hamble, Warsash, Bursledon and Swanwick. EC Wed. except Warsash Thurs. Hotel and restaurant Hamble, Warsash and Bursledon. Launching sites: (1) Warsash public hard, car park adjacent. (2) Hamble public hard, car park adjacent. (3) Swanwick Shore public hard (next to Moody's yacht yard) with car park adjacent. (4) At Bursledon on south-west side of bridge and at Land's End public hard with car park at the station ¼ mile distant. Buses from Warsash, Hamble, Swanwick and Bursledon. Station at Bursledon. Yacht clubs: R. Southern YC, Hamble River SC, RAF YC, Warsash SC.

SOUTHAMPTON

Admiralty Charts Nos 1905 and 2041

Double High Water *First HW Springs −00 h. 13 m. Dover. 'Young Flood' stand lasts from 1½ to 3 hours after local LW.*
Heights above Datum *MHWS 4m5. MLWS 0m5. MHWN 3m7. MLWN 1m9.*
Depths *Deep harbour for ships with draughts up to 50m2, shelving in the upper reaches of the Rivers Test and Itchen.*

SOUTHAMPTON WATER has been used by ships of all sizes from time immemorial. It is an almost straight stretch of water, measuring 6 miles from Calshot Castle to the Royal pier. Navigation is straightforward in well-buoyed and lit channels. There are anchorages available for yachts. The city provides almost everything required by yachtsmen. Local bye-laws require that yachts keep clear of steamers everywhere in the area. But the port's main appeal for visiting yachtsmen is as a place to pick up or land crews.

Approach and Entrance When entering Southampton Water the main channel lies between Calshot LV and Calshot BY north cardinal pillar buoy, and runs north-west close to Calshot Castle and its conspicuous radar tower.

Approaching from the eastward, keep well offshore between Hill Head and Hamble, as the shoal water extends a surprisingly long way from the shore. Whether coming from east or west remember the Bramble Bank, situated in mid-Solent. In spite of being such a well-known danger, yachts still go aground on this shingle shoal which may vary from year to year in depth and position. At the lowest springs it used to be the scene of an annual cricket match organized by Uffa Fox.

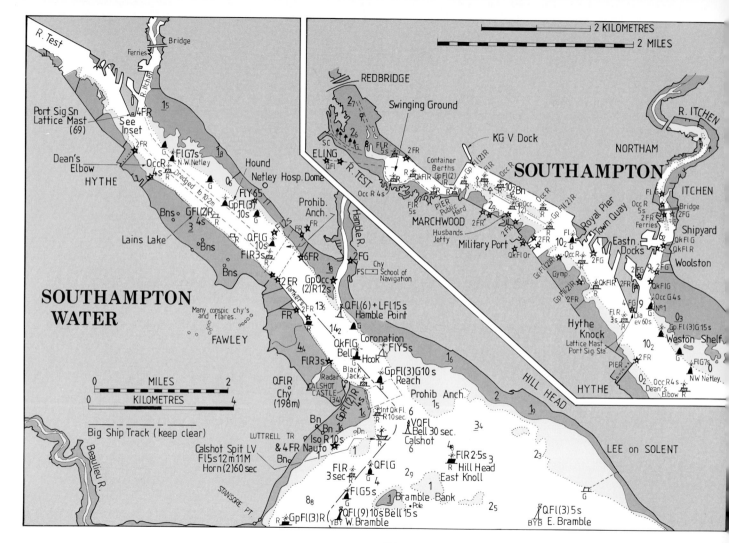

R. Test

Bridge
Ferries

REDBRIDGE

2 KILOMETRES

2 MILES

Swinging Ground

KG V Dock

R. ITCHEN

NORTHAM

SC
ELING
QFl

R. Test

Container
Berths
GpFl(2)

SOUTHAMPTON

Port Sig Sn
Lattice Mast
(69)

See
Inset

FlG7s
N.W. Netley

Hound

4FR

OccR
4s

Dean's
Elbow

HYTHE

Netley Hosp. Dome

Prohib.
Anch.

FlY65

GpFl(3)
10s

GFl(2)R

Lains Lake

Bns

Bns

Bns

QFlG
10s

FlR3s

SOUTHAMPTON
WATER

Hamble R.

2FR

2FG

Chy
FS School of
Navigation

6FR

2FR

GpOcc
(2)R12s

Many conspic chy's
and flares.

FAWLEY

FlR

FR

FR

QFl(6)+LFl15s
Hamble Point

Coronation

FlY5s

QkFlG
Bell

Hook

FlR3s

Black
Jack

GpFl(3)G10s
Reach

QFlR
Chy
(198m)

Radar

CALSHOT
CASTLE

GFl(2)R

Prohib. Anch.

MARCHWOOD

Husbands
Jetty

Military Port

Royal Pier
Town Quay

Eastn.
Docks

Woolston

Hythe
Knock

Lattice Mast
Port Sig Sta

HYTHE

Weston Shelf

NW Netley

Dean's
Elbow

ITCHEN

Bridge
Ferries

Shipyard

MILES

KILOMETRES

Big Ship Track (keep clear)

Beaulieu R.

STANSORE PT.

Bn

Bn

Iso R10s

LUTTRELL TR
& 4FR Nauto

Calshot Spit LV
Fl5s 12m 11M
Horn (2)60 sec

Int QkFl
R10sec

VQFl
Bell 30 sec.
Calshot

Prohib Anch.

Dn

FlR2·5s
R Hill Head
East Knoll

QFlG

FlR
3 sec

QFlG

FlG5s

Bramble Bank
Pole

QFl(9)10s Bell 15s
W. Bramble

LEE on SOLENT

QFl(3)5s
E. Bramble

GpFl(3)R

63. Calshot. Radar control at Calshot Castle to the right, Fawley power station chimney to the left.

Once within Southampton Water navigation is easy. Mud flats run off a long way on both sides. The deep ship channel is dredged to 10m2 and marked by red buoys on the west side, and by green conical buoys on the east side.

The docks will be seen from a considerable distance. Here there is the Port Signal and Radar Station at the junction of two channels, the Test river leading approximately north-west, and the Itchen river joining from north-north-east. The Test is the clearly-marked channel leading past the Ocean Dock, the Royal pier and the long line of the Western Docks to the Container berths.

If proceeding to moorings farther up the River Test, the Marchwood Channel may be taken. The entrance lies just north of the Middle Swinging Ground No. 2 R can buoy about 3 cables west-north-west of the Royal pier. The leading beacons will then be brought into transit at 298°. The front one is a white triangle on a dolphin and the rear a white diamond on a dolphin. The depth on the transit is 2m4 to within ½ cable of the front beacon. Close to starboard lies a long shoal marked on its far north-east side by a beacon and a pile. On the port hand from No. 2 buoy to Marchwood buoy there is shoal water almost as far as Husband's jetty, where it deepens to 2m and more for 3 cables. There are a great many moorings in this area. The shoal area in the Marchwood Channel lies from about ½ cable south-east of the first beacon nearly as far as the rear beacon and both beacons should be left close to port. There are many small craft moorings in the area in depths of 0m5 to 0m9. Immediately after passing the rear beacon a vessel is in deep water of the main channel dredged to 10m2, leading past the Container berths and Swinging Ground.

The Eling Channel, which is very narrow and dries out, is entered close south to the North-West Swinging Ground (Eling) buoy. It is marked by beacons with triangle topmarks on the starboard hand except at the junction with the Redbridge

64. Dock head and Port Signal and Radar Station at the junction of Test River to the left and Itchen River to the right.

Channel, which is marked by a YB south cardinal junction beacon. Near the entrance of Eling Channel there are two port hand beacons, south of which there are small craft moorings in 0m3. Power cables cross the channel, height 36m.

The River Itchen is commercialized in its lower reaches up to and beyond the Northam bridge, and is used only by yachts when proceeding to yards situated up the river. At the entrance the wide drying flats of Weston Shelf are left to starboard and the dredged area for the docks and basins is on the port side. Beyond the dredged area the channel carries 2m6 past the new Itchen bridge at Woolston as far as the end of the line of big moorings buoys ½ mile beyond the bridge. In this reach there is the port hand Crosshouse beacon (Occ R ev 5 sec.) starboard the Chapel beacon (Fl G ev 3 sec.). Beyond these are the channel runs between wide mud flats on either hand and the depths are variable up to Camper & Nicholson's, so that in the absence of local knowledge the depth is 1m1 which gives 1m6 at MLWS.

Lights Calshot Spit LV exhibits a Lt Fl 5 sec. 12m 11M. Fog signal 2 ev 60 sec., and the Calshot north cardinal pillar buoy, V Qk Fl bell 30 sec. The entrance between the two is thus as easy by night as by day. Southampton Water is marked by buoys with R Fl Lts on the port side and Fl G Lts on the starboard. The lights are so numerous that reference to the chart should be made.

Port Signal and Radar Station Call sign SPR (Southampton Port Radio) is available for communication on VHF Channels 16, 14 and 12.

Anchorages Where available these are generally remote from commercial activities, but it is possible in suitable weather conditions to anchor anywhere that can be found in Southampton Water clear of (a) prohibited areas, (b) shipping fairways and docks and their approaches and (c) moorings. The anchor should be buoyed. A riding light is necessary at night. Some of the positions for anchorage or moorings are: (1) *Between Calshot Castle and Fawley R buoy* temporary anchorage off the mud flats in moderate west to south-west winds. (2) *Hythe*. Large yachts lie north and south of Hythe pier. For smaller craft enquire at yacht yard or club for moorings, or anchor south of the pier. Yacht yard, hotel, shops, petrol, etc. EC Wed. (3) *Southampton*. There are Harbour Board moorings for large yachts off the Royal pier. (4) *Marchwood*. Many moorings south of the Marchwood Channel. Enquire at Husband's shipyard or Marchwood YC. Fuel and water at shipyard jetty; frequent launches to Southampton Town Quay. (5) *Container Swinging Ground*. Anchorage prohibited but at neaps there is just room to anchor close beyond No. 14 and the Eling buoys. (6) *River Itchen*. There are Harbour Board moorings for large yachts and on the east side of the river almost opposite Camper & Nicholson's there is Kemp's Shipyard who own the yacht terminal with alongside berths (2mo at MLWS and soft bottom) with fuelling, water and chandlery. Anchorage is possible in the Itchen River on the starboard hand out of the main fairway but serves little useful purpose. (7) *Netley*. Between the hard ½ mile north-west of Netley dome and the G and Y Bns marking a sewage outfall, keeping inshore of hovercraft testing area marked by Y buoys. Yacht yard at hard. Lee shore in prevailing winds.

Other Facilities Southampton, like Portsmouth, provides facilities of almost every kind for yachts, large or small. Ministry of Transport office. Customs and bonded stores. Weather Centre. Camper & Nicholson's large yacht builders and shipyard (also marine engineers, yacht agents, chart agency, compass adjusting, instruments and chandlery) and smaller yards and boat-builders. Shops of all kinds. EC Mon. Some Wed. Hotels, restaurants, car ferry service, hydrofoil to Cowes. Good train services including express 70 minutes to London. Buses to all parts.

Launching sites (1) From foreshore north of Hythe pier, (2) from ramp at head of Ashlett Creek, south of oil refineries, (3) from hard on north shore of Eling Creek, (4) Itchen River at Woolston hard on east side or up river at Kemp's Shipyard, (5) at public hard, Netley. Yacht clubs: R. Southampton YC, Southampton SC, Eling SC, Weston SC, Hythe SC, Marchwood YC, Esso SC, Netley Cliff SC.

BEAULIEU RIVER

Admiralty Chart No. 2040

Double High Water *at entrance. First HW Springs* −*oo h. 30 m. Dover.*

Heights above Datum *at entrance approx. MHWS 3m7. MLWS om6. MHWN 3m1. MLWN 1m6.*

Depths *About om6 LAT on the bar; within the river the depths are variable as shown on the plan, except near LW Springs, there is 1m8 up to the yacht harbour at Buckler's Hard but considerably more water in parts of the river.*

BEAULIEU RIVER is the most beautiful anchorage within the Solent. A long, straight channel leads between the mud flats to the river proper, most of which lies between deep woods on either hand. Four miles upstream lies the historic village of Beaulieu,

with its thirteenth century Abbey and twentieth century motor museum. The entrance is shallow but marked, and available to most vessels except at exceptionally low spring tides.

Approach and Entrance   From the west follow the line of the Hampshire coast, keeping ½ mile off the mud flats, until the tripod beacon, Qk Fl R, at the eastern end of Beaulieu Spit, the Lepe Coastguard cottages and a conspicuous white boathouse have been indentified. Continue until the leading marks come into line at 339°. The shallowest part of the approach channel is to seaward of the dolphin, so at LW pick up the transit line and stay on it from 2 cables out. The front is a white board with triangular top on the first port hand pile, and the rear, which is situated among dark green trees, has a similar white board with a triangular top but with a vertical black stripe in its centre. Do not confuse it with the RW diamond-topped telephone beacon 2 cables farther west. Follow the transit which leaves the dolphin close to port across a bar with om6. Within the entrance the river soon deepens and it is marked by red piles with can tops and red reflectors (even numbers) on the port hand and green piles (odd

65.   *Beaulieu River entrance. White leading marks in the centre.*

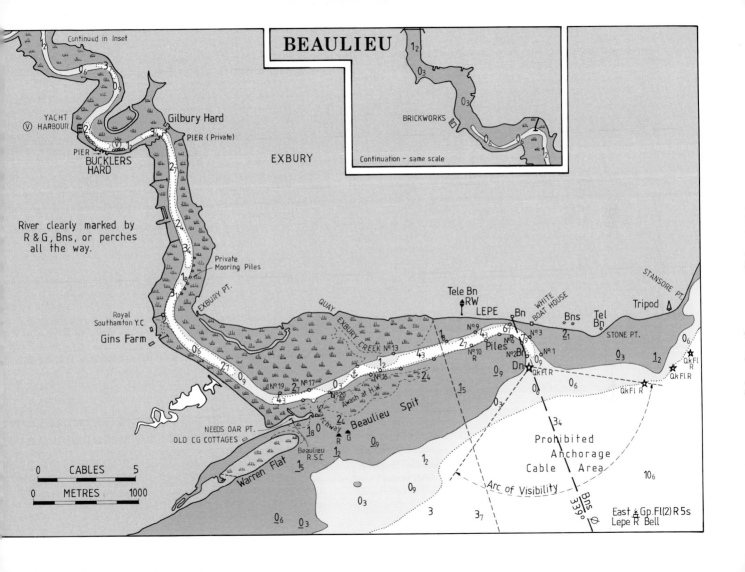

66. *Yacht Harbour and Buckler's Hard. (Photo : Aerofilms Ltd.)*

numbers) with conical tops and green reflectors to starboard. About a cable beyond the inner transit beacon there is a sharp bend in the river to the west-south-west, well marked by piles.

From the eastward leave three Qk Fl R beacons off Stone Point to starboard and do not steer direct to Beaulieu Spit dolphin near

LW springs, but steer to come on the leading transit over 2 cables south of the beacon.

Once beyond the first bend the channel continues to be marked by pile beacons and it is fairly wide to the next bend at Need's Oar Point. From here the river is marked by perches. There are a few shoal patches, as shown on the chart, which require attention at LW springs but, at most states of the tide, vessels of 2m0 draft have no difficulty in sailing up to the Yacht Harbour and ¼ mile beyond it.

Swashway provides a short cut off Need's Oar Point. It dries out at LW but carries about 2m4 at MHWS and is usually marked by two small round red buoys to port and three green to starboard. Approach the outer buoys from the south—not across the flats east or west—and proceed on 305° between them.

Light Beaulieu Spit beacon Qk Fl R. Vis 277°–037°.

Anchorage Owing to the large numbers of moorings, yachts may anchor only in the long reach between the prohibited anchorage west of the entrance and Need's Oar Point.

There are pile moorings near *Buckler's Hard* to accommodate about 100 visiting yachts, and other moorings temporarily vacant can sometimes be had on application to the HM, whose office is at the *Yacht Harbour Marina*. Here there are 100 berths and a yacht yard (tel. Buckler's Hard (059063) 200).

Facilities Water and fuel at the Yacht Harbour. At Buckler's Hard there are the Master Builder's Hotel, the Maritime Museum and a good village store, with deep freeze, which opens every day. There is also a taxi service. Grid-iron and launching site at Buckler's Hard or from beach at Lepe opposite the entrance to the river; both with convenient car parks. Yacht clubs: Beaulieu River SC at Need's Oar Pt and R. Southampton YC at Ginn's Farm. Nearest stations Beaulieu Road, or Brockenhurst 6 miles.

Admiralty Chart No. 2040

Double High Water *First HW Springs approx.* −00 h. 30 m. Dover.

Heights above Datum *MHWS* 3m4. *MLWS* 0m5. *MHWN* 2m8. *MLWN* 1m5.

Depths *About 0m9 on the bar, then 3m3 to Fishhouse Point. Within the harbour from 1m2 to 0m9 as far as Causeway Lake.*

THE HAMLET of Newtown was once the capital of the Island and vessels of all sizes used the river as a harbour. Romans sacked the town, and then in 1377 it was burnt to the ground by the French. Today only the old town hall and over-grown tracks through the trees, which were once busy streets, recall its importance. But, where once lay fourteenth-century sailing ships, the anchorage is now crowded in weekends during the season. The river, the marshlands and woods retain much of their original character. The National Trust owns the Estuary and much of the adjoining land and marshes which are the nesting places of countless sea birds. Landing at Fishhouse Point is not allowed during the nesting season, April to June.

Approach and Entrance The entrance to Newtown River is 3½ miles east of Yarmouth and ¾ mile eastward of Hamstead Point, which is the most pronounced headland between Yarmouth and Gurnard. It will be identified with certainty when the Hamstead Ledge G conical buoy is sighted. The bar lies ¾ mile east-south-east of this buoy.

Keep near a line joining the Hamstead Ledge buoy with another G con buoy, Salt Mead, until the leading marks are identified. They are inconspicuous and the R port hand buoy marking the 2m0 line off the entrance does not have the topmark

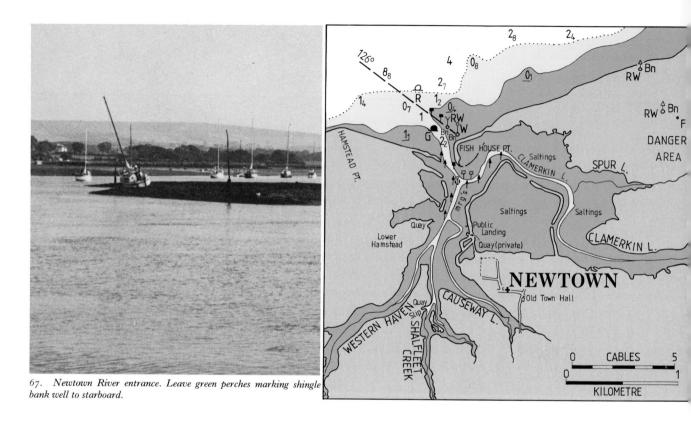

67. *Newtown River entrance. Leave green perches marking shingle bank well to starboard.*

advertised on the Admiralty chart and is no bigger than a dinghy-racing turning mark. The leading marks stand on the shore east of the entrance and consist of two posts, the outer one RW with a white 'Y' topmark and the inner one a white disc within a black ring. Alter course to 125° on these marks, and allow for a strong current across. Leave the bar buoy (R Sph) to port and the second

(G Sph) marking a gravel spit projecting towards the channel, to starboard. When the 'Y' post is close ahead, alter course for the entrance between the shingle points. There are a few perches on each side of the channel with R can topmarks to port and G painted ones to starboard. Here the tide conforms to the direction of the channel.

To starboard there is a shingle spit which is fairly steep-to, but beyond it is mud, while on the port hand a little farther in is another fairly steep shingle point, Fishhouse Point. Beyond this the channel divides; the port hand one is Clamerkin Lake, but the main channel runs in a SSW direction, both marked by perches.

There is a gravel reef to starboard opposite the junction of Clamerkin Lake and the main river, marked by three beacons, so keep to port after entering, before sweeping round into the centre of the river. In this reach there are usually yachts on moorings or at anchor which show the lay of the channel. Here the channel is very narrow at LW.

Anchorage The principal anchorage is between the junction of the main channel with Clamerkin Lake (where there is 2m7) and the junction with Causeway Lake ¼ mile farther south, where there is about 1m0 at LW. Several moorings occupy the best positions in about 1m8, so that the visitor will have to anchor where best he can, according to what space is available. The anchorage is rather exposed to north-east winds. Alternatively, there is anchorage at the lower end of Clamerkin Lake in 1m2 and rather more water farther up the lake where there are moorings, two of which are for visitors. Moorings can sometimes be obtained on application to the HM (tel. Calbourne (098378) 424). Dues help the upkeep of river and moorings; if not collected make a donation in the box beside the boathouse. Smaller craft that can take the mud at LW will find room farther up the main channel. There are no lights on the river or its approaches.

Facilities Water at tap at south end of footbridge and Lower Hamstead farm. Farm produce from farms at Shalfleet or Newtown, but there are no shops at Newtown.

There are a small slip and boatyard at Lower Hamstead and another small yard at Shalfleet Quay. Shalfleet is 2 miles from the anchorage and can be reached by dinghy. There are bus services to Newport and Yarmouth and a small shop and inn. Petrol, diesel and paraffin at Shalfleet Service Station on main road.

YARMOUTH

Admiralty Chart No. 2040

Double High Water *First HW Springs — oo h. 51 m. Dover.*
Heights above Datum *MHWS 3m1. MLWS om6.*
MHWN 2m5. MLWN 1m4.
Depths *Tide gauges are placed on the pier facing north for incoming vessels and on the dolphin facing south for vessels leaving the harbour. There is 1m3 in the entrance and from 2m3 to 1m3 within the harbout itself.*

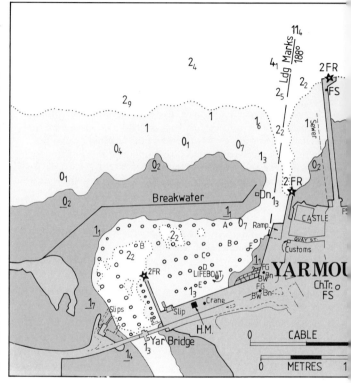

YARMOUTH is a good protected harbour for yachts at all states of the tide. The town itself is a beautiful one, especially viewed from seaward. It is one of the most popular ports in the Solent; so much so that yachts have sometimes to be refused entry in summer weekends.

Approach and Entrance Yarmouth can be located from a considerable distance by its conspicuous pier. There is plenty of water in the approaches from east or west off the pierhead, but there is a local tide rip situated near the Black Rock (marked by a G Con buoy) about 4 cables to the westward of Yarmouth pier. With sufficient tide small craft can pass inside the Black Rock (dries om8) by keeping the end of the Victoria pier (a cable east of Sconce Point) in line with the south side of Hurst Castle. This passage carries om4 but do not go north of the line until Black Rock has been passed.

The harbour entrance lies west of the pier, and there are leading marks, consisting of two posts surmounted by white diamonds with two horizontal black lines, on 187°, which indicate the best water in the approach channel. At the entrance there are a large dolphin (used for warping the ferry under bad conditions)

close to the end of the breakwater on the starboard hand and the ferry jetty on the port hand. Best water will be found by keeping on the port side off the jetty but stand out to avoid the slipway at its inner end, then bear to starboard towards the rows of piles. The HM usually gives berthing instructions from a boat,

68. *After passing the dolphin bear to starboard to the lettered line and numbered pile moorings as directed by the Harbour Master.*

otherwise make contact at his office on the fuelling point on South Quay. The harbour has rows of pile moorings designated by letters A–E with numbers for each berth, between which are narrow fairways and depths range from 2m2 to 1m3. There is little room for a yacht to tack so use auxiliary power, or warp into position. When the harbour is full a red flag is hoisted at a flagpole at the seaward end of the ferry jetty at the harbour entrance, or at night two R Lts Vert are exhibited from the same point. Yachts may then enter only with permission of the HM.

Lights There are 2 fixed R lights at the end of the long outer pier, F G Lts are on the two leading marks. There are 2 F R Lts at the end of the ferry jetty, which is left to port when entering. Two F R lights at the end of the groyne west of the South Quay mark the turn of the fairway towards the swingbridge.

Moorings and Anchorage Yachts berth alongside each other, between the mooring piles. The HM will indicate which berth to take. Each line of piles has a letter and each pile a number. It is forbidden to anchor in the harbour, but above the swingbridge (arrange time to open with HM) there is some room left clear of moorings in which to anchor in the river. Outside there is anchorage to west or east of the end of the pier, although the swell from passing ships causes some discomfort, and the anchorage is exposed to northerly winds. Bring up a little inside the line of the pier end if draught permits.

Facilities There are three yacht yards, marine engineer and scrubbing berths. Good yacht chandler and ironmongery. Water and fuel at New Quay. Customs Office alongside ferry ramp. Yarmouth is a compact little town with hotels and restaurants. Quay St shops include chandler, PO and bookseller. EC Thurs. Dinghy compound. Launching sites from dinghy slips at the Quay or from the ferry slip by arrangment with the HM; car park adjacent. Frequent car ferries to Lymington. Buses to Newport and connections with all parts. Yacht club: R. Solent YC.

LYMINGTON

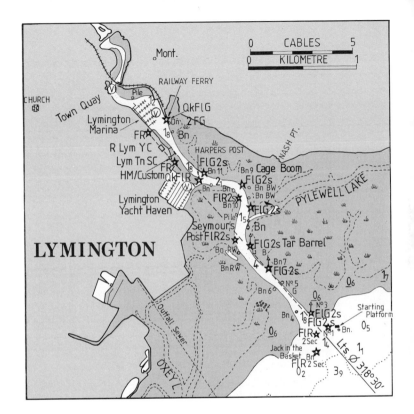

Admiralty Chart No. 2040

Double High Water   First HW Springs −oo h. 41 m. Dover.

Heights above Datum *MHWS 3mo. MLWS om5. MHWN 2m6. MLWN 1m3.*

Depths   *1m4 outside the entrance, then 2m4 in mid-channel to the Ferry Terminal. Depths then decrease to om9 off the Town Quay with a om3 shoal a cable short of it.*

LYMINGTON RIVER provides a good harbour for yachts at all states of the tide. Lymington itself is a small and charming Hampshire town, with excellent facilities of every kind including 750 alongside berths at two marinas and very active yacht clubs which have made it one of the most important racing centres in the Solent.

Approach and Entrance   The entrance lies about 2½ miles north-east of Hurst Castle. Whether approaching from west or east keep well away from the extensive shoal water. The first mark which will probably be identified is the starting platform for races on the east side of the entrance. Nearer, the red Jack-in-the-Basket beacon on the port hand at the mouth of the river will be seen. The Royal Lymington club house 1¼ miles up the river is also conspicuous. Once the entrance has been identified the rest is easy, as the winding channel is clearly marked by R piles with can topmarks on the port hand and G piles with triangles to starboard. There are two pairs of leading beacons on the mud in the Short Reach for the ferries, one BW north of Enticott Pile leading 007° for inbound ferries and a R one south of Seymour Post for outward bound ones. The big car ferries which have very

little room to manoeuvre in the channel have right of way.

Lights   Two red leading lights on pylons lead to the entrance at 318°, but it is better for yachts to follow the lights on the beacons: five Fl R or Qk Fl R to port and seven Fl G to starboard, with two F G at the ferry terminal.

69. *The Royal Lymington Yacht Club starting platform is conspicuous on the starboard side of the river entrance.*

70. *The Royal Lymington Yacht Club. The main channel to the Lymington Marina and Town Quay is on the extreme right.*

Anchorage Anchoring is prohibited in the river, which is fully occupied by Lymington Harbour Commissioners' moorings. These should not be picked up without permission. Arrangements for berthing, particularly for large yachts, should be made with the HM by telephone (Lymington (098378) 424). There are berths for upwards of 100 visiting yachts apart from marinas, and the following are the principal positions: (1) *On mooring buoys below the bridge* where there is about 0m9, but a soft bottom so that the keel sinks into the mud and yachts remain upright at low water. (2) *Alongside Town Quay* just short of the railway bridge, 50m long, up to six abreast with about 1m3 some 6m from the quay, i.e., third berth out. (3) Berths are often vacant at the marinas, the *Lymington Yacht Haven* in Harper's Lake or the *Lymington Marina* off the Berthon Yard. Contact on VHF Ch 37. (4) Anchorage outside river is possible in offshore winds and settled weather.

Facilities are outstanding. First-class yacht builders and repairers for all sizes of yachts. Leading international sailmakers for ocean racing and other classes and two smaller sailmakers. Customs. Brooks & Gatehouse electronics. Water at Bath Road pontoon and Town Quay and at marina pontoons where fuel is available. Hotels, restaurants, inns, banks and shops of all kinds. EC Wed. Stations at Ferry Terminal and Town linking with express service from Brockenhurst. Car ferries to Yarmouth. Bus services to all parts. Launching sites at public slipway adjacent yacht club, or at slipway at Town Quay. Car parks near. Yacht clubs: R. Lymington YC, Lymington Town SC.

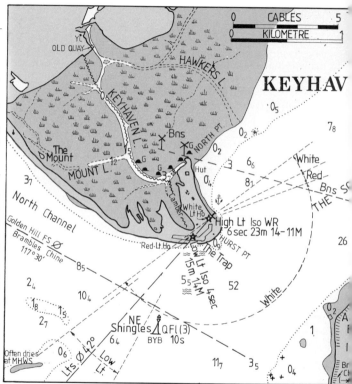

Admiralty Chart No. 2219

Double High Water *at Hurst. First HW Springs* −00 h. 55 m.
Dover.
Heights above Datum *MHWS 2m7. MLWS 0m5.
MHWN 2m3. MLWN 1m3.*
Depths *On the bar 0m3 but liable to alter. Once inside between
3 and 4 m. About 1m5 off Mount Lake, then gradually decreasing to
0m2 at the quay.*

THE ENTRANCE to Keyhaven is exposed to easterly winds, but in
normal conditions the river makes a very pleasant harbour for
small craft. It is so crowded with moorings that there is no room
left to anchor except near the entrance. The bar makes the
entrance rather inconvenient, for if a yacht arrives on the last of
the ebb she will have a longish wait for sufficient water to enter.

Approach and Entrance Keyhaven lies on the north side
of the Solent, 4 cables north-north-west of Hurst Point. If
crossing the Solent allow for the strong tidal streams across one's
track.

The entrance to Keyhaven Lake lies at North Point, the end of
the shingle spit extending from Hurst Point. The point is
conspicuous and stands out as a low sand and shingle promontory
against a background of mud flats. There are two leading marks
on the flats, each with 'X' topmarks on course 283°, but there is
only 0m3 at MLWS.

Shape a course for a position about ¼ mile north-east of the old
pier near Hurst High Light; then approach the entrance at about
west-north-west with Yarmouth open astern. A small G buoy to
be left to starboard at the entrance when course must be altered

very sharply as North Point comes abeam to leave its steep
shingle extremity about 10m to port and the second of the series
of Sph G buoys to starboard. The channel at first bears to south-
west and is at least 2m deep almost as far as Mount Lake; it is
clearly marked by the starboard hand buoys in the first reach and

71. Keyhaven Yacht Club and landing pontoon.

round the bend to north-west as far as Mount Lake. Above that there are one or two port hand R buoys but the trend of the channel can be judged by the line of yachts on moorings in the centre, or farther upstream, where it is very shallow, by a double line of smaller craft.

Anchorage The only anchorage in the Lake lies between North Point and the first of the private moorings which occupy the whole river farther up. There is a good anchorage in moderate westerly winds off the old pier near Hurst High Light. To the north of it the water soon begins to shoal so that it becomes necessary to take soundings and anchor farther from the shore. Close to the old pier the anchorage in Hurst Roads is tolerable

121

72. *Hurst Point and entrance to Keyhaven. (Photo : Brian Manby)*

even in strong south-west winds, but good ground tackle is needed in rough weather as there are strong tidal eddies.

Facilities   Poor landing on steps at the end of Keyhaven Old Quay, better at New Quay beyond the yacht club but little water at LWS. Boat-builder for repairs and laying up. Hard for scrubbing with 1m8 at MHWS. Water and fuel from boatyard. Gun Inn, general stores, PO. EC Thurs. Occasional buses. At Milford-on-Sea, 1 mile, usual facilities of a small seaside town. EC Wed. Launching sites at Keyhaven hards with car park adjacent. Yacht clubs : Keyhaven YC, Hurst Castle SC.

CHRISTCHURCH

Admiralty Chart No. 2219

Double High Water *at entrance. First HW Springs −02 h. 16 m. Dover, which is higher than the Second HW. Town Quay 25 m. later. HW at Neaps is variable, but Second HW is higher and may occur about +01 h. 00 m. Dover.*

Heights above Datum *(in harbour) MHWS 1m8. MLWS 0m4. MHWN 1m4. MLWN 0m6.*

Depths *About 0m1 on bar, but variable and may be lower in prolonged north and north-east winds. Off Mudeford Quay about 2m2. In the channel up to Christchurch there is considerable variation in depth—from 0m3 to 2m9.*

Owing to the shallow water over the bar 1m2 is about the maximum draught for entry at HW, except on exceptionally high tides or with local pilotage, which can be had by prior arrangement with Elkin's yacht yard. But once the difficulties of the entrance have been overcome, Christchurch harbour will be found an interesting place to visit. At Mudeford there is good bathing, and Christchurch itself is a beautiful old town, famous for its priory.

Approach and Entrance The entrance to Christchurch lies about a mile north of the conspicuous Hengistbury Head. The bar shifts frequently and varies in depth. Fresh onshore winds between south and east or heavy swell make the entrance dangerous, but in westerly winds some shelter is provided by Hengistbury Head.

There are two dangers when approaching from the west. Firstly the Christchurch ledges and secondly the Clarendon rocks off the shore on the south side of the entrance. From the

73. Christchurch entrance and Haven Quay.

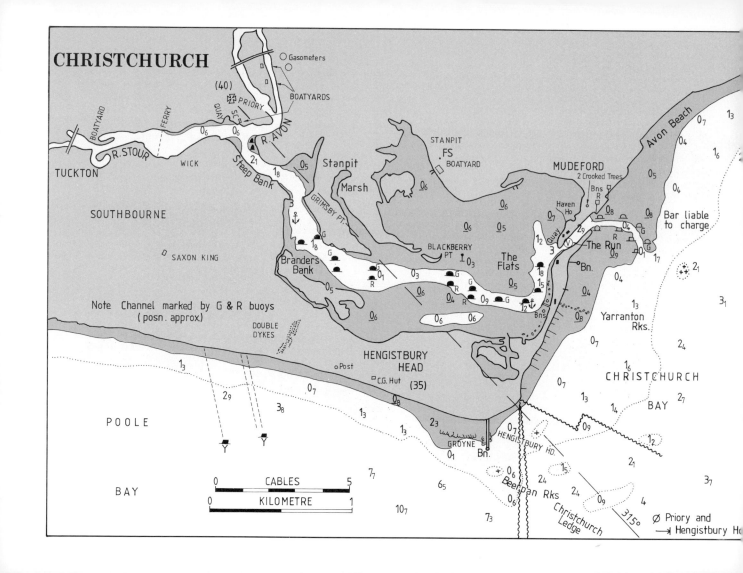

CHRISTCHURCH

Gasometers

(40)

PRIORY

BOATYARDS

QUAY

SC Bn

FERRY

BOATYARD

R. AVON

R. STOUR

TUCKTON

WICK

0·6   0·6

2·1

1·8

0·5

STANPIT

FS

BOATYARD

Stanpit
Marsh

Steep Bank

SOUTHBOURNE

3

MUDEFORD

2 Crooked Trees

Bns

R

Haven
Ho

0·5

0·4

Avon Beach

0·7

0·4

1·6

1·3

0·5

Bar liable
to charge

0·8

GRIMSBY PT.

SAXON KING

1·8

G

Branders
Bank

G

G

0·1

R

0·5

0·6

0·3

0·6

0·3

R

BLACKBERRY
PT

0·3

0·6

0·9

0·6

0·5

The Flats

1·2

0·7

1·5

1·8

1·5

Quay

2·9

3

R

0·4

V

The Run

0·9

G

1·7

0·1

Bn.

0·4

Note Channel marked by G & R buoys
(posn. approx)

DOUBLE
DYKES

G

G

R

R

0·4

0·9

G

0·5

1·2

Bns

0·8

Bn.

Yarranton
Rks.

1·3

3·1

HENGISTBURY
HEAD

Post

C.G. Hut

(35)

0·6

0·6

0·7

0·7

0·8

2·4

CHRISTCHURCH
BAY

1·6

1·4

2·7

1·3

POOLE

1·3

2·9

3·8

0·7

0·8

1·3

2·3

1·3

0·7

0·7

HENGISTBURY HD.

0·9

1·3

1·2

2·1

Y

Y

GROYNE

Bn.

0·1

315°

BAY

0   CABLES   5

0   KILOMETRE   1

7·7

6·5

0·6

0·6

Beerpan Rks

1·5

2·4

2·4

0·9

4

3·7

10·7

7·3

Christchurch
Ledge

Ø Priory and
→ Hengistbury Hd

74. Christchurch Sailing Club, the Priory in centre, Elkin's yard and fuelling station on right.

north-east there are no outlying dangers. From the North Head buoy at the end of the North Channel or from the seaward end of the Needles Channel head for the right hand edge of Hengistbury Head, keeping Christchurch Priory tower open to its right. Watch the echo-sounder. The channel across the bar in 0m4 is very shallow, narrow and varies both in position and depths, so a newcomer should arrive on a rising tide or wait at anchor outside the 2m0 line. The channel is marked by small Sph buoys, R to port and G to starboard, but these may drag after gales. There are two landmarks which assist in finding the buoys: Haven House at the quay on the far side of the entrance bearing about west by south and a conspicuous big house near the beach among trees opposite the outer pair of buoys. Once the outer buoys have been identified, the channel may be entered. At the innermost R buoy the channel bends sharply to port leaving the sea wall and the quay to starboard and the spit of submerged land to port. This

channel is known as 'The Run', where there is the maximum rate of stream (reputed to attain 9 kts on an exceptional spring ebb) and a depth of at least 2m0 at the quay.

Continuing up to Christchurch the channel is well marked by small Sph R buoys to port and G to starboard. The streams are much weaker but the depth is lower to the east of Branders Bank than it is on the bar.

Moorings and Anchorage   Christchurch Harbour is full of moorings. Christchurch SC has two visitors' moorings and Elkin's yard keep two deep-water moorings available. Yachts can anchor anywhere that room can be found but should keep clear of the centre of the buoyed channel and avoid anchoring in The Run as the stream is fierce. Multi-hulls and twin-keelers which can dry out have an advantage.

Facilities   Three yacht yards. Water and fuel at Elkin's jetty. Hotel, restaurants, banks, PO and many shops (EC Wed.) at

75. Christchurch. Shifting sands at entrance and Haven Quay top left. (Photo : Kitchenham Ltd.)

Christchurch. Launching sites: (1) Slipway at Christchurch Quay. (2) At sailing club, by permission. (3) At Elkin's yacht yard. (4) From beach on harbour side of Haven Quay. Car parks adjacent. Yacht club: Christchurch SC. Frequent buses and trains from Christchurch.

POOLE HARBOUR

Admiralty Charts Nos 2611 and 2615

Double High Water *at entrance. First HW Springs — 02 h. 36 m. Dover. At Poole Quay about 35 m. later. At Neaps the tides are weak and time of HW is almost unpredictable.*

Heights above Datum *Entrance MHWS 2m0. MLWS 0m3. MHWN 1m6. MLWN 1m1.*

Depths *3m7 on bar and in Main Channel to Poole Town Quay.*

POOLE is a busy commercial port with a large well-sheltered area available for yacht moorings, a new 350-berth marina at Parkstone and numerous channels providing interesting pilotage and anchor berths for small yachts. There are several privately-owned small islands; in the centre is the comparatively large Brownsea Island, owned by the National Trust and well worth a visit. There is plenty of water for yachts of average size in the main channels, which are clearly marked, but the upper reaches of the various branches are uneven in depth and mostly shallow so a large scale chart is needed for their navigation. Range of tide is small but the streams at springs are strong, especially in the entrance.

Approach and Entrance The prominent feature in the approach to Poole is the chalk Handfast Point, with Old Harry Rocks off it. The new Fairway buoy (safewater RW Fl 10 sec.) is 6½ cables NE of the Point. The bar buoy is situated a mile north-north-east of it; about 2 miles beyond the buoy will be seen the harbour entrance, with the conspicuous Haven Hotel on the east side.

There is an ugly sea on the bar (5m4) and in the Swash entrance channel during strong winds between south and east, particularly on the ebb, when the approach may be dangerous. On the ebb there is a tide rip off Handfast Point.

The entrance channel, named the Swash, runs in at 322° from

76. *Poole. The chalk cliffs of Handfast Point ¾ mile south-west of the Fairway buoy are easily picked out.*

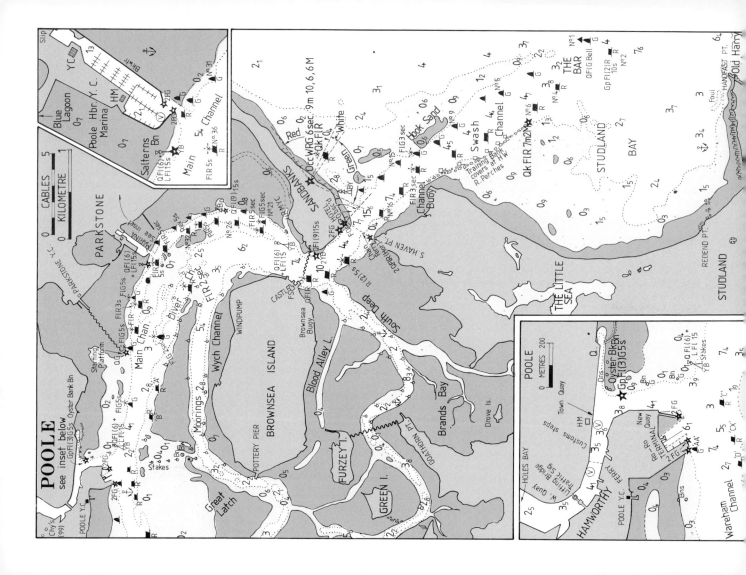

POOLE

see inset below

Chy's (99)
GpFl(3)G5s Oyster Bank Bn

POOLE Y.C.

PARKSTONE

P PARKSTONE Y.C.

Staffing Platform

Main Chan.

Moorings

River

Wych Channel

WINDPUMP

POTTERY PIER

Great Lated

BROWNSEA ISLAND

Brownsea Buoy

CASTLE

Blood Alley L.

GOATHORN PT.

FURZEY I.

GREEN I.

Brands Bay

Drove Is.

South Deep

S HAVEN PT.

SANDBANKS

OccWRG 6sec 9m 10, 6, 6,M

Red   Green White

QkFlR

HOTEL

Channel Buoy

QkFlR 7m2M

THE BAR

GpFl(2)1R 10s

HANDFAST PT.

Old Harry

Foul

STUDLAND

STUDLAND BAY

REDEND PT.

THE LITTLE SEA

STUDLAND

Swash Channel

Hook Sand

Training Bank covers at HW. R. Perches

Inset (top left)

Slip
YC
Bkwtr
Blue Lagoon
Poole Hbr. Y.C. Marina
HM
Salterns Bn
Main
Channel

QFl(6)+
LFl15s
FlR5s

Scale

CABLES 5 ... 0   5
KILOMETRE 1 ... 0

Inset (bottom right)

POOLE

METRES 0 ... 200

Oyster BkBn
GpFl(3)G5s

Town Quay
HM
Customs steps
New Quay
Ro-Ro
TERMINAL
FERRY

HOLES BAY
W. Quay
Lifting Bridge Traffic Sig
POOLE Y.C.

HAMWORTHY

Wareham Channel

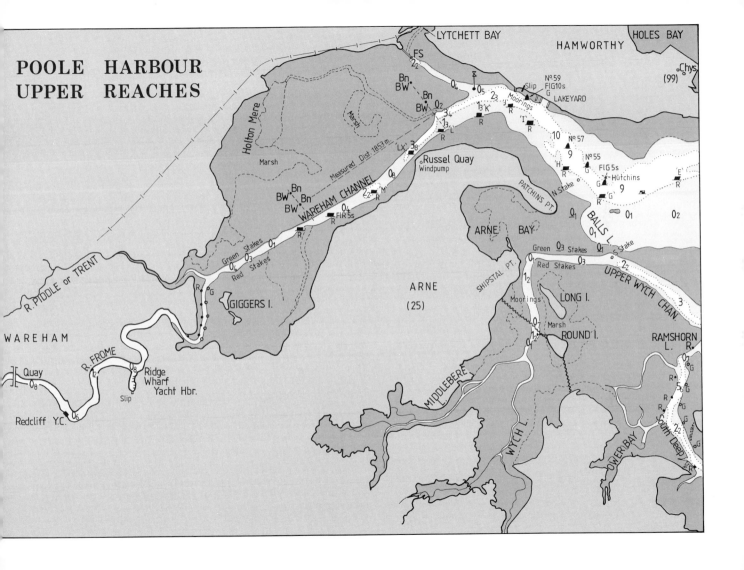

POOLE HARBOUR
UPPER REACHES

77. *The beacon at the end of the training bank on west side of the Swash channel and harbour entrance in background to right.*

the Bar buoy to the Channel R can No. 12 buoy between the training bank on the west side, and the Hook Sand G con No. 13 buoy on the east side. The channel is clearly buoyed with R can buoys (port) and G con buoys (starboard), but the buoys are close on the edge of the channel. There is a dolphin with light at the end of the training bank. Thereafter it is clearly marked by red posts with can topmarks. At the Channel Light buoy No. 12 (near the inner end of the training bank) alter for the entrance, leaving to starboard the Haven Hotel. A chain ferry crosses the entrance here. Care should be taken not to pass close ahead of the ferry when it is under way.

Inside the entrance the channel divides into two. One arm (South Deep) runs south-west, while the Main channel swings around between Sandbanks and Brownsea Island in a north-east direction and leads to Poole.

East Looe This channel affords a short cut off Sandbanks from the eastward. Find the R buoy (Qk Fl R) at the entrance. Approach it on about 300°, or at night within the white sector of East Looe Occ Shore Light, and leave it close to port. Then steer 245° to about $\frac{1}{2}$ cable off the Haven Hotel where the East Looe joins the Swash channel. Leave the ends of the groynes to starboard and keep well north of the inner G con (No. 19)

Swashway buoy. Least water about 0m4 at the east end, but the sands are liable to alter.

The Harbour The Main channel bears to north-north-east between North Haven Point beacon and the Middle Ground No. 20 YB south cardinal buoy, which is left to port. The channel is well marked by R can buoys with even numbers to port and G con buoys with odd numbers to starboard. The port hand buoys should not be passed closely. At Salterns YB Bn after passing the marina the channel is narrow and the beacon should be left close to starboard. On arrival off Poole enter the Little or Stakes channel leaving No. 43 YB south cardinal buoy to starboard. Then leave the Hamworth quay to port and three posts on the mud and a Fl G (3) ev 5 sec. light beacon to starboard before altering course again to enter the channel between quays.

In the other channels described below note that port hand stakes are painted red with red can topmarks; starboard hand stakes are green. Yellow stakes indicate oyster beds. When only one side of channel is marked (such as those between the Wych and Main channels) the stakes are placed on the western side. Stakes at channel intersections are surmounted by a circle and have the names of the channel on boards below their topmark.

The *Wych channel* lies on the north and north-west sides of

78.   *The east side of the entrance with conspicuous Sandbanks Hotel and block of flats. Brownsea Island to their left.*

Brownsea Island, whence it pursues a wandering course between the mud flats to Shipstal Point and then southward. It is deep and marked on the north side of the entrance by an intersection stake with a circular topmark and direction arms, one indicating the Wych channel and the other the Diver channel. It is then marked on each side by occasional piles on the mud but the bed of the channel becomes uneven towards the west side of Brownsea Island, and especially where the channel bends from south to north-west. It then deepens for $\frac{1}{4}$ mile before shoaling gradually to only om1 off Shipstal Point on the Arne Peninsula.

The *Diver or Middle channel* lies between the Main channel and the Wych channel and it is the shortest way to Poole. Leave the Middle Ground YB south cardinal No. 20 buoy east of Brownsea Castle about $\frac{1}{2}$ cable to starboard and steer for Salterns Bn No. 36 due north. After opening up the Wych channel and the stakes which mark it, identify the intersection stake already referred to and the Aunt Betty R can light buoy No. 54 (Fl R ev 2 sec.) about $1\frac{1}{2}$ cables north-west of it. Then steer to leave Aunt Betty and a stake close south-south-east of it to port to enter the Diver channel, which is marked by stakes and near its west end by

the G con Diver No. 49 light buoy (Fl G ev 2 sec.) where it joins the Main channel. The Diver channel carries 2m4 least water but at its entrance when approaching Aunty Betty 1m6 is crossed in the absence of local knowledge.

South Deep branches off to the south-west, west of North Haven Point, and is entered between No. 50A con G buoy to starboard and No. 18 R can buoy to port but do not round the port hand buoy sharply, as there is a gravel bank in the vicinity. Steer south-west until the stakes are located—green to starboard, red to port. South Deep is not difficult to follow and it is deep as far as and $\frac{1}{4}$ mile beyond Goathorn Point. The channel lies between mud flats with beautiful heath land and distant hills to the south. There are no lights.

The upper reaches of the various channels are marked by stakes and are navigable, but great care is required in keel yachts as the bottom is very uneven. They are ideal for centreboard and light draught craft.

Lights   By night the approach is easy. From the Fairway buoy, make for Poole Bar buoy (Qk Fl G Bell) and steer for the Channel buoy (Fl R 3 sec.) leaving the Training Bank beacon (Qk

131

79. *River Frome—approaches to Wareham, showing Ridge Wharf Marina at top.* (*Photo : Kitchenham Ltd.*)

80.   Poole Town Quay with Parkstone Yacht Marina top right. (Photo : Kitchenham Ltd.)

Fl R) well to port and the Hook Sand buoy (Fl G 3 sec.) opposite the Channel buoy to starboard. Then sail up the entrance towards Brownsea buoy (Qk Fl R) passing between the ferry hards (two F G (horizontal) to starboard and 2 Qk Fl R on the port hand). Leave to starboard North Haven west cardinal beacon (Qk Fl (9) ev 15 sec.). Altering course here, refer to plan and proceed up the main channel between R Fl buoys to port and G Fl buoys to starboard. Salterns pier south cardinal beacon (Qk Fl 6 ev 15 sec.) is left close to starboard.

Anchorages and Berths (1) Outside. There is excellent holding ground in *Studland Bay*, protected from westerly and south-westerly winds. Small village with hotels, PO and grocer about ¼ mile inshore. EC Thurs. (2) *Off Brownsea Island* most of the area is occupied by private moorings. Hail the launchman for advice or enquire at the R. Motor YC or at one of the yacht yards. (3) Moorings may sometimes be had inside the entrance on the east side in the *North Haven Lake*, off the yacht yard. Apply to boatman, yacht yard or yacht club. (4) *Poole Harbour YC Marina* at Salterns (220 berths). Turn off to starboard for it at No. 36 R can buoy (Fl R ev 5 sec.). It often has berths temporarily vacant. The guaranteed dredged depth is 1m5, but there are berths available for boats up to 2m3. Call the Dock Master from the reception berth just inside the entrance. (5) Alongside the *north quay in Poole town* where other yachts are berthed west of the steps. (6) *Cobb's Quay Marina* in Holes Bay. All facilities are there, but ask at HM's office the times of opening bridge— normally once every 2 hours. Depths at marina about 1m2

MLWS, 1m8 MLWN, but soft bottom allows deeper draught. (7) *Above Poole* off the Dorset Lake Shipyard in Wareham channel, where there are sometimes moorings for hire, and attendance. (8) *In west arm of harbour*, i.e. in South Deep, as far up as and a cable beyond Goathorn Point.

Anchorage may be found anywhere in Poole Harbour by choosing a position protected by land from the wind and free from moorings which are laid in all the best spots. In strong winds anchorage in open water areas may be uncomfortable for small craft, but shelter may be found at Poole Quay, or under a weather shore such as the Wych channel (protected from south by Brownsea Island) or off Goathorn Point (protection from west and south-west). For fuller information call Poole HM on Ch 16.

Facilities Yacht yards at Sandbanks, Parkstone and Hamworthy. Customs office. Water at tap or by hose on application at HM's office at Poole. Petrol at garages at bridge and quay where it is also available alongside in sealed cans or from all yacht yards and marinas. A refuelling barge is moored in Diver channel near Aunt Betty buoy. Diesel fuel in bulk from road tankers at Town Quay by arrangement. Ship chandlers. Yacht brokers. Sailmakers. Hotels and many shops. EC Wed. Launching sites: Lilliput Yacht Service, Sandbanks Rd: end of quay farthest from Poole Bridge by arrangement with the crane hirers. Public launching slip at Baiter, east of Fishermans Dock. Yacht clubs: Lilliput SC, R. Motor YC, Parkstone YC, Poole Harbour YC, Poole YC, Wareham SC, Redcliffe SC, East Dorset SC, Converted Cruiser Club.

SWANAGE

Admiralty Chart No. 2172

IN SETTLED weather and with winds between west-north-west and south-west there is a pleasant anchorage off the pier (2 FR Lts at its end). When approaching care should be taken to avoid Peveril ledges off the south extremity of Swanage Bay. The tide sets strongly across them. There is a R can buoy 4 cables off the Point marking the end of the ledges where there is a tidal race particularly on the south-south-west stream when the wind is contrary and it can be very rough. See Passage Data.

The anchorage is a cable west-north-west of the end of the pier in about 2mo, seaward of local moorings, with larger yachts farther out, but the holding ground has weed in parts and is not so good as at Studland Bay, which has the additional advantage of Poole near at hand as a port of refuge in case of a change of wind or weather.

Excellent hotels and shopping facilities. EC Thurs. Good sailing club (Swanage SC) which welcomes holiday membership. Launching site at slipway near pier with car park adjacent. Buses.

81.   *Conspicuous hotel left, pier centre, yachts at anchor on right.*

LULWORTH COVE

High Water *approx. − 04 h. 49 m. Dover.*
Heights above Datum *MHWS 2m1. MLWS 0m2. MHWN 1m4. MLWN 0m7.*
Depths *About 5mo in entrance ; 3mo in centre, shallows within 100m of the beach.*

LULWORTH COVE is a famous beauty spot and worth a diversion. There are good walks to the westward, but east of the cove there are gunnery ranges. Red flags are flown when firing is scheduled.

Lulworth should be visited only in settled weather and during offshore winds. A shift of wind to south or south-west, bringing with it a strong blow, as so frequently happens, will send a heavy swell into the cove. In such conditions power vessels, let alone yachts, may find it difficult to get out in safety. Therefore, clear out if the weather threatens to change and, if caught inside, apply to local boatmen for heavy anchors and cables.

Lulworth Gunnery Ranges There are two danger areas for shipping to the south of Lulworth and Kimmeridge. The one normally in use extends 5M out to sea and the outer, which is seldom used, extends out to 12M. Times of firing are published in local papers and notified to neighbouring HMs and yacht clubs who can supply leaflets giving the details. They can also be obtained from the Range Office, telephone Bindon Abbey

462721 ext. 819 or 824. When firing is in progress red flags and flag 'U' are flown by day and lights flashing red shown at night, at the huts immediately east of the cove on the summit of Bindon Hill and on St Alban's Head. Vessels may pass through the areas but passage must be made as quickly as possible and anchorage, fishing or stopping is prohibited. When the range is active, fast patrol boats are on station to keep yachtsmen clear of the area.

Approach and Entrance Lulworth is not always easy to identify from seaward. To the west there runs a series of white cliffs with curved summits. The entrance is just to the east of a sugar-loaf hill with an ex-coastguard hut situated upon it.

There are rocks on both sides of the entrance of the cove but those on the west extend farther than those on the east, so keep slightly east of the centre. Once past these rocks the fairway opens into the wide cove itself.

As may be expected, the wind is fluky or squally at the entrance, and often baffling when entering under sail.

Anchorage No anchorage outside. Anchor in about 2m4 on the north side of the cove where the holding ground is blue clay or on north-west in south-west winds. Avoid anchoring in the fairway to the beach landing of Lulworth village on the north-west side of cove.

Facilities Water at tap in car park or the beach café may oblige. Petrol and oil at garage. Small hotels. PO. Shops, EC Wed, Sat. Launching site from beach at end of road, with car park adjacent. Provisions at Boon's stores during summer months. Frequent buses in summer months.

82.   *Lulworth Cove. Enter east of midway in the entrance (Photo : Aerofilms Ltd.)*

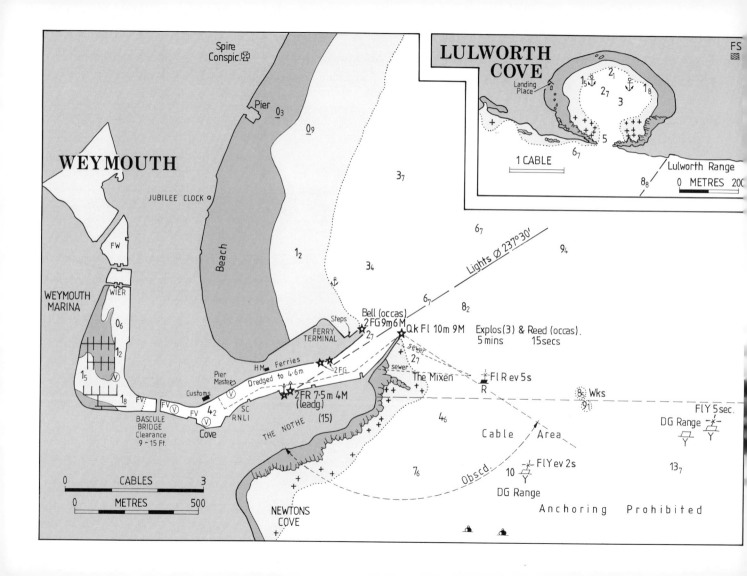

WEYMOUTH

LULWORTH COVE

FS

Spire Conspic. ✠

Pier 0₃

0₉

JUBILEE CLOCK ○

Beach

1₂

3₇

Landing Place

1₅ 8 2₁ 1₈

2₇

3

5

6₇

8₈

1 CABLE

Lulworth Range

0 METRES 200

WEYMOUTH MARINA

FW

WIER

0₆

1₂

1₅

V

1₈

FV

FW

6₇

Lights ∅ 237°30'

9₄

3₄

6₇

8₂

Bell (occas)
2FG 9m 6M

Steps

FERRY TERMINAL

2₇

Qk Fl 10m 9M

Explos(3) & Reed (occas).
5 mins   15 secs

sewer

2₇

HM Ferries

2FG

sewer

The Mixen

Fl R ev 5s

R

8₅ Wks

9₁

Fl Y 5 sec.

DG Range
Y   Y

Pier Master

Dredged to 4·6m

Customs

4₂

FV

V

SC RNLI

2FR 7·5 m 4M
(leadg.)

4₆

Cable   Area

FV

FV

Cove

THE NOTHE

(15)

BASCULE BRIDGE
Clearance
9 ~ 15 Ft.

0   CABLES   3

0   METRES   500

7₆

Obscd.

10 Fl Y ev 2s

DG Range

13₇

Anchoring   Prohibited

NEWTONS COVE

WEYMOUTH

Admiralty Chart No. 2268

High Water *—04 h. 38 m. Dover.*
Heights above Datum *MHWS 2m1. MLWS 0m2.
MHWN 1m4. MLWN 0m7.*

Tides *The tides are 4 hours flood, 4 hours ebb, and 4 slack
subject to the 'Gulder' as it is called, which is a small flood with a rise
of approx. 0m2 making its way into the harbour about ¾ hr. after the
first LW.*

Depths *The entrance, and north side, where ships berth is
dredged to 5m4. There is less water on the south side.*

WEYMOUTH, is a popular seaside resort with many historic
buildings along its quaysides. The harbour is sheltered but in
strong easterly winds the approach can be rough and there is
sometimes an uncomfortable swell in the area of the pierheads.

Approach and Entrance The harbour lies about ½ mile
north of the Portland Harbour breakwaters. The entrance is
between two piers. On the south is the Nothe Hill, and on the
north pier is the Pavilion. The Jubilee Clock—conspicuous—is
about ½ mile north along the front. Approaching from the
eastward a good transit is by bringing into line the two pierheads
on 273°. Several buoys will be seen and should be left well to port.
Three of these are light buoys; the outer three are Y (Fl Y ev 5
sec., Fl Y ev 10 sec. and Fl Y ev 2 sec.) D.G. Range buoys. The
closest inshore, off the Mixen rocks, marking the sewer outfall, is
a red can (Fl R ev 5 sec.). Then steer a cable off the entrance and

83. Entering Weymouth harbour. South pier and light with Nothe in background.

84. Weymouth harbour. Note white triangle leading marks to port.

round in between the two piers. There are two white triangular leading marks at $237\frac{1}{2}°$ on the south quay for ships but they need not be followed by yachts. Keep clear of the fairway in the outer part of the harbour when there are hauling-off warps across the harbour when a Cross-Channel ferry is about to depart.

Regulating Signals   From north pier a red flag over a green by day, or two red lights over green at night indicate entry or departure forbidden. Two red flags by day or three red lights by night indicate a vessel is leaving and no vessel shall approach or obstruct the entrance. Two green flags by day or three green lights by night indicate that a vessel is approaching entrance from seaward and no vessel may leave. When no signal is shown the entrance is clear. Within the harbour limits boats, whether under oars, sails or power, are to keep clear of the main channel, and not to obstruct or impede the passage of vessels entering or leaving.

Lights and Fog Signals   North pier, 2 F G. South pier, Qk Fl 10m 9M (obscured over Mixen rocks). Two F R leading lights on south side of harbour in line at $237\frac{1}{2}°$ lead in, open of the south pier light. Fog signals: South pier explosives (3) ev 5 mins. and Reed ev 15 sec. North pier, bell (very occasionally).

Anchorage   Visiting yachts may be hailed from the starboard side of the entrance or can contact the Pier Master's office on Ch 16 and will usually be directed to a berth in the cove. If the Pier Master's office is not manned or if there is a heavy swell, go

85.   *The Cove to which small yachts are usually directed and where they lie alongside in trots.*

right up the harbour and moor *alongside the Cove Quay* on the port side about a cable short of the bridge. This is the most popular berth for small yachts and is often crowded by yachts lying abreast. Anchorage outside the harbour may be found in settled weather and offshore winds in 2 to 3m about a cable north-west of the end of the pier, clear of the entrance and the turning space required by Channel Island ferries. Take soundings to find right depth, as shallow water extends a long way seaward. The depths of water alongside the Cove Quay wall vary from 0m1 to 0m4 at LAT, but a pontoon is usually positioned at the shallowest part. At a distance of 3m off the quay there is 1m0 increasing to 4m towards mid-channel. To the west of the Bascule bridge lies the 950-berth *Weymouth Town Marina*, mostly for small craft, but those with draughts up to 1m8 can lie afloat. The clearance under the bridge varies from 9–15 ft as shown on the tide gauge. Enquire locally about opening times.

Facilities   Yacht yards and chandlers. Customs Office. Water at cove and at quays. Fuel at quayside, by arrangement. Hotels, restaurants and shops. EC Wed. Main-line station—with trains to London and Southampton—and buses. Launching sites from slipway in harbour by prior permission of HM or at yards. Yacht clubs: R. Dorset YC, Weymouth SC.

PORTLAND

Admiralty Charts Nos 2255 or 2268

High Water — *04 h. 38 m. Dover.*
Heights above Datum *MHWS 2m1. MLWS 0m2.
MHWN 1m4. MLWN 0m7.*
Depths *Deep ship harbour except on its western side.*

PORTLAND HARBOUR lies in the bay formed by the mainland to
the north, the long narrow strip of the Chesil Beach to the west,
and the high peninsula of Portland to the south. From the east it is
protected by three big breakwaters which create a three sq mile
artificial harbour. This is primarily a naval base but it also
provides shelter for yachts, though it can be very uncomfortable
in gales or following windshifts. Within the harbour there are
numerous unlit floating targets, mooring buoys, etc., and chains
on the bottom. Frequent naval exercises are carried out from
Portland and in the adjacent waters with both submarine and
surface craft. Also night exercises often involve flares, Very lights
flashes, etc. The schedules are broadcast on Ch 14 at 0945 and
1645 daily.

Approach and Entrance Portland is easy to identify. It is a
high wedge-shaped peninsula that, viewed from seaward,
resembles an island. Its highest point (the Verne 44m) is at the
northern end; the southern extremity (the Bill) is low.

The principal danger to navigation in the approach to Portland
is the Race. This is the most dangerous disturbance on the whole
of the south coast, and the time of tide has to be studied, but it
does not affect yachts approaching from the eastward—see
Passage Data.

The harbour itself may be located behind its long stone
breakwaters, northward of the heights of Portland. There are
only two entrances in use: the East and North Ship channels.

Principal Lights and Fog Signals Portland Bill lighthouse
is a conspicuous white tower (41m) with a broad red band. To
seaward it shows Gp Fl (4) ev 20 sec. 29M over the sector 244° to
117°. Either side of these sector boundaries, the light's
characteristics gradually change towards the landward and
northern sector from Gp Fl (4) down to a single flash. A F R 13M
shows over the Shambles Bank (271°–291°). Diaphone ev 30 sec.
South-west end of outer breakwater : Occ R 30 sec. 5M obscured
seaward. *East Ship Channel :* 'A' Head Fl W 10 sec. 22m 20M
(north side); Fort Head inconspicuous Qk F R 2M (south side).
North Ship channel : 'C' Head Occ G 10 sec. 11m 5M (north
side); 'B' Head Occ R 15 sec. 11m 5M (south side).

Regulations Speed limit is 12 kts. Yachts should not
approach HM ships or jetties closely.

Sailing vessels and power-driven vessels of less than 20m
length shall not hamper the safe passage of large power-driven
vessels inside the harbour or its entrance.

Anchorage There is anchorage off *Old Castle Cove* in the
north-west of the harbour, with depths of 2 to 3m. Yachts should
anchor outside the yachts on private moorings, of which there are
many. It is better if possible to get use of a vacant mooring.
Enquire of the boatman or the Castle Cove SC at the top of a long
steep path. Visiting yachtsmen are usually permitted to use the
landing-stage belonging to the sailing club. There is water from a
tap on the shore. PO, shops and town are ¼ mile distant. To
Weymouth is a walk of over ½ mile or go by bus.

In strong southerly and south-west winds this anchorage is too
exposed. In this case bring up in the anchorage *to the west of the
R.3. Hard*, ½ mile west of Castletown, which is sheltered by
Chesil Beach and land from west and south winds, but even so
can be very rough during gales. Yachtsmen are allowed to land on
the RNSA (Portland Branch) pontoons close to the Castle and

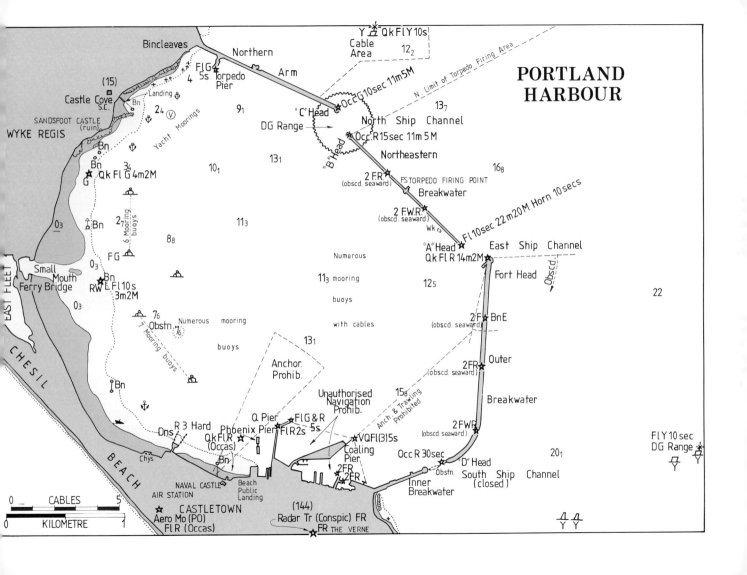

86. *Castletown Beach, the only public landing place on the south side of Portland Harbour other than the RNSA pontoons.*

enquiry can be made for possible use of a temporary mooring here. Castletown pier is private, and there is no public landing except on the beach just east of it. To the north and west of the pier there is a helicopter landing approach area: note the Prohibited Anchorage shown on the harbour plan. If in doubt contact the Naval Base on Ch 13 or 14

Facilities At Castletown. Water obtainable from Royal Breakwater Hotel or public houses. Fuel from garages at Victoria Sq. ¼ mile distant. PO and shops. EC Wed. Grocers Sat. Banks and wider range of shops at Fortuneswell, ½ mile distant. Yacht yards at Ferrybridge. Launching site: rather restricted but light boats can be launched from Castletown beach, road adjacent, or from beach adjacent to bridge at Wyke Regis which joins mainland to Chesil causeway. Yacht clubs: Castle Cove SC, RNSA (Portland Branch).

BRIDPORT

Admiralty Chart No. 3315

High Water *—05 h. 11 m. Dover.*
Heights above Datum *In approach approx. MHWS 4m1. MLWS 0m6. MHWN 3m0. MLWN 1m6.*
Depths *Bar within entrance between piers dries out. From 0m6 to 4m3 within harbour, but most parts dry out, except for the (3m3) coaster berths alongside and their turning area.*

WEST BAY, which is the port of Bridport, suffers from being a shallow artificial harbour which has a long narrow entrance. The entrance is dangerous in hard onshore weather. Once inside the harbour a yacht may be weather-bound waiting for fair conditions before attempting to leave, but this old West Country port is worth a visit, and offers a pleasant break on a passage across West Bay. There is some coastal trade.

Near LWS the inner sluice gates are opened and the entrance is scoured with the water released.

Approach and Entrance The approach to Bridport harbour is simple enough so far as outlying dangers are concerned, but the harbour entrance is unsafe in strong onshore

87. Bridport (West bay) entrance from south. (Photo : P. E. Payne)

winds, even at high water. Entry should be within 2 hours of HW.

When a vessel is expected and when there is sufficient depth a pilot flag is hoisted on the flagstaff above HM's office at the foot of the west pier; when the entrance is considered unsafe a black ball is hoisted. These signals are hoisted only for ships and not for yachts.

The only outlying shoals are the Pollock, 4m3, to the south-west, and the High Ground, 3m1, to the west. To steer between these shoals friom the west bring North Hill on east side of harbour in line with east pier at 075° true.

From south or east, steer straight for the entrance and, with sufficient rise of tide, enter, but beware of the backwash off the piers. The recognized line of approach is west pierhead and the distant Bridport Church tower in line at 011°. The bar lies within the entrance and dries out but carries 3m or more at MHWS. The channel is long and narrow (14m) and sailing craft without auxiliaries will need to be towed in during offshore winds.

Lights   The entrance should not be attempted by strangers at night. A Lt Iso R 9m 5M is established on HM's office on the west pier, but this serves only as a guide to the position of the harbour. When a coaster is expected pilot lights are exhibited: F G on east pierhead and F R on west pierhead, range 1M.

Anchorages and Moorings   (1) *Outside* the harbour in settled weather with offshore winds. Anchor about cable off the entrance in 2m4 clear of leading lines and sewer or to seaward in deeper water. (2) *Inside the harbour* consult the HM. He has no radio. Small yachts dry out at the west end of the harbour, or alongside the harbour walls. There are coaster berths (3m3) alongside northern end of the east quay where scour from sluice makes a deep hole. Apply to the HM for the use of one, which he permits when no coaster is expected. Otherwise berth at east end of harbour drying alongside quay, soft mud bottom.

Facilities   Water from hydrants near the quay. Diesel and petrol at local garage. Shops, hotels and stores. EC Thurs.

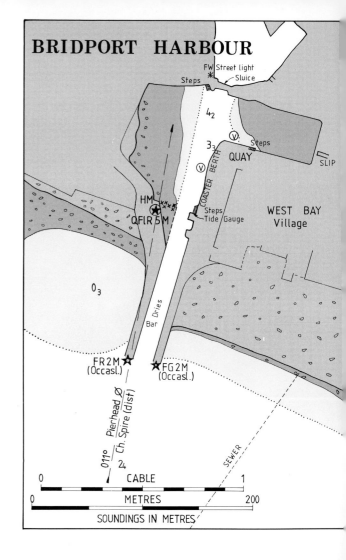

88.   At low water most of the harbour dries out except between the sluice and the coaster berth.

Scrubbing inside harbour; no yacht yard. Launching site: good
slip and adjacent car park. Good bus connections to Bridport (1½
miles).

LYME REGIS

Admiralty Chart No. 3315

High Water − *04 h. 53 m. Dover.*
Heights above Datum *in approach approx. MHWS 4m3.
MLWS 0m6. MHWN 3m1. MLWN 1m7.*
Depths *about 1m0 a cable east of the entrance, more to
seaward. Harbour dries out at LW and entrance is less than 1m0, but
there is 4m0 at MHWS.*

LYME REGIS and its harbour, known as 'The Cobb', are
picturesque and worth visiting, though crowded in the holiday
season. The harbour dries out, but a berth alongside the quay is
sheltered from all but gales between NE and SE. In strong
onshore winds the approach and entrance are dangerous when
the swell enters the harbour.

Approach and Entrance Lyme Regis is just east of the
centre of Lyme Bay, some 22 miles west of Portland Bill. The
approach is straightforward. The harbour lies immediately south
of a conspicuous green parkland, marking the scene of a recent
landslip. It is protected from the west by the long stone pier
known as The Cobb, which is forked at its eastern end. To
seaward of the outer fork is a post and R can topmark marking a
heap of large Portland stones, serving as a breakwater and
covered at half flood. There are also stones and rocks all along the
west and south of The Cobb.

The entrance to the harbour lies between the eastern end of the
inner fork of The Cobb and the southern end of the detached
breakwater which affords partial protection to the harbour from
the east. The entrance is narrow.

Steer for the post and topmark off the outer fork of The Cobb,

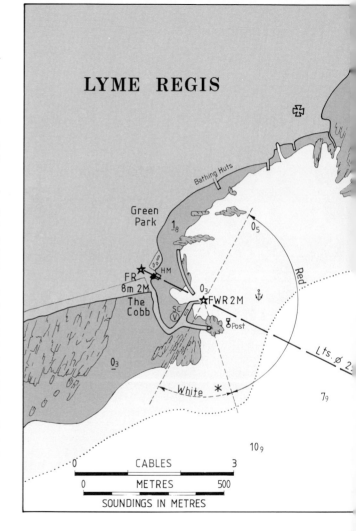

89. *Entrance of Lyme Regis harbour from the eastward.*

90. *Lyme Regis quay at high water, where there are temporary alongside berths for visitors beside the Sailing Club.*

leaving it about 50m to port and hold on until the harbour entrance is opened up. Then steer in, given sufficient tide to enter the harbour.

Leading Lights Front light on inner pierhead F W R 2M. Rear light on old lamp-post above the HM's office and slipway F R 2M. Lights in line lead in at 296°. The lights are weak and on approach are rendered inconspicuous by the many town lights ashore.

Anchorages and Moorings (1) Anchor *outside the harbour* in settled weather and offshore winds to the east of the entrance. The anchor symbol on the plan shows the most northerly position in about 1mo LAT, as the water shoals rapidly towards the shore. It is better to anchor in deeper water farther seaward if remaining for any length of time, especially at spring tides, but with less protection from the west. Take soundings to find the right depth, but it is better to consult the HM as the quality of the bottom varies. (2) Most of the harbour dries out and the moorings in the centre are for permanent occupants. *At the quay alongside the sailing clubhouse* there are mooring berths for twelve visiting yachts only, but it is advisable to contact the HM in advance to reserve a berth on VHF Ch 16, 14 or telephone 2137. The inmost berth dries about 1m3 at LAT on clean sand bottom and the outer 0m3.

Facilities Water at shoreward end of The Cobb. Fuel delivered for small fee. Hotels and shops. EC Thurs. Scrubbing can be arranged and small yacht repairs. Launching site, slip and car park adjacent. Dinghy park. Buses to all parts. Nearest station Axminster 6 miles. Yacht club: Lyme Regis SC and Lyme Regis Powerboat Club.

IN NORTHERLY or north-westerly winds and settled weather there is a delightful anchorage for small yachts off Beer, 5 miles east of Sidmouth. It is sheltered by Beer Head, a precipitous headland (130m) easily identified as the most westerly white chalk cliff on the South Coast before the red cliffs of Devon. The anchorage is on the western side of the small bay east of the Head, as close inshore as soundings permit. Approaching from the west, round Beer Head and follow the line of the cliffs, which have rocks at their base, until abreast of the road running down to the beach from the village with its conspicuous church tower. Approaching from the east give a wide berth to the headland on the east side of the cove, which has rocks extending over a cable off it, before turning into the anchorage. Land by dinghy on beach, which is steep. There are local fishermen and boatmen who will ferry to the yacht or attend to the dinghy.

With any forecast of change in wind leave quickly. Local fishing boats are hauled up on the beach out of danger. For yachts the nearest all-weather refuge is Brixham.

Facilities Hotels, shops. EC Thurs. Boat-builder. Launching site from the road leading down to the beach which is steep and suitable for launching.

Across Seaton Bay $1\frac{1}{2}$ miles to the east of Beer Roads, the RIVER AXE runs into the sea close west of Haven Cliff. The entrance runs NNE, but is extremely narrow and unmarked, so should be attempted only in calm weather and with local knowledge, preferably in a dinghy for the first time. Once inside, the river affords good shelter for boats drawing less than 1m5 which can take the ground at LW. Across the river $\frac{1}{4}$ mile from the entrance there is a low bridge, which impedes further navigation.

Facilities Axe YC, launching slip, boatyard, shops, hotels and PO. Occasional buses.

EXMOUTH

Admiralty Chart No. 2290

High Water *Exmouth Dock. −04 h. 53 m. Dover. At
Topsham ½ h. later.*
 Heights above Datum *Approaches MHWS 4m5. MLWS
0m5. MHWN 3m3. MLWN 1m7. Dock about 0m5 less.*
 Depths *The approach and sands are liable to change, and the
buoys are moved to conform. The depth of the bar is about 1m5 (2m0
MLWS). Within the harbour the bottom is uneven. There are deep
stretches off Exmouth town and south and south-west of Bull Hill
Bank, but on the west and north of the bank there are 1m5 patches.
The river tends to shoal towards Topsham and practically dries out
in the upper reaches.*

91. *Exmouth safewater fairway bell buoy.*

THE RIVER EXE has some 6 miles of navigable channel and is
worth visiting when cruising in the West Country. The only
harbour is a small tidal dock at Exmouth town but there are
several anchorages. It should not be regarded as a port of refuge
as the sands on the bar are liable to shift and there is a dangerous
sea during strong onshore winds, especially with the ebb running
against the wind. Under average conditions, however, the
approach and entrance are not difficult, being well buoyed.

Approach and Entrance The outer Fairway buoy (Sph
bell buoy RW vert bands) is situated ½ mile south-south-west of
Straight Point, which is a low promontory backed by red cliffs,
but should not be confused with the lower Orcombe Point a mile
westward. There are high cliffs between the two with ledges of
rock at their foot. Whatever the direction of the approach, make
for the Fairway buoy, but when coming from the direction of
Torbay or Teignmouth give a good offing to the Pole sands on the
south side of the entrance channel, which are extending eastward.

As stated, the entrance should not be attempted during strong
onshore winds especially if the ebb has started to run. The easiest
time to approach is half flood. This coincides with the turn of the
offshore stream to the west. The tidal streams in the offing are
weak but are very strong in the channel and the entrance. As the
sands are liable to shift after gales it is necessary to navigate up the
channel by the buoys (which are moved accordingly), leaving the
even-numbered R can buoys to port and the odd-numbered G
con buoys to starboard. The leading marks on course 305° are
difficult to pick up by day (FS on Customs House at rear and
black post on the sea-wall at the front) or by night, when they
tend to be lost in the town's lights. Some of the port hand buoys
are very close to the Pole sands so they should not be approached
too closely. The streams run like torrents after the last port buoy
(No. 10) has been passed and it is best to keep on the starboard
side of the fairway.

The River Off Exmouth the river takes a sharp turn to the

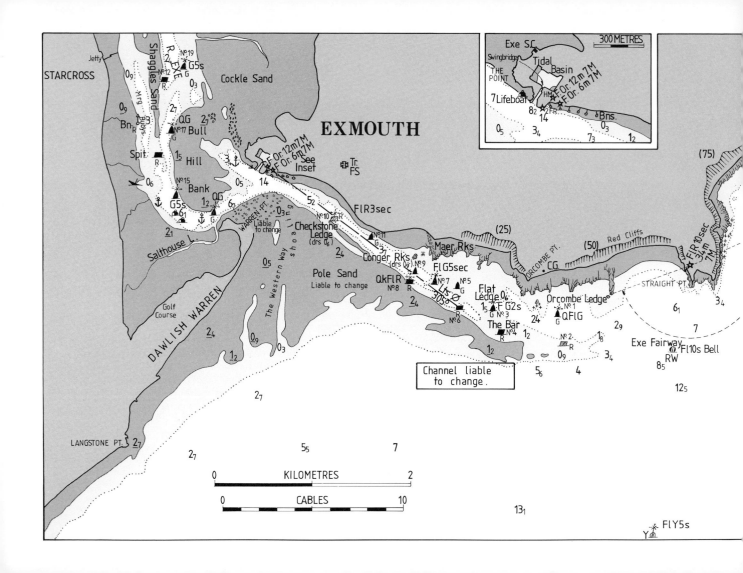

STARCROSS

Jetty

Shaggles Sand

R.EXE
No 19
G5s
G

Cockle Sand

EXMOUTH

0.9

0.9

Bn
R

Mrg
Buoys

0.3

No 12
R

2.7

No 17
Bull
QG

2.7

Spit
R

1.5
Hill

0.6

No 15
Bank
G5s
G
6.1

0.6

1.2
QG
G

6.7

Golf
Course

DAWLISH WARREN

LANGSTONE PT.
2.7

Salthouse L.

2.1

WARREN PT.
Liable
to change

0.3

The Western Way
shoaling

0.5

2.4

0.9

1.2

0.9

0.3

2.7

F.Or.12m7M
F.Or.6m7M
See
Inset

14

Tr.
FS

4.5

0.5

5.2

No 10
R

Checkstone
Ledge
(drs 0.6)

FlR3sec

No 11
G

2.4

0.3

Conger Rks
(drs)
No 9
G

Pole Sand
Liable to change

QkFlR
No 8
R

2.4

305°

FlG5sec
No 7
G

Maer Rks

No 5
G

Lt.

(25)

Flat
Ledge
1.5
F.G2s
G
No 3
G

No 6
G

The Bar
No 4
R

1.2

1.2

2.4

0.6

QFlG
Orcombe Ledge
No 1
G

1.2

No 2
R

1.2

Channel liable
to change.

1.8

0.9

5.6

ORCOMBE PT.
CG

(50)

Red Cliffs

(75)

FlR10sec
34m
7M

STRAIGHT PT.

6.1

3.4

Exe Fairway
Fl10s Bell
RW

2.9

7

3.4

8.5

12.5

13.1

FlY5s

5.5

7

0   KILOMETRES   2

0   CABLES   10

2.7

2.7

INSET

Exe SC

Swingbridge

THE
POINT

Tidal
Basin

F.Or.12m7M
F.Or.6m7M

7 Lifeboat

HM
8.2
14
2F.R.

300 METRES

Bns

0.5

3.4

0.3

7.3

1.2

92. View from No. 7 buoy heading seaward approximately east-south-east, with Orcombe Point in centre and Straight Point beyond.

south-west between Bull Hill Bank in the middle of the harbour and the Warren sands which form a continuation of the Warren (the low point on the south side of the entrance). The main flood sweeps past Exmouth in a north-westerly direction and accordingly course should be altered sharply to port well before reaching the dock in order to get into the stream between Bull Hill Bank and the Warren Sands, and in particular to avoid the shoals extending easterly from Bull Hill Bank. The reach of the river south of the Bull Hill Bank is called the Bight and is marked by two starboard hand buoys and by mooring buoys on the port hand. The channel follows round Bull Hill Bank northward and bends, leaving the R spit buoy and the Shaggles Sand to port and No. 17 buoy close to starboard. Course (see Imray Laurie Norrie & Wilson Chart Y No. 45) should then be towards the Lympstone Church to the north-north-east, passing between No. 12 R port hand and No. 19 G starboard buoys. The channel then bears in a north-north-west direction towards Powderham, leaving to starboard No. 21, No. 23 G buoys and perch, soon bearing north-north-east again leaving to port Powderham Pool and No. 14 R buoy. Then follow the buoys in a shoaling channel with depths as low as 1m5 in parts nearly to Turf Lock. Above Turf Lock the channel is marked by beacons on either side as far as Topsham.

When proceeding from Exmouth up the river a considerable saving of distance can be made by passing through the Shelly Gut. This is a shallow channel on the east side of Bull Hill Bank but it can be used only with local knowledge as the sands are steep-to on either side and the channel is intricate.

The Starcross channel lies west of the Shaggles Sand and carries 0m9 to 2m1 as far as Starcross. It is entered at the Shaggles Spit R buoy (leaving it to starboard). Although the channel is unmarked except by a beacon on the port side, the best water can be located by the larger yachts lying on moorings in it.

The Western Way   This is a drying swashway between the Pole sands on the eastward side and the Warren Sands on the western side. It requires local knowledge and a shallow draught boat.

Lights   Straight Point Lt Fl R 10 sec. 34m 9M.

The approach is marked by Fl or Qk Fl G Lts on the starboard hand (which is the easier side to follow) and by Lts on two buoys (Qk Fl R and Fl R 3 sec.) on the port hand. There are two Lts, F Or 7M, near the Customs House and the dock which lead in line at 305°; but the transit crosses the outer end of the Pole Sands and is only of service from No. 6 port hand buoy (no light) to the Checkstone No. 10 port hand buoy Fl R 3 sec. Within the harbour there are the starboard hand light buoys.

93. *View after passing No. 10 buoy and heading towards the dock with Exmouth seafront on right.*

Anchorage and Moorings (1) Temporary anchorage outside, off the entrance west of the Fairway buoy in calm weather. (2) *Exmouth dock*. This is approached through a narrow entrance where ferries berth, and is spanned by a swingbridge which has to be opened by arrangement with the HM—on Ch 16 during office hours or by telephone on Exmouth 72009. The basin is tidal and the north-west side dries out and is occupied by boats. HM's office is on the south side of the bridge and with his permission yachts berth at the south-east quays if these are not occupied by coasters. Depths about 1m2 alongside quay but less water in centre. Keel yachts will partially dry and there are a few ladders. When entering allow for the very strong streams setting across the entrance. (3) Anchor (if room can be found clear of moorings) *beyond the entrance to the dock off the Point* in 3m, clear of the lifeboat. Five-knot tidal stream at spring tides and rough when a fresh wind against stream. (4) Large yachts may anchor clear of the fairway in the *Bight between Bull Hill Bank and Warren Sands*. (5) *West of Bull Hill Bank* outside the small craft moorings. (6) Anchorage off *Starcross*, south-east of the pier in 0m6 to 2m1 but best positions occupied by private moorings. Enquire at club as to possible temporary vacancy. Well sheltered from west. Water, and some facilities. EC Thurs. Ferry to Exmouth. Main line station. (7) There is a mooring area between the perch, No. 25 buoy and *Lympstone Sand* which is approached from No. 23 buoy and stated to have an approximate depth of 1m0 at LW. (8) Small craft can anchor in 1m5 south of landing stage at *Turf*, clear of the coasters' fairway, or north of No. 25 buoy.

Exeter Canal The canal is 5 miles (8 km) long and is entered at Turf Lock. Least depth 3m3. Locked basin at Exeter.

Facilities at Exmouth. Boat-builders and repairers. Customs. Water by hose at dock. Petrol and oil. Hotels and shops. EC Wed. *Launching sites*: (1) Ramp south of harbour entrance near HW, where yacht club puts a wooden ramp over the soft sand in summer months, little room in road for cars and trailers but car park on the pier. (2) Beach north of harbour entrance. (3) By arrangement with yacht yards. (4) At Lympstone, 2 miles north of Exmouth ramp, for launching near HW. Yacht clubs: Exe SC, Starcross YC at Powderham Pt, Starcross Fishing and Cruising Club at Starcross, Topsham SC, Lympstone SC. Station and bus services.

TEIGNMOUTH

Admiralty Chart No. 26

High Water *approaches* −05 h. 11 m. *Dover.*
Heights above Datum *MHWS* 4m8. *MLWS* 0m6.
MHWN 3m6. *MLWN* 1m9.
Depths *About 0m3 on the bar; deep pool off Ferry Point, then
depths in the fairway over 2m up to Shaldon bridge.*

TEIGNMOUTH is an attractive little seaside town. The harbour on
its west and south-west side is well sheltered but the streams are
fast so that it is best to obtain moorings if possible. The entrance
is difficult for strangers and the bar makes it dangerous during
onshore winds and when a swell is running.

Approach and Entrance The entrance to the River Teign
lies to the northward of the Ness, a bold red sandstone headland
with pines at its summit, which is easy to identify. The Ness and
the Pole Sands projecting eastward from it flank the south side of
the river entrance, and the Spratt Sands lie on the north side. The
sands on the bar are constantly shifting and in some years steep
sandbanks build up. Without a pilot or assistance from those with
local knowledge the entrance should not be attempted by
strangers, except with the utmost caution in settled weather
during offshore winds and on the last quarter of the flood. The
following directions form a rough guide to the entrance but
should not be relied upon owing to the shifting sands.

Approach from the southward with the *inner* end of the pier
bearing about north magnetic. Before the Ness comes abeam
identify the leading marks above the Point (grey stone tower at
front, black pillar at rear) on a transit of 334°. This will lead over
Pole Sands at a point which dries 0m3, thence into deeper water
west of the bar and south of Spratt Sands.

To the west will now be seen the white beacon with a black base

94. *The Ness (red sandstone) and to right the white beacon.*

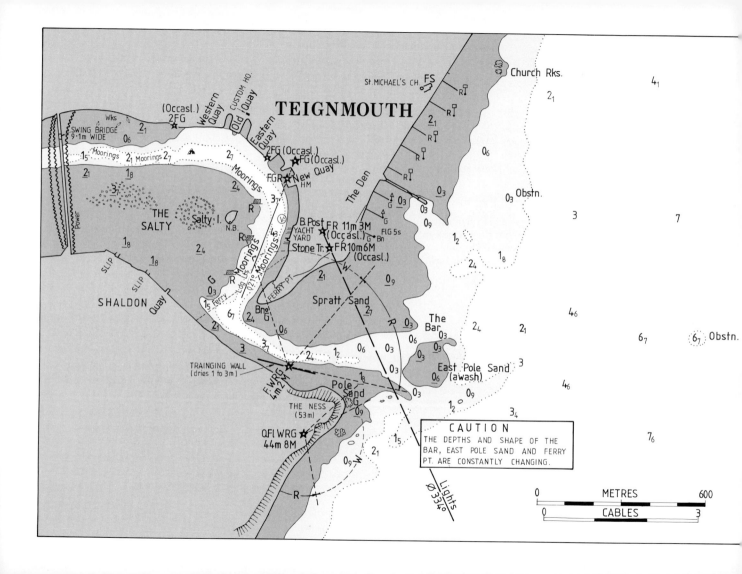

TEIGNMOUTH

St.MICHAEL'S CH. FS
Church Rks.

SWING BRIDGE
9·1m WIDE

Wks

(Occasl.) 2FG

Western Quay

CUSTOM HO.

Old Quay

Eastern Quay

2FG (Occasl.)

FG (Occasl.)

New Quay

HM

FGR

Moorings

Moorings

THE SALTY

Salty I.

N.B.

R

R

Ldg. Lts.

0·210° Moorings

Moorings

SHALDON

SLIP

SLIP

Quay

Ferry

Ferry Pt.

Bn

G

G

R

B.Post FR 11m 3M
(Occasl.)

Stone Tr.

Spratt Sand

Yacht Yard

FR 10m 6M
(Occasl.)

Bn

Flg 5s

The Den

The Bar

The Ness
(53m)

Pole Sand

G

R

TRAINING WALL
(dries 1 to 3m)

Fl.WRG
4m 2M

QFl WRG
44m 8M

East Pole Sand
(awash)

Obstn.

Obstn.

Obstn.

R

Lights Ø 334°

CAUTION
THE DEPTHS AND SHAPE OF THE
BAR, EAST POLE SAND AND FERRY
PT. ARE CONSTANTLY CHANGING.

METRES
0   600

CABLES
0   3

Power

95. *Close up of the conspicuous white light beacon.*

(Phillip Lucette) on the north-west side of the Ness, on a training wall which is covered before half flood. When this beacon bears between 250° and 258° steer about 40m off it, taking soundings to skirt the north side of the Pole Sands. An alternative and more direct approach is from the east steering for the white beacon (which is conspicuous) keeping a steady bearing 254°, distant 4

cables and proceed as before. In either case it is sensible in tidal calculations to assume that an area drying 0m6 will be crossed, as a stranger may not find the best water and the sands are liable to change.

At this beacon follow the chart round the green beacon off Ferry Point on the north side of the channel. Note that the sands

96. In the reach east of The Salty with New Quay on left and yacht yard on starboard hand, off which there is a visitors' mooring.

have crept southward from the point so the beacon should be left 100m clear to starboard. Here the stream runs very hard. Once past Ferry Point alter course quickly to starboard at 021° and steer for the end of the New Quay leaving the three red can buoys well to port.

The whole of the centre of the harbour is occupied by 'The Salty' flat; the river runs round to the east of this. Pilotage is now easier because the flats are marked by port hand buoys, while the starboard shore is fairly steep-to. After passing the third red port hand buoy keep on the starboard side of the channel on the line of New Quay until rounding into the straight E–W reach, north of The Salty, leading to the bridge. Here the direction of the channel can be judged by yachts lying on moorings, keeping close to the larger ones for the best water.

Lights   There is a sector Lt (Qk Fl W R G) on the Ness and F R leading lights on 334° over the eastern extremity of Pole Sands, but strangers should not attempt the entrance at night; the leading lights are intended for pilots and those with local knowledge.

Anchorage and Mooring   Anchoring is possible outside Teignmouth harbour 1 to 2 cables south-east of the pier end or a cable south-east of the Ness in settled weather and offshore winds, taking soundings to find a suitable depth. Within the harbour it is difficult to anchor as the streams are strong and there are moorings and chains on the bottom in all the best parts. The only possibility is at neap tides on the edge of The Salty near the second and third red buoys. Accordingly it is necessary to try to find a vacant mooring. There is a visitors' mooring off the yacht yard on the east side of the channel in deep water. Moor fore and aft to two white buoys with a 15m spread. Enquiry can also be made of the HM at New Quay as to the possibility of moorings' being temporarily vacant. Call on Ch 16 or by telephone on 3165.

Upper Reaches   The river above Shaldon bridge is navigable as far as Newton Abbot at high water by small craft with local knowledge.

Facilities   Water from New Quay. Fuel and chandlery but Shaldon better for this purpose. Yacht yard with patent slipway up to 36m long and 2m7 draught, and two small boatyards. Several hotels and restaurants. Good shops. EC Thurs. Launching site for dinghies at Shaldon. At Teignmouth launching is possible at the end of Lifeboat Lane and Gales Hill, also at Pellew Steps, and there is a launching site at the yacht yard. Ferry to Shaldon. Yacht clubs: Teign Corinthian YC, Shaldon SC. Buses and mainline station.

TORQUAY

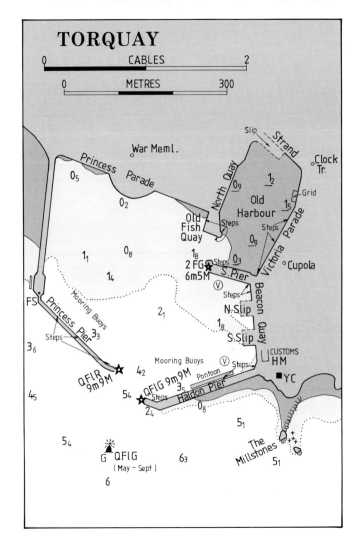

Admiralty Chart No. 26

High Water −05 h. 08 m. Dover.

Heights above Datum MHWS 4m9. MLWS 0m7. MHWN 3m7. MLWN 2m0.

Depths *4m2 just within the entrance. Inside the outer harbour there is over 3m alongside the Haldon (east) pier, and the Princess (west) pier. In the southern part of the harbour the depth is over 2m, but the inner harbour dries out except at the end of the south pier.*

TORQUAY lies in the north-western corner of Torbay, well sheltered, except from strong onshore winds. The town is a large and popular seaside resort and over-crowded during the holiday season.

Approach and Entrance Approaching from the eastward, the church tower on high ground at the back of Babbacombe Bay and the spire of the Roman Catholic church will first be seen. Torbay will next be identified with Hope Nose and the Ore Stone (32m) and Thatcher (41m) rocks on the north side and Berry Head on the south. Entering the north side of the bay note that there is a sunken outlier about 90m south-west of Ore Stone, and the Morris Rogue (0m8 over it) 1½ cables south-east of the East Shag (11m) rock.

From the southward there are no outlying dangers. The entrance is 61m wide, and within the outer harbour there is plenty of water for yachts. There is not much room for manœuvre, so enter slowly and be prepared to meet excursion vessels, which are frequently leaving the harbour.

Lights South of the entrance a G con buoy Qk Fl G (April/Sept.). On the Haldon (east) pierhead a Qk Fl G; on

97. *Torquay harbour and entrance showing Princess Pier (left), Haldon Pier (right) and south pier of the inner drying harbour. Moorings for yachts are shown and also the dinghy slips in the outer harbour and the slip in the inner harbour. (Photo: Aerofilms Ltd.)*

Princess (west) pierhead a Qk Fl R; on the inner pier there are two F G Vert.

Anchorage and Moorings (1) *Outside*, in offshore winds, good anchorage off the Princess pier in 3m6 to 4m8 or near the end of the Haldon pier in 2m4 to 2m7 or more to seaward but keep clear of the fairway. (2) Inside the harbour, moor to buoy as directed by the HM, or berth temporarily *alongside Haldon pier.* Large yachts lie inside to east and west of entrance, smaller ones farther in. The outer piers are in constant use by pleasure and excursion vessels in summer months, but yachts sometimes lie alongside the wall in inner harbour and dry out. The HM can be contacted during office hours on Ch 16 or by telephone on 22429.

Facilities Water near dinghy landing on east of outer harbour or in quantity at Haldon or south piers. Petrol, diesel oil and chandlery at south pier. Boat-builders. Scrubbing by arrangement. Launching site at all states of tide on slip east of outer harbour with car park adjacent; also at slipway in inner harbour, 3 hours each side of HW, by permission of the HM. Hotels and restaurants of all grades. Excellent shops. EC Wed. or Sat. Mainline station. Buses to all parts. Ferry to Brixham. Yacht club: R. Torbay YC.

PAIGNTON

PAIGNTON has a very small harbour on the west side of Torbay, north of Roundham Head, with its prominent red cliffs. From the east quay with its Lt Fl R 7m 3M there is a rocky outcrop running due east, the seaward extremity of which is marked by a R lattice beacon with a spoil ground topmark. Approach from north-east is simplest.

The harbour dries out and is crowded with moorings but there is good anchorage in offshore winds north-east of the entrance within easy reach of the harbour by dinghy. Facilities are good and the HM can sometimes arrange a berth where a visiting yacht can dry out alongside the quay.

BRIXHAM

Admiralty Chart No. 26

High Water — *05 h. 11 m. Dover.*
Heights above Datum *MHWS 4m7. MLWS 0m7. MHWN 3m4. MLWN 1m9.*
Depths *The outer harbour is deep but the inner harbour dries out at Springs almost to the end of the New pier.*

BRIXHAM is an historic fishing port but the famous sail trawler fleet has been replaced by motor fishing vessels. The innumerable sea-gulls bear witness to this continuing activity. The big outer harbour is easily accessible at all states of the tide, which makes it one of the best yachting centres in the West Country. Brixham YC welcomes visiting yachtsmen from recognized clubs and has its own landing steps and boatman. The harbour is sheltered except from the northward and Torbay provides a fine sailing area with weak tides which is exposed only to the eastward.

Approach and Entrance Brixham lies a mile west of Berry Head, which is a headland, sloping at 45°, easily identified. The harbour entrance is wide but the end of the breakwater should not be rounded closely when approaching from east as trawlers and tripper boats may be leaving harbour and hidden by the breakwater. Speed limit is 5 knots.

Lights Berry Head Lt, Gp Fl (2) 15 sec. 58m 18M. At end of breakwater Lt Occ R 15 sec. 3M.

Anchorages (1) *Outside in Brixham Roads* in about 7m, or small yachts can anchor in fine weather outside to the east of the breakwater, close in towards Shoalstone Point. (2) *Inside on west side of the harbour* as indicated on the plan, between moorings and just clear of fairway. Inevitably there is often considerable wash

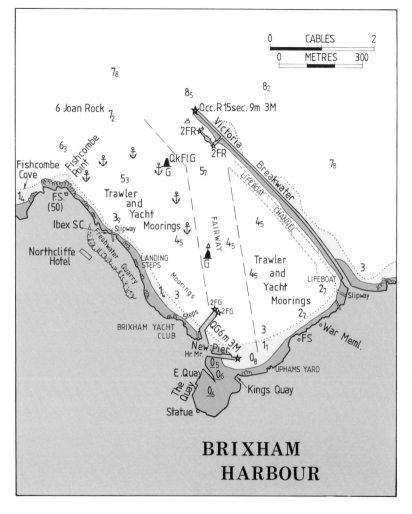

BRIXHAM HARBOUR

from passing trawlers and excursion boats near the fairway, so it is preferable to be close to the land near the entrance in reasonable weather. (3) Small yachts can anchor in *Fishcombe Cove* (just west of the headland at entrance) but this position can be dangerous if the wind freshens anywhere north to north-east. (4) In the south-east corner of harbour *near the lifeboat slip*.

There are a few visitors' mooring buoys in the harbour, but if none is found vacant apply to HM or the boatman at the yacht club. Yachts should be reported to the HM within 24 hours of arrival. In the event of gales from the north-west (which can occur suddenly if the wind veers at the end of a southerly gale) or north, shelter should be sought at Torquay.

Facilities Brixham is particulary well provided with facilities for visiting yachts. There are banks, hotels, restaurants and shops of all kinds (EC Wed.). Upham's is a large yacht yard with four slipways and 10-ton hoist. Two other boat repairers. Two scrubbing grids 2m4 draught and eight scrubbing berths 3m0 draught by arrangement with HM. Also crane lift 4 tons at quay head. Compass swinging by arrangement with HM. Sailmakers. Water is obtainable by permission at the yacht club steps or at the New pier where diesel oil is also obtainable. Customs Office. Yacht chandlers at quay and at Upham's. Launching sites: from south-east corner of outer harbour at all states of tide, breakwater hard slipway and from new slipway at Freshwater Quarry. Frequent buses to all parts and excursion boats to Torquay and Paignton. Yacht clubs: Brixham YC, Ibex SC.

98.   *View of Brixham Harbour facing north-west towards Torquay. From left the inner harbour and breakwater. The new pier and fish market with Brixham Yacht Club beyond it.*

DARTMOUTH

Admiralty Chart No. 2253

High Water   −05 h. 15 m. *Dover.*
Heights above Datum *MHWS 4m8. MLWS 0m4. MHWN 3m6. MLWN 1m8.*
Depths   *Deep water channel as far as Dittisham, but beyond there are considerable variations in depth.*

DARTMOUTH is one of the best-protected harbours on the South Coast. Shelter inside can be found in any weather and, if weatherbound, small yachts will find plenty of water to be explored within the harbour. Dartmouth is a town of character and the upper reaches of the Dart are beautiful. At HW navigation is possible as far as Totnes, some 10 miles up the river, in a vessel of up to 4m draught. Dartmouth is one of the West Country harbours offering the advantage that there is always room for visiting yachts either at anchor as directed by the HM or at the three marinas.

Approach and Entrance   Dartmouth lies between the two promontories of Berry Head and the Start (see photographs Nos. 10 and 11 in Passage Data section), being 5 miles from the former and 7 miles from the latter. The entrance is not conspicuous from seaward, but it can be located by the conspicuous 24m daymark (elevation 170m) above Froward Point, east of the entrance, and the craggy Mewstone Rock (35m) and associated rocks.

The entrance is deep and well marked but there are dangers on each side. On the east side there are rocks to the west of the Mewstone; the Verticals (dry 1m8) and the West Rock with a depth over it of 0m9. South of Inner Froward Point is the Bear's Tail (dries 0m6) and 2¾ cables west of the Point is Old Castle Rock (with 1m8 over it), to the SW of which is the G con Castle Ledge buoy. From about 3 hours flood to 3 hours ebb the stream sets towards these dangers, which should be given a wide berth. Approaching from the eastward keep the East Blackstone Rock (which is ½ mile east of Mewstone) well open of the Mewstone until the G con Castle Ledge buoy comes in line with Blackstone

99.   *Dartmouth Day Beacon bearing north, distant 1 mile.*

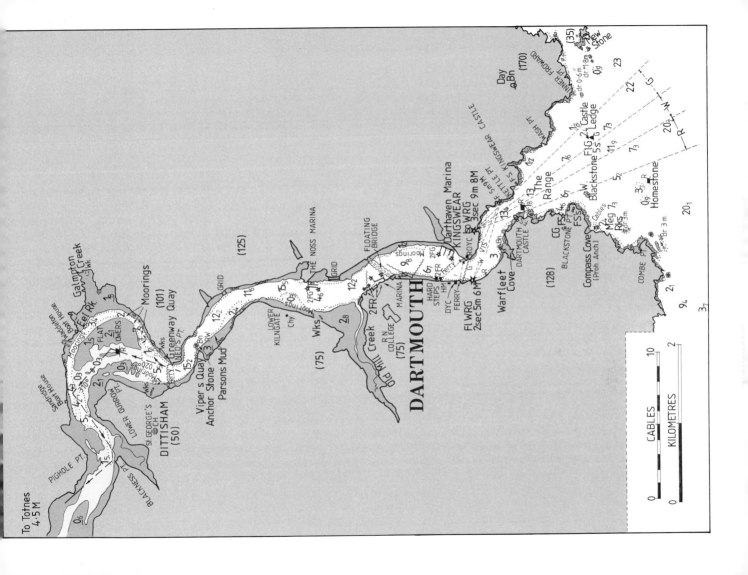

Point on the west side of entrance.

On the west side of the approach there are rocks a cable off Combe Point and 3 cables off this Point is the Homestone (with om9 over it) marked by R can buoy. To north-north-east of this Point are the Meg Rocks which dry 3mo. Off Blackstone Point there is the Western Blackstone Rock, which can be seen as it is 2m high, and should be given a clear berth.

Between these dangers the fairway is wide and the approach is easy, except in strong south or south-east winds when a heavy swell runs into the harbour, reaching at times as far as the lower ferry. Meeting an *ebb* tide it can cause an ugly sea for boats and small vessels. In the narrows there are two rocks to avoid on the west side opposite Kingswear Castle, the Checkstone (om3 over it) and the Kitten rock (1m8 over it) south-south-east of the R can Checkstone buoy, which lies off the ledges on the western side. The Kitten rock is on the edge of the fairway, so when approaching the narrows keep well east of it and steer to give a good berth to the Checkstone buoy. The wind is often baffling and fluky in the narrows and their approach, but navigation is straightforward after passing the Checkstone by keeping to the middle of the fairway.

Lights Enter in white sector of Kingswear light on east side of harbour. Iso W R G 3 sec. 9m 8M, W 325°–331°, G 325°–318°, R 331°–340°. The green sector covers dangers to starboard and the red those to port. Alter course to port when white sector (289°–297°) of Dartmouth harbour light (Fl W R G 2 sec. 5m 6M) is entered and steer for it; thence steer up river between the shore lights of Dartmouth and Kingswear. When leaving Dartmouth keep on a stern bearing in the white sector of the harbour light. When the white sector of Kingswear light is entered steer out on it, leaving Castle Ledge buoy (G 5 sec.) to port.

Anchorage and Moorings (1) *Outside* there is temporary anchorage in settled weather in the range but there is often an uncomfortable swell. It is prohibited in the area between Blackstone Point bearing 291° and Combe Point bearing 343° owing to cables which emerge seaward from Compass Cove. (2) Anchorage available east of *main channel opposite Dartmouth*

100. The Mewstone and associated rocks from the southward.

166

101. *Entrance to River Dart. (Photo : Aerofilms Ltd.)*

102. Battery Point and Dartmouth Castle on west side of narrows. (Photo: C. Sergel)

103. Dittisham, 3 miles up the River Dart on the west side.

between line of large buoys and small craft moorings, but beware ground chain along line of large buoys. The Royal Dart YC has six moorings, which may be used by visitors on application to the Club. (3) *Dart Harbour and Navigation Commission moorings.* These are marked DHC and are available on the east side of the harbour and for smaller yachts on the Dartmouth side, on application to the HM. Berthing for short periods is allowed alongside the embankment wall, where there is also a scrubbing grid. Both embankments dry out at springs; the upper one beyond the ferry pontoon (two F R at each end) also at neaps. (4) Alongside at the *Darthaven Marina* just upstream of Kingswear Railway Station. Contact on Ch 37. (5) Moorings and berths are available at *Dart Marina* above floating bridge on west side, with petrol, diesel oil, water, yacht yard, hotel and all facilities. The same organization also has berths alongside the marina up river off Noss Works. (6) *Off Parsons Mud* on the west side of the river between small craft moorings south of the Anchor Stone, but note that cargo ships proceed all the way up the river and the channel must be kept clear at all times. (7) *Greenway Quay,* Dittisham. Some visitors' moorings off Ferry Boat Inn at Dittisham and off Stoke Gabriel. Anchor off Ferry Boat Inn below moorings. Fresh water tap on quay in front of inn. LW landing pontoon at Dittisham for dinghies. Small passenger ferry operates between Dittisham and Greenway. Scrubbing alongside Greenway Quay by arrangement with ferry operator. Yacht yards in Galmpton Creek. Also anchorages off the upper boathouse between Sandridge Point and Galmpton Creek and upstream beyond Blackness Point.

Upper Reaches   (a) If proceeding up river from Dittisham to the east of the Flat Owers Bank, keep all mooring buoys close to starboard to avoid the mudbank. (b) When there is sufficient depth of water to navigate to the west of the Flat Owers Bank, steer for the boathouse at Waddeton until the R buoy is abeam to

port, then alter course to port and steer for the upper Sandridge boathouse. When the upper Sandbridge boathouse is abeam to starboard, alter course for Blackness Point, keeping Higher Gurrow Point fairly close to port. When Blackness Point is abeam to port, alter course for Pighole Point and leave all moorings close to starboard after passing Pighole Point. (c) If proceeding beyond Stoke Gabriel, when Mill Point is abeam, alter course for the middle of the wood on the south bank of the river. Off the entrance to Bow Creek there are R and G channel buoys, then steer for the R buoy off Duncannon. The river is marked with buoys and beacons to the end of the Fleet Mill Reach after which the best water is approximately in the centre of the river to Totnes.

Make fast alongside in the Mill Tail which is the left hand channel on arrival at Totnes. The main river has two trots of moorings and a visitors' mooring is sometimes available by arrangement with the Totnes Boating Association. The Mill Tail dries out, the bottom being mud to a depth of about 0m5 and then sand. Attractive old town with castle. Boatyard. Chandlery. Hotels and restaurants. Shops.

Facilities   Water by arrangement at Harbour Office or at any marina. At Dittisham public standpipes. Fuel at marinas and from a barge moored in the middle of the river between the upper and lower ferries. Hotels and restaurants, good shopping centre—EC part Wed. part Sat. Customs House. Yacht yards, chandlers and all facilities. Yacht clubs: R. Dart YC (Kingswear), Dartmouth YC, Dittisham SC. Launching sites: public slipway at Kingswear next R. Dart YC, except near LW. Slipway at Dartmouth dinghy basin, 2 hours each side HW or at any tide from slipway alongside upper ferry slipway, provided ferry is not obstructed. The nearest rail connection is at Paignton 7 miles away. Buses to all parts.

SALCOMBE

Admiralty Chart No. 28

High Water — *05 h. 38 m. Dover.*
Heights above Datum *MHWS 5m3. MLWS 0m7.
MHWN 4m1. MLWN 2m1.*
Depths *On the leading marks the bar normally has a depth of
1m5, but immediately east of the transit there is only 0m7 and the
depth on the bar sometimes changes. Beyond the bar there is a deep
channel as far as Tosnos Point in the 'Bag'. Above Tosnos Point up
to Heath Point there is upwards of 2m with local knowledge, but
strangers may not find more than 1m2 in parts. The estuary then
shallows, but at three-quarters flood it is possible for vessels of 2m7
draught to navigate up to Kingsbridge, some 3 miles above Salcombe.*

VISITING yachtsmen consider this lovely well-sheltered estuary
to be one of the best of the West Country ports. It offers
anchorages and visitors' moorings, and is ideal for day sailing and
boating of all kinds, and for family bathing, picnics and walks.

Approach and Entrance The entrance is a simple matter
with sufficient rise of tide on the bar and in the absence of strong
onshore winds or swell.

The entrance is just to the east of Bolt Head, and some 3 miles
west of the Prawle. Boat Head is a remarkable promontory with a
spiked skyline. There are two islets, the Mewstone (19) and Little
Mewstone (5), off the Point. A stranger might find some
resemblance in profile between the Bolt and the Start, but the
latter is a far longer headland and has a white lighthouse on it.
(See Passage Data.)

Strong southerly winds meeting the ebb at the Bolt set up
overfalls which can be avoided by entering from farther east. The
only dangers in the approach are rocks to the west near the
Mewstones, which should be given a fair berth, and on the east
side of the Rickham Rock, which has 2m7 over it, and rocks near
the coast farther eastward.

Whether approaching from west or east it is simplest to alter
course northward about ¼ mile east of the Bolt. Now sail
northward past Starehole bay where the remains of the wreck of
the barque *Herzogin Cecilie* lie in the north-west corner under the
high cliffs.

A headland on the north-east corner of this little bay with a
detached rock (the Great Eelstone) will be observed. The
Cadmus Rocks (0m3) lie south of Great Eelstone and must be
avoided. The bar is situated about 2 cables north of the Great
Eelstone Rock and the line of approach leaves the Great Eelstone
about 1½ cables to port. The leading marks on course 360° consist
of a RW beacon with RW cage topmark on the Poundstone Rock
(dries 4m) and a RW beacon with a diamond topmark, situated in
front of the left-hand edge of a big red-roofed house with two
gables (see plate 99). If they cannot be located, a compass bearing
on the left-hand edge of the house should suffice even if not
affording the best water. There is also an approach across the bar
farther to the east with a white house in line with the Poundstone
beacon at 327°, but this is not recommended except in calm
weather and near the top of the tide.

The bar is dangerous in strong onshore winds especially
against an ebb tide, and has only 0m7 over it and less in some
years. The bar should not be attempted under these conditions,
nor should it be crossed when a swell is running in until there is
ample tide over it. It is here that a lifeboat was lost. The entrance
and bar are protected by land from the west and in normal
conditions present no difficulties.

Once over the bar continue on the leading line leaving to port
the Bass Rock (dries 0m9) off Splat Point, and to starboard the
Wolf Rock (dries 0m6) marked by a G con buoy. As the

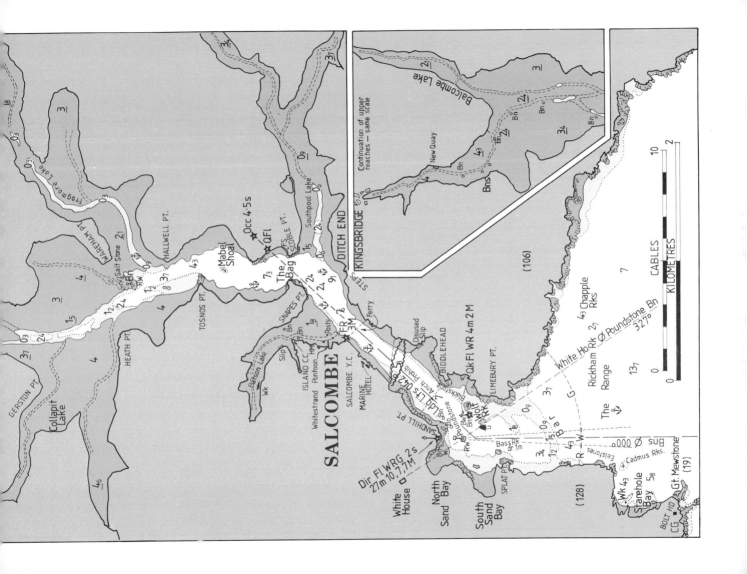

104. *The leading beacons almost in tangent with the left side of the red-roofed house with two gables.*

Blackstone Bn Lt comes abeam to starboard, alter to leave to port the Poundstone and two beacons off Sandhill Point and proceed on 042° up the middle of the wide fairway.

Lights At Sandhill Point directional Lt Fl WR G 2 sec. 27m 10, 7, 7M. Keep in the narrow white sector. When Blackstone beacon (Qk Fl WR, R 218°–048°, W 048°–218°) changes from red to white the Wolf Rock has been cleared. Hold on course for $\frac{3}{4}$ cable until the leading lights up the river come into line at 042° but no farther. The front is Fl W 1$\frac{1}{2}$ sec. and the rear Fl W 3 sec.; they are situated near Scoble Point on the east side of the Bag. They lead as far as the port hand ferry landing light F R and anchorage. It is possible to continue on the transit to the Bag by bringing the rear light just open to the right of the front one when passing Snapes Point, given sufficient moonlight to avoid the

numerous yachts on moorings. On leaving Salcombe and proceeding down channel the cut of the W R sectors on the Blackstone beacon Qk Fl Lt provide an additional safeguard from shallow water on the south-east side. The cut in the sectors can also be used when entering once clear of all the Blackstone Rocks if the leading lights cannot be picked out among the riding lights.

Anchorage and Moorings (1) *In the range outside* the bar during offshore winds in settled weather, in depths as convenient. (2) *Outside in Starehole Bay* in 4 to 6m but avoid the wreck a cable off the north-west corner. (3) Large yachts usually bring up *off the Marine Hotel*, but it can be rough here in strong south-west winds. (4) Off the mud flats between Salcombe and *Snapes Point*. (5) *Off Ditch End*, on south side of the channel east of Salcombe. Convenient landing here, then short walk to ferry boat landing,

172

105.   Salcombe as seen from the entrance of Southpool Lake.

but visitors' moorings now occupy best positions. Take soundings to find position between deep channel and steep edge of the sands. (6) *In the Bag*, about ¾ mile north-west of Salcombe, but if anchoring take care to keep clear of many existing moorings. (7) In the pool beyond shallow entrance of *Frogmore Creek* in 1m8. (8) *Moorings*. Salcombe is well provided with visitors' moorings with large white buoys numbered V1 to V22 which commence off the Marine Hotel and are situated each side of the fairway. All are capable of handling at least a 20-ton vessel and three between Scoble Point and Ditch End can accommodate 100-ton ships. These can be used with permission of the Harbour Office or from his staff patrolling in launches marked 'Harbour Master', who can also find other moorings for visitors. He can also be contacted on VHF Ch 16 or by phone at 2951. Under no circumstances anchor near the fairway in the vicinity of the town.

Creeks   The arms and creeks provide a pretty and interesting cruising area for dinghies and shallow draught boats at HW, but the large-scale Admiralty chart is desirable.

Southpool Lake, which joins the main channel opposite Salcombe, has uneven depths and the pools are occupied by moorings.

Frogmore Creek, which joins on the east side above Tosnos Point, also has an uneven bottom with depths ranging from a pool with 1m8 shallowing farther east to 0m3.

The upper reaches of the main channel are marked by posts on the mud on the port hand above Gerston Point and are navigable at HW to Kingsbridge.

Facilities The principal facilities for visitors are centred near Whitestrand Landing Pontoon. HM's office (with VHF Ch 16 and 14). Water, diesel oil, petrol and chandlers near by. Water also from water boat if bucket hung in rigging. Six yacht or boatyards. Grid. Launching slip 2 hours each side HW, and car park, though often crowded. Customs House opposite the Salcombe Hotel. Banks, hotels, restaurants and a good range of shops. EC Thurs. Hourly bus service to Kingsbridge. Yacht clubs: Salcombe YC. The Island Cruising Club invites visiting yachtsmen to use its clubhouse at the north-east end of Salcombe. In rough weather, when dinghies are uncomfortable or unsafe, visitors may use the Club's launch service between Salcombe and the Bag by prior arrangement with the Club Office (tel. 2445).

HOPE COVE

Admiralty Chart No. 1613

THE CHARMING village of Inner Hope lies in the cove just to the northward of Bolt Tail. It affords fair anchorage for yachts and small ships during winds from north-north-east to south in depths ranging from 10 to 2m. Run in on a bearing of 110° towards the old Lifeboat House, and anchor before closing the line of the breakwater wall bearing 030°. There are some ledges in the inner cove, and there is a drying harbour for boats formed by a breakwater. Three hotels. Village. EC Thurs. Bus to Kingsbridge (9 miles). Stores. PO.

YEALM RIVER and NEWTON FERRERS

Admiralty Chart No. 95

High Water *− 05 h. 37 m. Dover.*
Heights above Datum *Entrance MHWS 5m4. MLWS 0m7. MHWN 4m3. MLWN 2m1.*
Depths *0m4 on the leading line S over the bar with 1m4 just south of the transit, but sands are always liable to change : thence not less than 2m1 to Yealm Pool.*

THE YEALM is one of the most beautiful but often overcrowded harbours on the South Coast. The anchorage is sheltered and the entrance easy, except in strong onshore winds. Newton Ferrers is not so well provided with facilities as Salcombe, for example, but no cruise on the South Coast would be complete without putting into this secluded river.

Approach and Entrance The entrance is rough in strong onshore winds from the south-west, but under normal conditions with adequate tide it is easy enough. The approach is made across Wembury Bay, which lies between Wembury Point on the north and Yealm Head on the south-east. From Wembury head there are rocks and ledges extending ½ mile south towards the conspicuous Mewston Island (59m). On the south-west side of the Mewstone lies the Little Mewstone Rock (15m) which has an off-lying rock 50m off it awash at LW. Altogether the rocks or shoals extend 2 cables south-west of the Mewstone. In this vicinity there are tide rips when the wind is across the stream. A quarter of a mile eastward of the Mewstone lie the Inner (dry 3m0) and Outer Slimers (1m5).

Approaching from the northward or westward the Mewstone

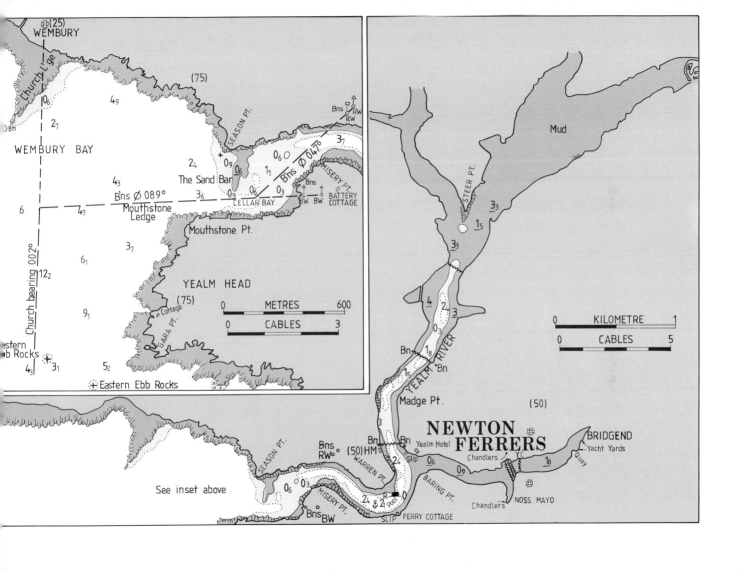

106. The Mewstone from south-west. This conspicuous islet lies on west side of Wembury Bay.

should be rounded at a distance of $\frac{1}{4}$ mile before standing north-east into Wembury Bay to pick up the leading marks, taking care to leave the dangerous Outer Slimers (dry 1m5) to port.

When the entrance of the river is opened up, a white cottage will be seen between trees near the summit on Misery Point (the inner point on the south side of the river) and below it, above Cellar Bay, a pair of leading beacons at 089° each topped by white triangles with a vertical black line. Bring these into line. After leaving Mouthstone Ledges to starboard keep 40m south of the transit, steering nearer the rocky shore on the starboard hand.

Approaching from the south or eastward keep at least 3 cables off Gara Point to clear the Eastern and Western Ebb rocks (awash). Then come on to the leading mark which is the square tower of St Werburgh's Church (about a mile east of Wembury Point) bearing 002°. The Ebb rocks will be left close to starboard,

107. The first pair of leading marks are situated above Cellar Bay south of Misery Point in line at 087°.

108. Ferry Point. Newton Ferrers. The Yealm Hotel and landing behind yacht in foreground. Continuation of Yealm River to the left, Newton Ferrers Arm to the right.

but 005° gives better clearance. Hold on until the leading marks in Cellar Bay have been identified. Then alter course to their transit and proceed as before.

The bar lies south and south-east of Season Point with least water of 0m4 on the transit of the triangle-topped leading marks above Cellar Bay. When about 1½ cables off the lower leading mark course has to be altered to port to the next leading beacons which will be seen to the north-east on the hillside to the right of a clump of trees about 3 cables east of Season Point. These are white boards with a R Vert line and lead through the first bend in the channel at 047° but cross an inner arm of the bar with only 0m6, although slightly better water may be found close to starboard of their line. After that the river is clearly defined and it is merely necessary to keep near mid-channel taking care to leave to port the R can buoy on the north side of the Pool. Note from the harbour plan that the deep channel is very narrow (50m) off the eastern extremity of Warren Point with only 0m3 on its west side and 0m4 on the east.

Above Warren Point, the Newton Ferrers creek opens out on the east side and becomes Newton Ferrers Arm. It is wide but dries out at LW. The River Yealm itself continues above Warren Point first in a north-north-west direction and then bears through north to north-east. The bottom is uneven, with depths of 3m4 to 1m8 for over $\frac{1}{2}$ mile, but with shallower patches as far as Shortaflete Creek.

Anchorage and Moorings The Yealm has become so popular that moorings are laid in all the best parts, and there is now no clear area left for anchoring in the Pool except in the fairway. If the HM does not make contact he can be reached by phone at Newtown Ferrers 872533. Holding ground in parts of the river is poor and yachts should lay out two anchors, which should be buoyed if close to moorings. (1) *Anchor outside* in settled weather only, south-west of Misery Point off Cellar Bay in from 0m3 to 1m2 beyond the junction of leading lines, sheltered from east and south. (2) Anchor in the pool *west of Warren Point*. Moorings are available on application to the HM, including a trot south of Madge Point where yachts moor fore and aft and lie several abreast. Note that anchoring is prohibited between the lower limit of oyster beds north of Madge Point and the upper limit east of Steer Point.

Facilities Water at private tap by Ferry Cottage near slip, or free at tap on ferry steps under Yealm Hotel. Stores, chandlery and PO at Newton Ferrers and Noss Mayo, also petrol and oil. EC Thurs. Scrubbing can be arranged. Two boat-builders. Hotels. Yealm YC opposite Noss Mayo. Newton Ferrers Sailing School, whose boats should be given consideration when under instruction. Launching sites: (1) Slip for launching at Bridgend Quay 2$\frac{1}{2}$ hours either side of HW. (2) At the Brook, Newton Ferrers, same hours. (3) Also at Riverside road west 3$\frac{1}{2}$ hours either side of HWS or 4$\frac{1}{2}$ hours at HWN. HM at Newton Ferrers. Buses to Plymouth.

PLYMOUTH

Admiralty Charts Nos. 1900, 1901, 1902 and 1967

High Water *Breakwater* −05 h. 49 m. *Dover.*
Heights above Datum *Devonport : MHWS 5m5. MLWS 0m8. MHWN 4m4. MLWN 2m2.*
Depths *A deep water harbour used by large ships. In the fairway the R. Tamar has least depths of 2m4 as far as Cargreen, 1$\frac{1}{2}$ miles above the bridge at Saltash. Thereafter shoal-draft boats can continue to Gunnislake, 16 miles from the breakwater.*

PLYMOUTH is a naval and commercial port. The well-known anchorages are rather too exposed for small yachts in bad weather, but shelter can be found in the docks or up the rivers, with frequent bus services connecting with centre of the town. Cawsand at the west entrance and the Yealm River to the east are two of the pleasant alternative anchorages in the area.

Inside the harbour is the River Tamar running northward above Saltash, which is navigable and sheltered—the clearance under the high-tension wires 4 cables south of Cargreen is 30m, but looks less. The Tavy joins the Tamar about 1$\frac{1}{4}$ miles above Saltash. This is a pretty river and though yachts cannot pass under the bridge it is navigable by small craft at HW, but note high-tension wires, 12m clearance. Below Saltash the St German's (or Lynher) River joins the Hamoaze and extends in a westerly direction. The river is deep for about 2 miles and is navigable. Large-scale charts are required for navigation in these rivers. Plymouth harbour has developed greatly of recent years as a yacht and dinghy centre and there are more yacht and sailing clubs than in any other south-west centre.

The harbour is under the jurisdiction of the Queen's Harbour

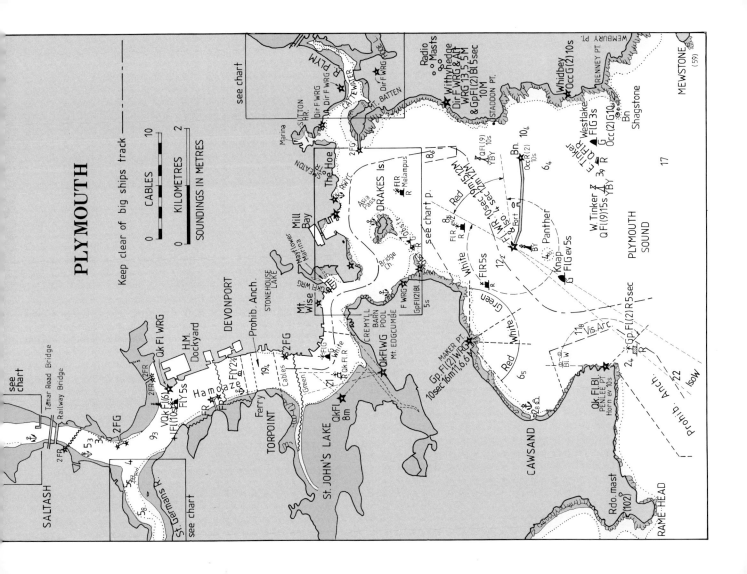

PLYMOUTH

Keep clear of big ships track ---------

CABLES

0   1   10

CABLES

KILOMETRES

0   2

SOUNDINGS IN METRES

see chart

SALTASH

Tamar Road Bridge
Railway Bridge

2FR

St Germans R.

see chart

5₃
3₃
2FR
5₅
4₄
5₆
6
5₈

2FR
2FR
2FG
9₃
VQkFl(6)
+Fl(10)s
Fl Y5s
QkFl WRG
H.M. Dockyard
DEVONPORT
Prohib. Anch.
STONEHOUSE LAKE
2FR
Fl Y2₄s
Cables
21
19₄
Hamoaze
2FG
2FG
Ferry
TORPOINT
QkFl 8m
St JOHN'S LAKE

White
(Green)
Fl G
QkFl R
CREMYLL
BARN POOL
Mt. EDGCUMBE
QkFl WRG
MAKER PT.
Gp.Fl(2) WRG
10sec 16m11.6.6s

23₂
Fl R

Mt. Wise
MILLBAY
Mayflower Marina
QkFl WRG
GpFl(2)Bl 5s

F WRG
GpFl(2)Bl
5s

White
F WRG

Red
White
Green
Red
White
6₅
11₆
Vis.Arc.
2₄
Bl
22
IsoW

CAWSAND

Qk Fl.Bl.
PENLEE PT.
Horn ev 10s
23₂

Prohib. Anch.

RAME HEAD

Rdo. mast
(102)

Mill Bay
SEATON
The Hoe
RWYC
Asia Pass
DRAKES Is.
Fl R
Melampus
Bridge Ch.
18₁
see chart p.
Red
Fl R
8₂
Fl(9)
QFl(9)
10s
YBY
10₄
Fl W.R
M2-120sec
M2-120sec

Marina
2FG

SUTTON HR.
Dir F WRG
Dir F WRG
Dir F WRG
MT. BATTEN
see chart
PLYM

Radio Masts
Withyhedge
Dir F WRG
WRG 13.5.5M
& GpFl(2) Bl 5sec
10M
STADDON PT.

Whidbey
OccG(2)10s
RENNEY PT.

WEMBURY PT.

E. Tinker
Westlake
Fl G 3s
Occ(2)G10.
Bn
Shagstone
17
MEWSTONE
(59)

Fl R5s
12₄
FlR
R
Knap
G FlGev5s
Panther
4₆
BY
Bn.
OccR(2)
10s
6₄
W.Tinker
QFl(9)15s YBY
PLYMOUTH SOUND

Port
8₁
Fl(9)
Gp.Fl(2) R 5sec
Fl R
6₅

109. Plymouth breakwater at high water and West Head lighthouse. Staddon Heights in background.

Master. There are bye-laws prohibiting anchoring in many places, principally in the main fairways. Yachts over 20m in length are subject to control by the Traffic Signals displayed from the Longroom Port Control Station west of Millbay docks and Flagstaff Steps Signal Station during the movement of large vessels between the Sound and Hamoaze. Full details of the signals are contained in the *Channel Pilot* and the Dockyard Port of Plymouth Order 1975.

All small vessels are required to keep clear of large ships which can only navigate in the deep water channels, especially warships. The Longroom Port Control Station keeps a constant VHF watch on Ch 16.

Approach and Entrance Plymouth Sound lies between Penlee Point on the west and Wembury Point (off which lies the Mewstone) on the east. Within the Sound is a long low breakwater in the centre with channels each side of it. The principal approach to the harbour is through the western channel

but the eastern channel is equally navigable.

The Eddystone Rocks and Lighthouse are situated 10 miles off the entrance, and a course of 024° from the lighthouse leads to west breakwater head, which soon becomes conspicuous. From the westward a vessel will first pass Rame Head which appears as an almost conical promontory with the ruins of a chapel at its summit. A mile and a quarter east is Penlee Point, a low headland with a turreted beacon tower. The Draystone rocks (over most of which there is 1m8) extend $\frac{1}{4}$ mile to the south-east of Penlee Point, and are marked by a R can buoy. The western entrance lies only $1\frac{1}{2}$ miles ahead between Mount Edgecumbe and the breakwater. If the wind is light and off the land there are often pockets of calm or variable winds. After passing through the western entrance, Drake's Island will lie to the northward, distant $1\frac{1}{4}$ miles. The main fairway leads north-east and is marked on the port hand by the R New Grounds and Melampus can buoys towards the famous Plymouth Hoe and thence through the Asia

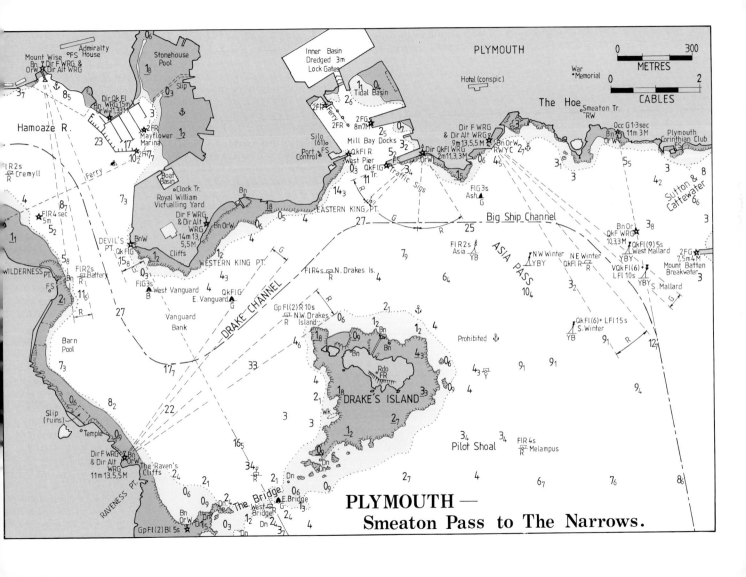

110. Royal Western Yacht Club of England (with flagstaff) and Plymouth Hoe.

Pass. Yachts need not keep to the big ship fairway and can leave the buoys on the wrong side by reference to the chart (see plan).

There is a short cut with 2m1 to the Hamoaze between Drake's Island and the Mount Edgecumbe shore known as 'The Bridge'. This channel is marked by a R can port hand buoy and G con starboard hand buoy. As there are the remains of several dolphins in the vicinity of the entrance of the channel steer for it on course 332°, pass between the buoys and continue for 150m, until leaving a R buoy to port, after which the main Drake Channel is soon entered.

From the eastward the Mewstone (59m) and the rocks south-west of it will be left to starboard. Next the Shagstone, off Renney Point (a nearly square rock 1m2 high marked by a black and orange beacon surmounted by a cone), should be given a good berth as the tide may be setting across the rocks between it and the

shore. Continue northward passing between the breakwater (unlit beacon at east extremity) and Staddon Point, leaving the coastline to starboard until the channel between Drake's Island and Mount Batten is approached. Here course may be altered to take the Asia Pass or the Smeaton Pass or, if bound for the Barbican or Cattewater, hold on to Mount Batten breakwater end leaving it to starboard and the Mallard Shoal buoys to port. The channels are used by large ships, so yachts need not adhere to them.

Lights At night enter by the western channel in the white sector of the West Breakwater Lt W R 10 sec. 19m 15–12M (W 262°–208° R 208°–262°). Bell 15 sec. The lower light in the window of the same structure Iso W 4 sec. 12M is useful if coming from the west of south-west as the sector (031°–039°) leads straight to the breakwater head leading past Draystone

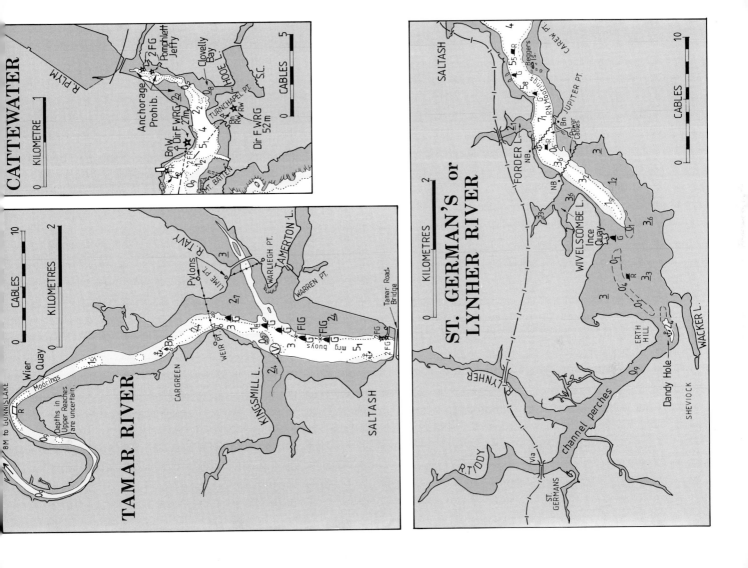

CATTEWATER

KILOMETRE

R. PLYM

2 FG
Pomphlett Jetty
Clovelly Bay
HOOE
Anchorage Prohib.
BnW
Dir F WRG 27m
TURNCHAPEL PT.
Bn
RW RW
Dir F WRG 52m
MT. BATTEN
S.C.

CABLES

TAMAR RIVER

8M to GUNNISLAKE
Wier Quay
Moorings
Depths in Upper Reaches are uncertain.
Bn
CARGREEN
WEIR PT.
Pylons
LIME PT.
R. TAVY
WARLEIGH PT.
TAMERTON L.
WARREN PT.
KINGSMILL L.
mrg buoys
FIG
FIG
FIG
FIG
SALTASH
Tamar Road-Bridge
2 FG

CABLES
KILOMETRES

ST. GERMAN'S or LYNHER RIVER

SALTASH
CAREW PT.
Beggers Is.
Jupiter Moorings
Bn JUPITER PT.
River Cables
FORDER L.
NB.
WIVELSCOMBE L.
Ince Quay
G
R
LYNHER
ERTH HILL
Dandy Hole
channel perches
Via
ST. GERMANS
R. TIDDY
SHEVIOCK
WACKER L.

KILOMETRES
CABLES

buoy (Gp Fl (2) R 5 sec.) south-east of Penlee Point. Keep a look-out for the Knap and unlit buoys. Within the harbour the edge of the cut of the white/red sector of W Breakwater Lt leads to the Melamphus buoy (Fl R 4 sec.) after which refer to buoys (Fl R port and Fl G starboard as marked on the plan on p. 183). Within the harbour there are many directional lights, but these are intended for deep-draught ships and, although their characters are shown, some of their sectors have been omitted on the small-scale plan as their use is not necessary for the pilotage of smaller craft. At Mill-bay entrance the lights at west pierhead are Qk R and at east pierhead Qk G, with 2 FG at the end of Trinity pier on your starboard hand and 2 FR at the end of RO/RO terminal right ahead. For traffic signals see (9) below.

Anchorages and Moorings As Plymouth is a large harbour, the selection of an anchorage depends on wind direction and weather conditions. It is always wise to buoy the anchor. (1) *Outside.* Cawsand Bay is an excellent anchorage in winds from south-west to north-west. It has gradually shelving shores and offers good holding ground. (2) *Off the north side of Drake's Island.* Good holding, but exposed in unsettled weather. (3) Moorings or anchor berths on application to the Royal Western YC, or anchorage outside them in reasonable weather. (4) *In the Cattewater* (the easterly channel to the north of Mount Batten). Either off the Barbican on eastern side leading to Sutton Pool, or apply to Sutton Yacht Harbour on Ch 37, 16 or 12 for a pontoon berth, depths up to 2m1 MLWS. Moorings sometimes available on application to the yacht yard in Clovelly Bay, west of Turnchapel Point. (5) *Anchor in Barn Pool*, which is a bay sheltered from the west by Mount Edgecumbe. The bay is very deep, so work in well towards the shore and let go in about 4m5. Here also buoy the anchor as there is wreckage on bottom. Reverse eddy close inshore. (6) *Off Cremyll*, near the ferry, but the stream is strong. (7) *Off Torpoint* in the Hamoaze above the ferry-landing and sewer outfall, marked by a noticeboard in 3m0.

Avoid fouling moorings. (8) *Mayflower Marina* in Stonehouse Pool north-east of Cremyll. Deep-water berths for craft up to 21m length overall; forty-five visitors' berths. Contact on Ch 37. (9) *Mill-bay dock.* Subject to permission of the Dock Master (east side of entrance) on Ch 16 craft drawing up to 7m9 may lock through 2 hrs either side of HW into the inner basin and lie alongside the quay. Entry signals: 3 B balls or 3G Lts Vert. Departure signals: 4 B balls or 3 R Lts Vert. Waiting trots in outer basin. There is complete shelter in the basin, all facilities and dock police in charge. Mill-bay dock is the best place for preparing to 'go foreign'. Provisions and bonded stores near by, and Customs. Local shops and not far from centre of town. If leaving the yacht, arrangements for caretaking may be made.

Tamar River (for upper reaches see Y Chart No. 51) Above Tor Point the river continues wide and deep and there are naval and reserve ships at moorings. Two miles up the river St German's River joins it on the west side, and $\frac{3}{4}$ mile beyond it is spanned by the high railway bridge and the road suspension bridge at Saltash. The entrance of the River Tavy lies 1$\frac{1}{4}$ miles above the bridge, and here the River Tamar channel is narrow with depths as low as 1m8 near the starboard hand buoy, with wide expanses of shoal water on both sides. At Weir Point the river is spanned by high-tension cables with a clearance of 30m5. At a distance of 1$\frac{1}{2}$ cables beyond the Point the best water 1m5 is only about 50 metres wide and a visiting yacht may cross a shoal in only 0m9, but the river deepens to about 4m5 off Cargreen. Above Cargreen the channel requires local knowledge, as the best water is narrow between unmarked mud shoals. High-tension cables (19m2 clearance) span the river 1$\frac{1}{4}$ miles beyond the village. The pretty upper reaches are navigable by shallow-draught boats near HW. Principal achorages: (1) *Saltash* on west side below or above the bridge in 6m or more. Anchorage prohibited in vicinity of water mains and cables. Facilities at Saltash. (2) *Off Cargreen.* Water, facilities and inn.

St German's or Lynher River (see Y Chart No. 49)   The river is entered on the west side of the Tamar nearly $\frac{3}{4}$ mile south of Saltash bridges, leaving to port a R can buoy marking the flats and Beggars Island. It is buoyed as far as Forder Lake off which there is 1m8. Beyond this the bottom is uneven and nearly dries at LAT $\frac{1}{2}$ mile east of Earth Hill except for the Dandy Hole. Above Earth Hill the river is navigable in the dinghy or in shallow-draught boats near HW. Principal anchorages: (1) *Off the bay east of Jupiter Point* but little room clear of Royal Navy moorings. (2) *South-west of Forder Lake* in 1m0 to 3m0. (3) *In Dandy Hole* in 1m5 to 4m2 on south side of river south of Earth Hill and north of Warren Wood. This anchorage can only be reached at half flood, and soundings should be taken to find the edges of the pool. Two anchors necessary to restrict swinging. No facilities.

River Tavy   This shallow river is not available for yachts as it is spanned near the entrance by high-tension lines (12m0 clearance) and by a railway bridge. There are extensive mud flats, but the river is pretty and navigable by dinghy or on the flood by shallow-draught low-masted boats.

Facilities at Plymouth   Plymouth provides all facilities for anything from a dinghy to a man-of-war and the amenities of a large town and resort area. There are several yacht yards of which Mashford's at Cremyll is best known. Yacht clubs: R Western YC of England, R. Plymouth Corinthian YC, West Hoe SC, Mayflower SC, Laira SC, Tamar River SC, Saltash SC, Torpoint Mosquito SC, Cawsand Bay SC. Launching site: the City Council has built a dinghy park alongside the Mayflower SC, Barbican, which will accommodate about 300 dinghies. The Royal Western YC and RPCYC have also a private slip for club members. Express railway services. Good bus services.

LOOE

Admiralty Chart No. 147

High Water $-05h.\,53\,m.\,Dover.$
Heights above Datum   *Outside MHWS 5m4. MLWS 0m6. MHWN 4m3. MLWN 2m0.*
Depths   *Harbour and entrance dry at LW. In anchorage 1m8 to 3m6.*

LOOE lies some 9 miles west of Rame Head and about 8 miles east of Fowey. The harbour approach and entrance dry at LW; Looe is not recommended in unsettled weather, as the entrance becomes dangerous in strong onshore winds and gales. The harbour itself is unsuitable for any yacht that cannot take the ground or lie against a quay. The anchorage outside is a good one during offshore winds and is partially protected from the south-west by Looe Island. Though crowded with visitors in summer months, the town is pleasant, and hiring boats and motor trips form a local summer industry.

Approach and Entrance   Looe is easy to locate because Looe Island (St George's Island) is conspicuous off the entrance. The principal danger in the approach from the westward are the Ranneys Rocks which extend south-east and eastward of Looe Island. To clear them keep the beacon on Gribbin Head open of the cliffs at Nealand Point (west of Polperro) until the pierhead bears 305°, when steer for it. There are tidal rips south of Looe Island and the Ranneys which in bad weather may be avoided by keeping farther to seaward. There is no passage suitable for strangers between Looe Island and the mainland. Approaching from the eastward, leave to starboard the YB Knight Errant south cardinal buoy (unlit). Course may then be shaped from the buoy to the harbour entrance at 305°. On near approach to the harbour entrance keep clear of the Needles Eye, Chimney Rock and other rocks south of the entrance, and of the Pen Rock to the north. See chart for soundings. Just within the harbour entrance it dries 1m4. Wait for sufficient tide. Off east quay there is a reverse eddy on the flood. There is a coastguard station on east side, from which storm signals are exhibited. A red flag is flown from a flagstaff when conditions in the bay are dangerous to haul boats ashore.

Lights Lt Occ W R 3 sec. 8m. 15, 12M at end of pier. Fog siren (2) 30 sec. sounded during fog when fishing and other vessels are at sea. Sectors: W013° to 207°; R to 267°; W to 313°; R to 332°; obscured elsewhere. Approach at night in W sector 268° to 313° between the two R sectors.

Anchorage and Harbour Anchorage in the roadstead is good during settled weather in winds between west and north. There is wash from passenger launches and motor boats, as the roadstead is much used by pleasure boats. To avoid this and because the ebb runs fiercely out of the harbour, anchoring to northward of the scour of the tide from the harbour entrance may be found better, say, with the pierhead bearing about west by north, but keep well clear of the Pen Rock which lies a cable north-east. Depths range from 1m5 to 3 or 4m farther seaward. At neaps it is possible to bring up much closer in.

Within the harbour there are long quays with 3m0 to 4m0 MHWS on the eastern side and 1m8 to 3m3 MHWS on the western. The harbour is often crowded by fishing vessels and other boats, but the HM on the East Quay will direct to a berth.

Facilities Water at quays or fish market. Fuel and oil. Hotels and restaurants. Many shops. EC Thurs. Boat-builders and repairers and scrubbing. Launching site and car park on east side near flagstaff. Station and bus services. Yacht club: Looe SC.

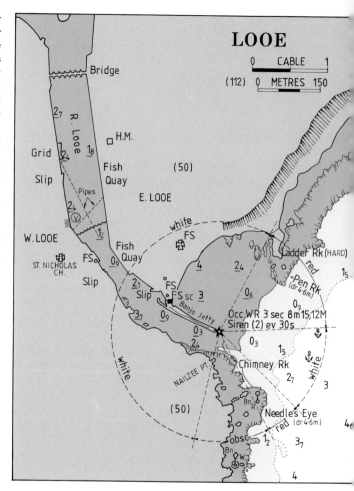

III. Looe showing entrance, river and west quay. Yachts should anchor seaward of the launches in foreground. (Photo : Aerofilms Ltd.)

II2. The harbour entrance dries out at low water.

POLPERRO

Admiralty Chart No. 1267

High Water   − *05 h. 54 m. Dover.*
Heights above Datum *approx. MHWS 5m4. MLWS 0m6.
MHWN 4m3. MLWN 2m0.*
Depths   *Harbour dries out but has 3m3 at MHWS and 1m5 at
MHWN. Deepens to 2m5 in anchorage outside.*

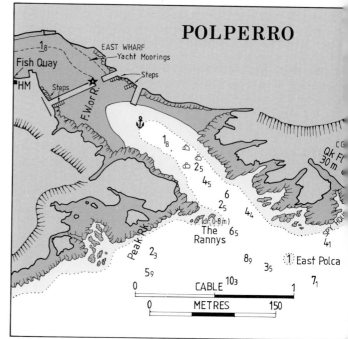

POLPERRO is one of the Meccas of the Cornish tourist industry. It
is a small drying harbour 3 miles west of Looe and 5 miles east of
Fowey. It lies at the end of an inlet between the cliffs extending
about 3 cables in a north-westerly direction, and is protected by
an outer pier and two inner piers between which is the entrance.
This is only 9m8 wide and in bad weather closed by a hydraulically-
operated harbour gate. Polperro is a fishing village principally
engaged in mackerel, pilchard and line fishing. There is no new
chart of the harbour. The plan and soundings are based on a
survey by Captains Williams and Bell, R.N., in 1857, coupled
with observations by the HM. There appears to have been little
alteration during the last 120 years, and trawlermen confirm the
soundings have not changed.

Approach and Entrance   Approach should be made from a
south-east direction when the harbour piers open up. As is shown
on the plan, there are rocks extending to the Rannys (dry 0m8)
off the headland on the west side of the entrance and there are also
rocks at the foot of the cliffs on the east side. There is deep water
up to the entrance of the inlet except for a rocky patch named the
East Polca which lies a cable south-east of the entrance and has a
depth of only 1m0, but can be ignored in good weather with
sufficient rise of tide over it. A rocky patch about 30m north-east

of the Rannys can also be disregarded as this has a depth of 2m5
over it. When the promontory on the west side comes abeam the
mid-channel depth is about 4m5 gradually shoaling to 2m5, 1m8
and 0m1 off the outer pier. To approach on a lee shore is
dangerous in fresh south-east or southerly winds or when a swell
is running in. Once within the entrance the inlet is protected from
south-west through west to north-east.

113. Polperro approach, anchorage and drying harbour. (Photo : Aerofilms Ltd.)

114. Polperro and harbour breakwater near low water.

Keep in mid-channel when within the inlet and approach the harbour entrance (with sufficient rise of tide) leaving the outer pier well to starboard and steering mid-way between the inner piers.

Lights and Signals Spy-house Point east of the harbour entrance. Qk Fl W R 30m 8M; W 060°–288°, R elsewhere. On west pierhead F W 4m 4M. When the harbour entrance is closed, a R Lt is substituted for W at the pierhead and by day a B ball is hoisted. Strangers should not attempt to enter at night.

Anchorage and Harbour A few mooring buoys are laid just outside the harbour for mooring while waiting for the tide. There is also just room to anchor although the deep part of the

channel (2m5) is only about 25m wide. There are moorings inside the harbour but these are of use only to yachts equipped with legs, as the harbour dries out at least 0m6 MLWS. Yachts up to 12m in length are welcome in the harbour and at East Wharf there is a set of visitors' fore-and-aft moorings 18m apart, which dry at LW on hard bottom against wooden posts. Steel ladders to quay.

Facilities Water at fish market and on the quays. Fuel from Pearce Garage Ltd. in village. Several small hotels. Shops. EC Sat. but usually open during summer months. Frequent buses to Looe and occasional to Polruan and Fowey. HM is usually to be found at the Fish Quay on the south side of the inner harbour. Launching site on sloping beach at head of harbour.

FOWEY

Admiralty Chart No. 31

High Water −05 h. 55 m. Dover.
Heights above Datum *MHWS 5m4. MLWS 0m6. MHWN 4m3. MLWN 2m0.*
Depths *At least 6m is maintained in the channel from sea to Wiseman Stone.*

FOWEY is an attractive West Country port. It has a good deep harbour, available at all states of the tide. Large ocean-going ships load up to 1½ million tons of china clay annually from berths either side of Upper Carn Pt. It is sheltered from gales except from the SW. At such times there is a swell in the harbour, but shelter will be found farther up the river. The upper reaches offer pleasant dinghy excursions, though a look-out should be kept for squalls from steep slopes and sudden openings.

Approach and Entrance Approaching from the eastward there is the dangerous Udder Rock (dries 0m6) situated 3 miles east of the entrance. This is marked by an unlit YB south cardinal bell buoy, and there are no dangers between this rock and the entrance except drying rocks off Pencarrow Hd. Fowey would not be very easy to identify from seaward but for the daymark on Gribbin Head, 1¼ miles south-west of the entrance. The Gribbin Beacon is a red and white tower 25m6 high standing at an elevation of 76m2 on a lofty headland, and is a conspicuous landmark when approaching from any direction.

From the westward avoid the Cannis Rock (dries 4m3), some 4 cables south-east of Gribbin Head. There are dangers south of the head so far as the Cannis Rock. There is a YB south cardinal (Qk Fl (6) + LFl ev 10 sec.) bell buoy off this rock, but to clear

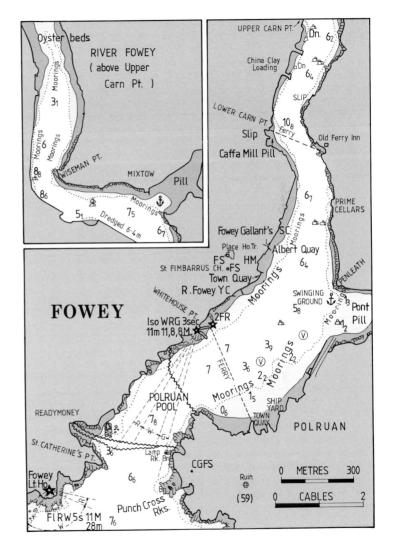

115. River Fowey. Polruan Pool in foreground and Pont Pill Creek to right. Fowey town opposite on west bank of river. (Photo : Aerofilms Ltd.)

the danger keep the cross on Dodman Point open southward of Gwineas Rock.

Once past the Cannis alter course for the entrance, but as there are rocky ledges off the shore west of the entrance give this side a good berth until close to the entrance. Here the only dangers are the Punch Cross ledge on the east side, marked by a white cross (which should be given a berth of at least 60m) and the Lamp Rock marked with a white beacon nearly a cable beyond it and the Mundy Rocks opposite on the west side. Fowey is considered a good port to run for, but the entrance is of course very rough during onshore gales, and the seas break heavily in the approach with an ebb tide running against strong southerly winds. However, there is no bar to worry about.

Lights Approach in the W sector of Fowey lighthouse. Lt Fl W R 5 sec. 28m 11M until the W sector of Whitehouse Point Lt (Iso W R G 3 sec. 11m 11, 8, 8M) within the harbour is picked up. Then enter in this sector. Once within the harbour the shore lights will be seen and there are 2 F R lights on Whitehouse jetty.

Anchorage and Moorings The river and harbour are under the control of the HM, who endeavours to meet the

116. Polruan Pool is crowded with moorings. Buoy the anchor if room is found to anchor temporarily near them.

requirement of owners, though in the high season the most convenient berths are not always available. The harbour is used by large ships, and yachts must not anchor in the fairway, but on the eastern side or in the swinging ground which lies off Pont Pill. Anchorages and then only with HM permission on Ch 16: (1) *The Royal Fowey YC*, which welcomes visiting yachtsmen, has five moorings on the Polruan side. If one is picked up temporarily the yacht must not be left unattended until application has been made and permission given by the Club. Yachts may not anchor off the Club. (2) *The area off Polruan* is crowded with moorings but it is sometimes possible to find a space for temporary anchorage out of the fairway clear of vessels on moorings. There are chains on the bottom so that anchors must have trip lines and it can be rough on the ebb tide in strong south-west winds. (3) Just clear of the many moorings *at Pont Pill*, but it is essential to keep well clear of the swinging ground used by big ships. (4) *In the pool above Wiseman Point* a secure anchorage, though during gales there are fierce squalls blowing down from the hills. Unfortunately it is so crowded with moorings that it is usually difficult to find space to anchor. Enquiry can be made locally as to

117. Fowey Town. The Royal Fowey Yacht Club and landing is at the sea wall below the church.

the possibility of hiring a mooring temporarily. When proceeding up to Wiseman Pool keep a good look-out for commercial traffic and car ferries.

Upper Reaches No difficulties are presented in sailing up the river as far as $\frac{1}{2}$ mile above Wiseman Point, but yachts may find the wind heads and is fluky in some reaches. Near Bodmin Pill the channel becomes narrow and shallow and most of the river dries out at LW. It is navigable by shallow draught boat at HW as far as Lostwithiel, as are Penpoll and Lerryn creeks on the east side. These reaches are pretty but are best explored by dinghy.

Facilities Landing at Town quay, Fowey Gallants SC at Albert quay, R. Fowey YC or Polruan quay, where water may be obtained. Tide permitting, fuel may be obtained alongside at Polruan, but only in cans on the Falmouth side. Hotels and good shops. EC Wed. Customs, HM and Lloyd's agent. Three yacht or boatyards. Scrubbing by arrangement at Mixtow Pill hard. Yacht clubs: Royal Fowey YC and Fowey Gallants Club. Buses. Station at Par 4 miles away. Launching facilities at Caffa Mill car park. Limited facilities at Polruan and at the Bodinnick Ferry Slipway, by arrangement with C. Toms & Sons. At Polruan there are small shops and hotels.

194

CHARLESTOWN and PAR

Admiralty Chart No. 31

High Water −05 h. 55 m. Dover.
Depths 4m3 at MHWS and 3m0 at the entrances, maintained by dredging inside Par and by the operation of lock-gates at Charlestown. Both outer harbours dry out completely at low tide.

LYING at the head of St Austell Bay, both these ports are primarily occupied in the china clay trade. For yachts Par can only be regarded as a temporary port of refuge, but Charlestown has a few available alongside berths inside the locked harbour and has the advantage of being only 1½ miles from St Austell.

Approach No attempt should be made to enter either port except by day in offshore winds or calm. Gribbin Head to the east, with its conspicuous R W daymark (104), and Black Head to the west mark the limits of St Austell Bay. Once inside the bay, Par can be seen for miles by reason of its large white sheds and many chimneys and cranes. Run in on a northerly course, leaving the R Bn with W diamond topmark marking Killyvarder Rock a cable to starboard.

Charlestown will be identified to the east of the houses of St Austell itself. The outer harbour entrance should be approached on a course of 287°, lining up a white patch on the harbour wall with the right-hand edge of a row of cottages showing through the pierheads.

Traffic Signals	Par	Charlestown
Harbour open	—	By night—G Lt
		By day—R ensign
Harbour shut	By night R Lt	By night R Lt
	By day—R flag	By day—B shape

Both harbours maintain watch on Ch 16 when ships are expected (usually one hour either side of HW). Yachts must make prior arrangements to visit either port. If not on VHF, telephone Par 2282 or St Austell 3331. Fuel, fresh water and provisions are available.

118. Charlestown (St Austell) provides a limited number of snug alongside berths for yachts. Normally coasters are berthed on the north side (L) of the locked harbour.

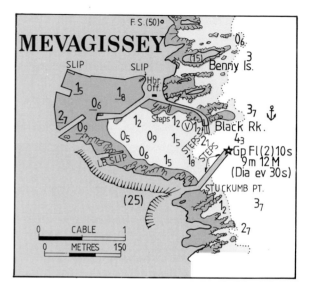

Admiralty Chart No. 147

High Water −05 h. 55 m. Dover.
Heights above Datum *MHWS 5m4. MLWS 0m7. MHWN 4m3. MLWN 2m0.*
Depths *2m1 at entrance, 1m5 to 0m9 in the centre of the harbour. The inner dries out from 0m6 to 1m5 and more in some parts.*

MEVAGISSEY is a pretty Cornish fishing village, overwhelmed by tourists in the summer. It has an inner harbour which dries on all low tides, while the outer harbour partially dries. It is well sheltered by the land from prevailing winds from south-south-west to north-west. The northern pier protects it from the north except in very rough weather, but winds from any easterly direction bring in a swell. It is a bad harbour in strong onshore winds and gales. Fowey, only 7 miles distant, or Falmouth 14 miles, are the nearest ports of refuge.

Approach and Entrance The harbour is situated at the south side of Mevagissey Bay, a mile north of the low Chapel Point, 3½ miles north of the precipitous Dodman Point, and 2 miles south of Black Head. The Gwineas (8m high) and Yaw (dries 0m9) rocks lie south-west of Chapel Point, and are marked by an E cardinal BYB bell buoy (Qk Fl 3 ev 5 sec.), some 2 cables south-south-east of the Yaw. The entrance is easy in moderate weather, but it is only 50m wide, and there are rocks off the northern arm of the pier and a strong backwash when a swell is running. It should not be attempted in strong onshore winds.

Anchorage Anchor in outer harbour in 1m5, provided the wind is not onshore. In selecting position anchor clear of the moorings and do not obstruct the fairway, which is in constant use by fishing vessels. The best position is on the north side of fairway, but anchor fore and aft to prevent swinging into the fairway. The HM will give directions. With strong easterly winds the outer harbour is untenable for yachts, due to swell.

Light Gp Fl (2) W 10 sec. 9m 12M from lighthouse at end of pier. Diaphone ev 30 sec. in fog.

Facilities Water at quay. Diesel oil, petrol, etc. at Marine Garage at inner harbour. Several small hotels and many shops. EC Mon. or Thurs. but some shops always open. Buses to St Austell, where there is a station. Boat-builder at Mevagissey, also yacht-builder at Portmellon, ½ mile southward. Coast Guard and storm signals.

119. *Mevagissey at half tide. (Photo : Aerofilms Ltd.)*

Admiralty Chart No. 1267

THIS little bay, ½ mile south of Mevagissey, provides a good, though rather narrow, temporary anchorage between the headlands. It is pretty and may be used during offshore winds in settled weather, taking soundings to find best position. There is a good yacht-builder (G. P. Mitchell) in the cove, and yachts are launched over the sea wall.

PORTSCATHO

Admiralty Chart No. 154

A SMALL drying harbour on the west side of Gerrans Bay, situated about 3 miles north-east of St Anthony Head. It has a steep slip suitable for launching boats about 1½ hours each side of HW. During offshore winds and settled weather there is a temporary anchorage outside.

Admiralty Chart No. 32

High Water   +*06 h. 12 m. Dover.*
Heights above Datum   *MHWS 5m3. MLWS 0m6. MHWN 4m2. MLWN 1m9.*
  Depths   *The eastern entrance channel is deep and the western over 5m; Black Rock lies between the two and uncovers about half tide. The main channel River Fal has plenty of water for yachts as far as Maggoty Bank north of Ruan Creek.*

FALMOUTH, the historic Cornish port in the days of sail, is the most westerly of the deep-water natural harbours of the South Coast. The harbour and the neighbouring rivers and creeks provide one of the best centres for day sailing in the south of England. Falmouth itself is primarily a commercial port, equipped with big dry docks, but it is rapidly developing as an important yachting centre with first-class facilities of all kinds. In bad weather it is the most westerly large port of refuge on the south coast of England.

Just within the harbour entrance is St Mawes, which offers clean anchorages in beautiful surroundings. It has something of the attraction of Benodet on the Brittany coast. Between the Falmouth and St Mawes sides of the harbour is the northern arm, the River Fal which is pretty and provides interesting cruising and day sailing. It forks 5 miles up, the northern creek (Truro River) leading to Truro and the eastern one, Ruan Creek, forming a shallow continuation of the River Fal.

Approach and Entrance   The approach to Falmouth from the west or south is safe under the lee of the land in westerly and south-westerly winds after passing the Manacle Rocks. It is also

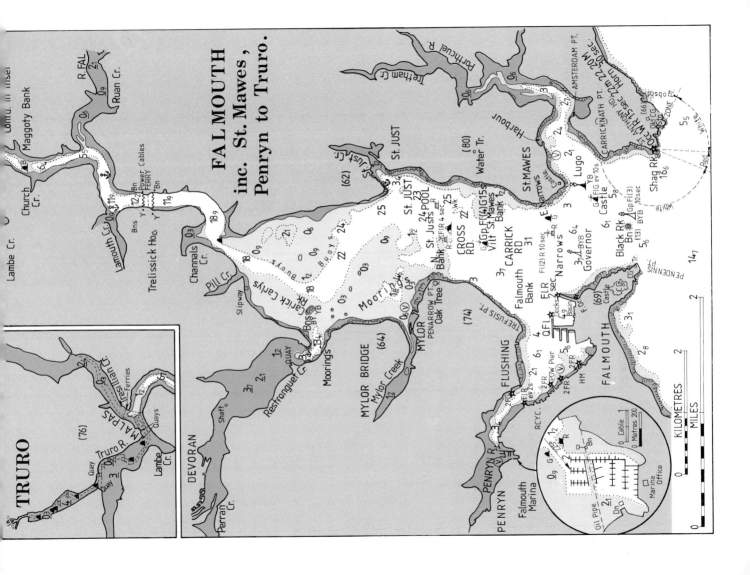

120.   On the right is the eastern breakwater and docks. On the left is Falmouth inner harbour extended from the docks past the yacht club to Greenbank Quay facing Flushing. Beyond is the Penryn River. (Photo : Aerofilms Ltd.)

121. Royal Cornwall Yacht Club slipway on left. Greenbank on right. Yacht moorings extend from Prince of Wales Pier to yacht club.

sheltered from the north, though steep seas may be found in the approach during strong winds.

The entrance lies within Falmouth Bay between Pendennis Point on the west and St Anthony Head to the east. It is a deep, easily navigated entrance but can be very rough during onshore gales blowing against an ebb tide.

Approaching from the eastward give the Dodman Point a berth of about 1½ miles, to clear the overfalls which in bad weather break over the ledges (The Field and The Bellows) some 6 to 7m deep. Also keep well away from Nare Head, for there are

dangerous rocks (The Whelps, which dry 4m6) south-west of the Gull Rock. This rock is very conspicuous, being an islet 38m high, situated just over ½ mile east of Nare Head. Off the next point (Creeb Point) there are patches with only 3m7 to 4m6. Here there are also overfalls in bad weather on these shoals known as 'The Bizzies'. Finally, if rounding St Anthony in very bad weather the overfalls over the rocky patches (with only 7m over them) can be avoided by keeping over a mile offshore, before altering course for the entrance.

In the entrance itself the only danger is Black Rock, which

122.   Falmouth Yacht Marina on the Penryn River upstream from Greenbank.

123. Mylor yacht moorings and harbour on the west side of River Fal.

124. Trelissick ferry landing on River Fal east bank.

uncovers at half tide. The rock is marked by a conspicuous black stone beacon, with globe topmarks, and a BYB buoy (Gp Fl (3) ev 10 sec.) on its east-south-east. Black Rock lies a little westward of

mid-channel and can be passed on either side, but the main channel is the eastern one.

After leaving Black Rock to port, big ships also leave the West Narrows buoy Gp Fl (2) R 10 sec. to port and turn to the westward through the 5m8 dredged channel if proceeding to Falmouth docks. Most yachts can steer direct from off Black Rock in a least depth of 3m to join the dredged channel off the end of the Eastern Breakwater Docks Fl R 2 sec. 20m.

On the eastward side within the entrance lies the entrance to St Mawes Harbour. To enter this leave the G con Castle buoy (Fl 10 sec.) to port and steer between this and Carricknath Point (the point on the south of St Mawes River entrance). About 3 cables north-west of the Point lies an unlit YB south cardinal buoy marking Lugo Rock—which is dangerous, as there is only 0m6 over it.

Lights   St Anthony Head. Lt Occ W R 15 sec. 22m, 22 20M. W from 295° to 004°, R to 022°, covering Manacles Rocks. W 022° to 172°. Fog Signal: Horn 30 sec. The Black Rock BYB east cardinal buoy carries a Lt Gp Fl (3) 10 sec. When entering at night give a good berth to St Anthony to clear the Shag Rock and leave the Black Rock buoy to port, after which follow lights as shown on chart. A sharp look-out should be kept for unlit buoys, including the Governor and other buoys off Falmouth.

Anchorage and Moorings   (1) *Outside*: good holding ground, protected from west, suitable for large ships. (2) *Carrick Road* (centre of harbour) and beyond. This is used by large vessels, but there is a big swell in southerly gales. (3) *St Mawes Creek*. In offshore winds or settled weather there is a delightful anchorage about a cable south-east of St Mawes harbour in 1m2 to 2m4. Soundings should be taken as the depths shoal towards the shore and also in the direction of the harbour. Tide is not strong inshore. Drying berths alongside quay in harbour but not much room. Water, fuel, hotels and shops. EC Thurs. Boat-builders. Ferries to Falmouth. Yacht club: St Mawes SC. In bad

125.   *St Mawes Harbour and (centre) Polvarth Point and Porthcuel River. (Photo: Aerofilms Ltd.)*

weather with onshore winds proceed up river beyond Amsterdam Point. The area is crowded with moorings but the club has a mooring and if enquiry is made locally there is a possibility of finding a private mooring vacant. Likewise beyond Polvarth Point the Porthcuel river is full of moorings, so little anchorage is

left clear of oyster beds. (4) *Falmouth, off the town*, temporary anchorage by permission of HM from his office or on VHF Ch 16 or by telephone to Falmouth 312285, but buoy the anchor, as the bottom is foul and there are moorings and chains. The Royal Cornwall YC has seven moorings for visiting yachts. Apply to the

126. St Mawes harbour and quay.

Club for use of one. Temporarily at Custom and North quays for provisioning, etc., where there is about 2m4, half flood to half ebb. Fresh water hydrant at North quay and shops at hand. (5) *Falmouth Yacht Marina* half a mile beyond Greenbank quay has 250 berths with a 2m0 dredged approach channel, marked by R and G buoys with leading marks of W diamonds on Bl boards. Call on Ch 37. Secure to any pontoon at the seaward end on arrival. Fuel, including diesel, chandlery and repairs all available. (6) *Restronguet Creek* on moorings in deep hole west and south of Restronguet Point; avoid shallow patch at the entrance to creek. (7) *Mylor Yacht Harbour* consists of a small inner dock which dries, and an area north-east of it with over 220 swinging moorings, and depths ranging from 2m4 at the outer end down to 0m9 off the dock. There is about 1m5 LAT in the approach on the leading marks of three prominent trees centre of field to right of Mylor Creek with St Just village dead astern, but strangers best await more water. Facilities including chandlery near inner harbour. Yacht clubs: Mylor YC and Mylor SC. (8) *St Just.* Anchorage during north and east winds just inside point, also many moorings. (10) There are numerous anchorages in bays and bights in suitable wind conditions (some of which are mentioned below) but keep clear of oyster beds.

The Upper Reaches The upper reaches and creeks of Falmouth harbour offer interesting day sailing but Admiralty

Chart No. 32 is desirable. At HW it is possible to navigate in the narrow buoyed channel as far as Truro where there is a quay, but at LW the river dries out below Malpas Point, south-east of which there are moorings and anchorage. On the western side of the main Fal channel are Mylor Creek (already referred to) and Restronguet Creek (dries out except for deep hole inside entrance). Yacht club: Restronguet SC. On the eastern side there is St Just Creek with 3m4 to 1m5 in anchorage and moorings area, but which dries out opposite the church. Ruan Creek, which is the eastern fork of the River Fal joining Truro River, is navigable for a short distance and there is anchorage near the entrance and small craft moorings farther east.

The Penryn River west of Falmouth carries over 2m and is buoyed for ½ mile above Greenbank Quay, as far as Boyers Cellars and the entrance channel to Falmouth Yacht Marina. At high water is navigable up to Penryn where there are quays and facilities.

Facilities at Falmouth Water from North quay, from Flushing quay or (by permission) from the yacht club. Petrol, oil and diesel from Falmouth Yacht Marina. Excellent shops including chart agents. EC Wed. or Thurs. Many hotels of which the Greenbank is near the yacht club moorings and anchorage. Yacht builders and repairers. Falmouth Boat Construction Ltd., up the Penryn River north-west of Flushing, has a fuel pontoon that is accessible at half-tide. Chandlery at yard and also at Falmouth Chandlers at Penryn. Customs. Railway station. Buses to all parts. Ferries to Flushing and St Mawes. Yacht clubs: R. Cornwall YC, Flushing SC.

Launching Sites in Falmouth Harbour (1) *At Falmouth*, Grove Place Dinghy Park, in south-west corner of harbour. Launching hard accessible at all times except lowest spring tides for vessels up to about 7.5m long. Car park immediately adjacent. Changing-rooms available at dinghy park. At Falmouth Yacht Marina. (2) *At St Mawes*, slipway at the harbour, which dries out. (3) Up the river *at Porthcuel* on east side of river, where road runs to slipway and beach. (4) *At Mylor* adjacent to the dockyard, car park, and at Mylor Bridge at end of creek, 1 hour each side of HW. (5) *At Trenewth*, south side of Restronguet Creek, road terminates at hard by sailing club. (6) Just west of the entrance of *Pill Creek* (¾ mile north-east of Restronguet Creek) slipway and car park.

HELFORD RIVER

Admiralty Chart No. 147

High Water *Entrance +06 h. 10 m. Dover.*
Heights above Datum *Entrance MHWS 5m3. MLWS 0m6. MHWN 4m2. MLWN 1m9.*
Depths *Deep water in the approach; 3m1 on the bar, a mile inside the river. Beyond Navas Creek the river soon shallows and the bottom is uneven.*

HELFORD RIVER is very beautiful, and is one of the favourite yachting harbours of the West Country. The entrance is simple, the depth of water adequate for most small yachts and it is usually possible to get a mooring or find room to anchor. It is protected by land from all directions other than easterly. Helford River and its various creeks offer a splendid expanse of water at HW for exploring in a dinghy and for picnics.

Approach and Entrance When coming from Falmouth keep on or east of stern transit of the conspicuous Observatory tower at Falmouth in line with Pennance Point until Bosahan Point (on south side of river) is well open of Mawnan Shear (on north side of entrance). This will clear the dangerous Gedges Rocks, which lie south of Rosemullion Head on the north-east of entrance and are marked by a BYB east cardinal buoy.

From the eastward keep in centre of entrance, but before approaching Bosahan Point give a good berth to the Voose rocks, marked by a beacon, some 4 cables eastward of Bosahan Point.

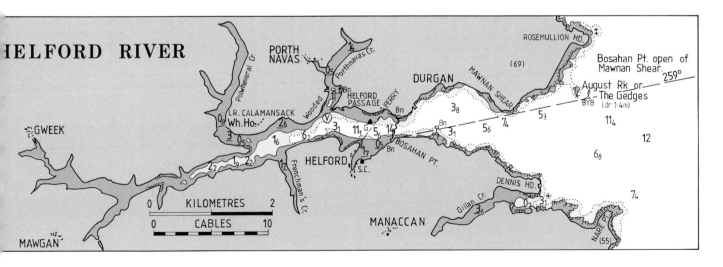

127. Helford River facing west. Right Mawnan Shear, Durgan Bay, Helford Passage, Porth Navas Creek. On left Bosahan Point, Helford Creek and Point. (Photo : Aerofilms Ltd.)

128. Helford Creek and Village.

Proceed through the 'narrows' and then avoid the shoal marked by a G buoy on the north side of the river opposite Helford Creek.

The leading marks up the river as far as Navas Creek are a white cottage in a group of buildings at Lower Calamansack which should be kept just open of the wooded point at Lower Calamansack. Entry is not difficult, even if these marks are not located, by keeping on the south side of the river off the ledges and leaving the G buoy, mentioned above, to starboard.

When coming from the west and south keep well clear of Nare Point and Dennis Head.

Lights   None.

Anchorage and Moorings   (1) *Off Durgan* anywhere clear of moorings in 1m3 to 3m4, exposed in easterly. (2) *Off Helford*. Excellent moorings off Helford River SC or yacht yard on buoys marked with a black cross for visitors, with dues payable at shop at Helford Point. Or anchor if room in 3m0 to 8m0. Strong stream. The mud south is very steep-to in places. Avoid cable crossing river near Bosahan Point, position marked by beacon on each side. (3) On moorings, if any available, across the bar in pool just *inside Navas Creek* in 1m5 to 2m2. (4) On north side of river south of the bar and oyster buoys *off entrance to Navas Creek*. There are oyster beds in Navas Creek and off and west of its entrance and elsewhere, on which vessels must not anchor or ground. (5) In settled weather and offshore winds, in *Gillan harbour* (on south side of entrance) in 1m4 to 3m1 — poor holding ground and avoid the sunken rock in the middle of entrance. If in doubt call the HM at St Keverne 442.

Facilities   Yacht club: Helford River SC welcomes visitors and has excellent facilities. At Helford there is a landing place at Helford Point (west of the creek), where water may be obtained from a tap at the shop. Boat-builders, and boats for hire. It is a short walk from Helford Point to the village, where there is a PO and shop; provisions and diesel may be obtained.

A ferry for pedestrians crosses the river from Helford Point to the Ferry Boat Inn at Helford Passage on the north side of the river, which is a hotel with restaurant. Provisions obtainable here. On this side of the river, water may be obtained from a tap at cliff, 180m east of entrance to Navas Creek and also at Durgan. Buses to Falmouth from top of hill at Trebah, north of Durgan. Boat-builders and repairers at Helford and Porth Navas. Launching site at Helford Passage where road runs to water's edge by inn. Car park belongs to the inn. At Porth Navas there are dinghy landing, club, bar, shop, water, fuel and minor repairs.

COVERACK

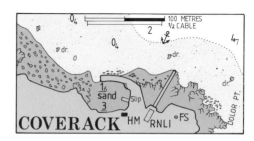

Admiralty Chart No. 777

High Water *+06 h. 07 m. Dover.*
Heights above Datum *MHWS 5m3. MLWS 0m6.*
MHWN 4m2. MLWN 1m9.

COVERACK COVE lies 5 miles NE of the Lizard, between Black Head and Lowland Point. The dangers in the approach from the south are The Gunthens which lie 2 cables off Chynhalls Point and cover at high water. To the north there are ledges and rocks off Lowland Point, the most dangerous being the Dava rock, which extends 2 cables south of the Point, as it is awash at half tide. To the NE lie the notorious Manacle rocks marked by a BYB east cardinal bell buoy Qk Fl (3) 5 sec. which must be given a good berth.

On the south side of the cove there is a small harbour, which is formed between the land and the pier, leaving an entrance 21m wide. It dries out completely but at MHWS it has depths of about 3m5. It is crowded with small craft by day but there is a berth at night for one yacht up to 5 tons alongside, preferably twin keeled. It is better to anchor outside, given settled weather and offshore winds where it is sheltered from the west, but exposed from the east.

Facilities Hotel and shops. EC Tues. Launching site on concrete ramp to firm sand. Water from hotel and fuel (in cans) from the garage.

129. Coverack Harbour. There is one berth for a small yacht against the quay but a good anchorage to seaward in suitable weather.

PORT MULLION (PORTH MELLIN)

Admiralty Chart No. 777

High Water *Lizard +05 h. 52 m. Dover.*
Heights above Datum *Lizard MHWS 5m3. MLWS 0m6.*
MHWN 4m2. MLWN 1m9.

THIS little harbour lies at the head of Mullion Cove, some 5 miles north-west of the Lizard. It is formed by two breakwaters,

between which is the narrow entrance. The harbour dries out and could be used by berthing alongside the breakwater or quay, but only in exceptionally settled weather, with offshore winds. The cove and harbour are exposed to winds from all westerly directions, and, as even swell from the west causes a surge within the harbour, it would be an awkward place to be caught out by a change in the weather. The narrow entrance and harbour have been extensively rebuilt recently.

The anchorage in the cove is safer, provided it is used only in settled weather and offshore winds. It is open to the Atlantic from the west, and should be left immediately if the wind shifts or a shift is forecast to that direction. Anchorage can be found in the

130.   Mullion Island on right, harbour to the left off the dip in the hills. Note the conspicuous hotel on the left.

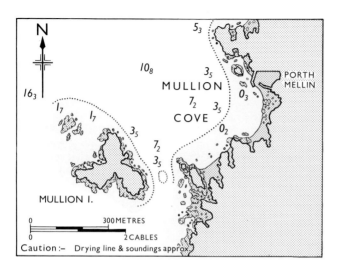

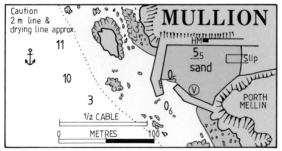

131. Mullion harbour which dries out at low water.

cove, taking soundings and bring up in 3 to 4m with the end of the harbour breakwater bearing approximately east Mag. The bottom is sand and rock. This anchorage is partly sheltered from the south-west by Mullion Island, but not sufficiently to make it a safe anchorage in winds from this direction.

There is a café at Port Mullion where some stores may be obtained. Road leads to steep beach where launching possible at HW. Car park. There are shops, a garage and 'pub' at Mullion village, situated at the end of an uphill walk of a mile from the pretty little cove. EC Wed. Launching site on hard beach exposed below ramp.

PORTHLEVEN

High Water + 05 h. 51 m. Dover.
Heights above Datum *MHWS 5m5. MLWS 0m8. MHWN 4m3. MLWN 2m0.*
Depths *There is 1m2 in the approach and 2m3 in centre of the entrance north-west of pier, but dries out above the lifeboat house.*

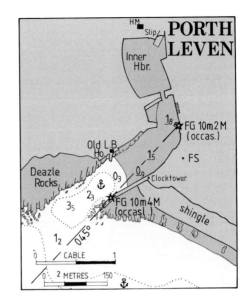

THIS small tidal harbour is situated 8½ miles north-west of the Lizard and may be located by a clock tower, a flagstaff and the white houses in the background, which are conspicuous from a considerable distance. The approach and entrance are open to the west, south and south-east. The port is now used principally by small fishing vessels. Porthleven is rarely visited by yachts. It provides only drying berths alongside the quay in the inner harbour.

Approach and Entrance The entrance lies between the rocks off the pierhead on the south-east side and the Deazle Rocks on the north-west side. It is considered a difficult entrance

132. Porthleven outer harbour near high water. Rocks dry at low water either side of entrance.

213

133.   Porthleven harbour near LW. Fishing vessels lie near centre of outer harbour. With sufficient tide pass between the short inner piers to the inner harbour if HM has a berth available. (Photo: Aerofilms Ltd.)

because it is only 60m wide and the Deazle Rocks are not marked by buoys or beacons, nor are there clear leading marks to the centre of the entrance. It would be undesirable for a stranger to attempt the entrance without local advice except by day under particularly favourable conditions in offshore winds and in the absence of swell.

Approach should be made on a course parallel with the long inner side of the pier, but about 20m north-west of it on the line of soundings 3m5 to 1m5 on the plan. This course crosses a bar formation (which is liable to change) in about 1m2 LAT. At the entrance there are ledges of rock extending about 50m or more off the pier and from south-west to south-east. The entrance thus lies between these rocks on the east side and the Deazle Rocks on the west. There is 2m3 at the entrance but it soon shallows within.

Fishing boats will be seen on moorings in the centre of the outer harbour but most of these nearly dry out at MLWS. Fishing boats proceed in or out of the harbour fairly frequently, and if in doubt advice may usually be obtained from one of them. When the harbour is closed this is indicated by the hoisting of a red ball on the flagpole at the inner end of the pier.

Lights   There is an Occas F G Lt 10m 4M which is situated about 30m from the pierhead. A second Occas Lt F G has been placed on the east side of the harbour vis 057°–075°. Approach at night would be dangerous for strangers.

Harbour   Except near the entrance the outer harbour dries 0m9 to 1m8, and there are rocks fringing the foot of the pier. The inner harbour can be closed with baulks of timber in bad weather. It dries out completely, but by arrangement with the HM there are berths alongside the quay where yachts can lie with about 3m at MHWS in the deepest berth.

Facilities   Water, fuel and some stores. EC Wed. Boatbuilders. Two small hotels. Good bus service to Penzance and Falmouth and district. Launching sites: trailed boats of any size from ramp, slipway at the head of the inner harbour for launching small craft by hand near HW.

ST MICHAEL'S MOUNT and MARAZION

Admiralty Chart No. 2345

High Water   +05 h. 50 m. Dover.
Heights above Datum   MHWS 5m6. MLWS 0m8. MHWN 4m4. MLWN 2m0.
Depths   *The harbour dries out but there is about 3m3 at MHWS.*

St Michael's mount, with the castle at its summit, is one of the strangest and most romantic looking formations off the south coast of England. From AD25, when it was used by Mediterranean merchants as a base for tin trading, its long and varied history is of great interest. It is now National Trust property and it is well worth making a point of sailing there if the weather is suitable.

The Mount is conspicuous from seaward. There is a small drying harbour at the north end which is formed between two piers and there is anchorage to the westward of the entrance.

Approach and Entrance   Approach may be made with the aid of the large-scale Admiralty chart from the direction of the Gear Rock beacon off Penzance steering on the line to the north end of the harbour breakwater at 074°. The principal dangers in the approach are the Hogus Rocks which form a large expanse of reef to the north-west of the harbour, and the Outer Penzeath Rock, with less than 2m over it, which lies about 3 cables west-south-west of the Hogus Rocks. These dangers are left to port. Nearly a cable south-south-west of the Mount lies the Maltman Rock which dries 0m9, but this needs to be considered only if approaching from south or south-east. The various rocks have no beacons to mark them and some yachtsmen consider that the

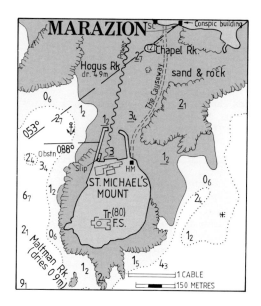

134. St Michael's Mount from the north at harbour entrance.

135. The harbour at St Michael's Mount.

harbour should not be attempted by a stranger without the aid of a pilot. However, in reasonable weather with a leading wind and an accurate compass the approach is safe enough.

The approach gradually shelves from 8m to 2m a cable west of the entrance. Depths then rapidly fall and the bottom dries out northward of the west pier. Do not leave the pier more than $\frac{1}{2}$ cable to starboard as the Hogus Rocks lie only a cable north of it. Then enter with sufficient rise of tide.

Alternatively, approach may be made from the south. Keep well away from the rocks extending south of the Mount. Then follow up the west side at a distance of about one cable, but note a rock (2m1 over it) and an obstruction (2m4 over it), dangerous in

a bad sea or swell. When the pierhead bears 060° alter towards the anchorage with Chapel Rock bearing 053° in the transit with a conspicuous building or, with sufficient tide, steer direct for the pierhead and enter.

Lights Approaching from Penzance steer 088° on the division of the red and white sectors of Penzance south pier light (Iso 2 sec.) leading south of the dangers to the northward and a little south of the entrance to St Michael's harbour. There are no lights at the harbour so strangers should not attempt the passage at night.

Harbour and Anchorage There is a pleasant anchorage in 2m7 about a cable west of the northern end of the west pier, which can be used in settled weather sheltered from north through east to south-east. The entrance between the piers is 30m wide and the harbour dries from 1m5 to 3m0. The HM will direct a visiting yacht to a drying berth, usually alongside a ladder on the west quay, and the east quay is used by the ferries and launches.

Facilities There are no facilities on the island except water and a café (open Mondays to Fridays in summer months), which supplies some provisions, but all facilities are available at Marazion, ½ mile to the northward. This can be reached across the causeway at LW or by dinghy or ferry at HW. Water, fuel, hotels, banks, shops. EC Wed., but some shops open on all days. Yacht club: Mount's Bay SC. Facilities for dinghy racing. Launching site: at the west end of Marazion on beach, with car park and garage adjacent. Frequent bus services.

Admiralty Chart No. 2345

High Water   *+ 05 h. 50 m. Dover.*
Heights above Datum   *MHWS 5m6. MLWS 0m8. MHWN 4m4. MLWN 2m0.*
Depths   *There is about 1m8 close to the seaward end of the south pier. Thereafter the outer harbour dries out completely, except close alongside the south pier where the depth outside the locks is 0m6. There is usually not less than 4m2 of water in the inner basin, which is open for about 2 hours before HW to HW.*

PENZANCE is a commercial harbour but it is also frequently used by yachts as the westernmost port offering shelter in bad weather. It is also a useful port of departure for the Irish Sea and the Scillies. In strong winds from the south and especially from south-east it is dangerous to run for shelter at Penzance owing to the shoaling water in the approach and because the lock-gates cannot always be opened. Mount's Bay is very exposed to winds from these quarters.

Approach and Entrance Penzance lies in the north-west corner of Mount's Bay some 15½ miles north-west of Lizard Point. A yacht coming from the eastward should keep 2 to 3 miles off the Lizard in rough weather (see Passage Data) or in a fresh wind against the tide, to avoid the overfalls and should shape a course outside the Boa shoal (3 miles west of the Lizard). On nearer approach to Penzance Bay there are shoals to the southward of Cudden Point which are clear once west of the transit of the tower on St Michael's Mount and Ludgvan church on high ground 1 mile inland on 340°.

Coming from the westward after passing the Runnel Stone,

follow up the coast keeping a mile offshore as far as St Clement's Island. Leaving the island about 2 cables to port make good 020° leaving Low Lee BYB east cardinal buoy to port, where bring Penzance South pierhead bearing 350° and steer for it. Give a good berth to Gear Rock ½ mile south of the pier (which is marked by an unlit Black Bn with cage topmark) and to the Battery Rocks to south-west of the pier. Then round in towards the pierheads. Note that at LW springs there is only about 1m8 east of the south pier and see 'Depths' for water within harbour. Four cables north-east of the entrance lie the Cressar Rocks marked by a BW beacon.

Lights Penzance south pier lighthouse has a Lt Iso W R 2 sec. 11m 9, 8M. Approach in the W sector. The R sectors on each side cover the outlying dangers, but the western edge of the white sector cuts close to Gear Rock.

Tidal and Docking Signals 4m5 least depth off pier. By day, a ball on flagstaff; by night, a R Lt. *Dock-gates open*: by day, 2 balls, horizontal: by night, 2 R Lts Vert. *Dock-gates closed or not to open*: by day, 2 ball Vert; by night, R Lt over G. When the dock-gates are open a F G Lt is shown on north side of the lock-gate and a F R on south.

Anchorage One of the HM's staff at the dock-gate may direct yachts to a berth. Or contact on VHF Ch 16. The large outer harbour on the north side dries out. Here there are many moorings for dinghies and small craft, which can take the bottom at LW. Keel yachts can dry out alongside the Albert Pier, which is the safer location outside the basin; or afloat on the South Quay, subject to the prior rights of the ferry. It is far better to enter the inner basin, where there is usually about 4m2 of water. The gates open from 2 hours before HW to HW. In strong southerly gales the seas break over the south pier of the basin, so the north pier is the better for shelter, although here there is often coal dust.

Waiting for tide, anchor outside about 2 cables south-east of

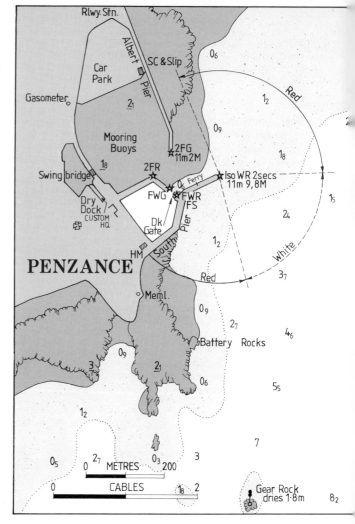

136. Penzance. Note lock-gates to inner basin. In the background, outer harbour dries out alongside Albert Pier.

the south pierhead, weather permitting.

Facilities Water on all quays. Customs. Two boatyards; scrubbing at hard in outer harbour. Fuel in SW corner of locked basin; chandlery and sailmaker in the town. Many hotels, restaurants, shops of all kinds. EC Wed. Yacht club: Penzance

SC. Launching site: dinghies may use the slipway at the outer harbour approximately from $3\frac{1}{2}$ hours before to $3\frac{1}{2}$ hours after HW. Station and buses to all districts. Passenger ferry and helicopter service to Scilly Isles.

Admiralty Chart No. 2345

High Water +*05 h. 50 m. Dover.*
Heights above Datum *MHWS 5m6. MLWS 0m8.*
MHWN 4m4. MLWN 2m0.
Depths *The entrance has been dredged to 3m9 and to a least depth of 2m5 on both sides of the new quay, which divides the harbour in two. A coaster drawing 3m3 can lie alongside the north pier. Either side of the newly-dredged channel the harbour shallows progressively farther to the NW with 1m8 at the third tier and drying at the end.*

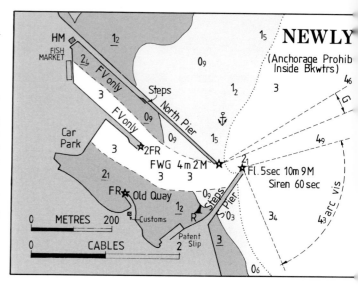

NEWLYN is a sheltered harbour but southerly and south-east winds can bring a heavy swell outside, and the approach would be very dangerous in a south-east gale. It is inconvenient for yachts not equipped with legs, as it is a busy fishing port with limited room to lie afloat alongside. It is prohibited to anchor anywhere in the harbour. The HM always endeavours to find a place for a visiting yacht, but this is difficult during the pilchard season in June, July and August. Then the harbour has to accommodate many fishing vessels from elsewhere in addition to its own fleet. The south pier has 3m9 at its extremity, but should not be used by yachts as it is reserved for commercial vessels.

The best way of visiting Newlyn in offshore winds is to anchor outside in Gwavas Lake and enter the harbour by dinghy.

Approach and Entrance Coming from any direction follow the instructions given for Penzance, but alter course for Newlyn when the harbour entrance bears 270°, distant about ¾ mile. Enter between the pierheads, when a small R spar buoy will be seen ahead. This marks the end of a slipway, and course should be altered to starboard to leave the buoy to port. The west side of

the harbour dries out, but there is a dredged channel with a least depth of 2m5 parallel with the new pier to within 35m of the inshore end of the Old Quay.

Lights South pier lighthouse: Lt Fl 5 sec. 10m 9M, 253° to 336°. Fog siren 60 sec. North pier F W G 2M, 238° to 248°, W over harbour. Slipway spar buoy has R W Scotchlite reflectors.

Anchorage and Harbour (1) Outside in Gwavas Lake in offshore winds; east of the south end of the north quay, clear of the fairway in 2m1 or more farther seaward. Good holding ground and well sheltered from south-west, through west to north-west. (2) Lay inside alongside outer half of North Pier or abreast of other vessels but apply to HM for berth least inconvenienced by movements of fishing vessels. Contact the

137. Newlyn. Visitors may be put on west side of New Quay.

HM on Ch 16 or telephone Penzance 2523. The best water is 3m3 at the outer end but the berths are in frequent use by the big fishing vessels. A cable from the entrance the depth alongside North Pier is 0m9 LAT plus 0m8 at MLWS, +2m0 at MLWN. Legs necessary when not alongside as no room elsewhere to lie afloat. Owing to the increasingly large number of fishing vessels based at the port, masters or owners of visiting yachts are asked to keep sufficient crew on board to move the vessel if requested by fishing boats. When the local fishing fleet is forced to return through stress of weather all berths at Newlyn are required by them and yachts are asked to seek shelter at Penzance.

Facilities Water by hydrants at all berths. Diesel oil hydrants and petrol at Ridges on the quay. Customs House. Two ship and yacht repairers, J. Peak & Son and H. N. Peak. Slipway up to 27m4 keel, 6m4 draught available on application to HM.

Three small hotels. Shops. EC Wed. Frequent buses to Penzance and elsewhere. Station at Penzance. Launching sites: by arrangement with HM only.

MOUSEHOLE HARBOUR

Admiralty Chart No. 2345

High Water *+05 h. 50 m. Dover.*
Heights above Datum *MHWS 5m6. MLWS 0m8. MHWN 4m3. MLWN 2m0.*
Depths *Dries out at LW. At MHWS there is about 4m8 and MHWN about 3m5. Bottom gravel on rock.*

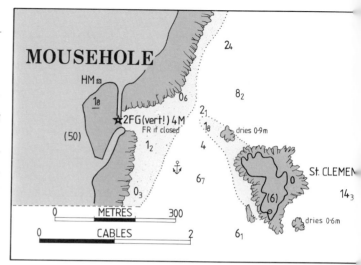

MOUSEHOLE HARBOUR is a small drying harbour formed by two breakwaters leaving an entrance only 11m wide. The harbour is well protected except in strong winds between NE and SE. The harbour entrance can be closed with baulks of timber during strong onshore winds. The harbour and village are picturesque and much frequented by artists. There is an anchorage outside during offshore winds.

Approach and Entrance Mousehole is situated $1\frac{1}{4}$ miles south of Newlyn and lies west of the small St Clement's Island, which makes it easy to locate. St Clement's Island is fringed with rocks as shown on the plan, and the easiest approach to the harbour is from the southward, following parallel with the line of the Cornish coast to port, and passing rather west of midway between the shore and St Clement's Island. Once the middle of the island is abeam the water between the island and the harbour is clear of dangers, apart from rocks fringing the seaward sides of the breakwaters. Depths in the approach vary from 6m7 when St Clement's Island is abeam down to about 0m5 off the entrance, where with sufficient tide final approach should be made when the centre bears 270°, distant $\frac{1}{2}$ cable.

Lights Two F G Lts are exhibited on the northern pierhead, but when the harbour is closed a R Lt is substituted.

Harbour and Anchorage Yachts dry out alongside the inner sides of the breakwaters; the deepest berths are near the entrance. The HM will give instructions for berthing, but the harbour is often so crowded that it is difficult to get alongside. The HM's telephone is Mousehole 511. The anchorage outside provides good holding ground. It is sheltered by the land from north and west and St Clement's Island provides partial protection from light east winds, but it is open to south and south-east, which are dangerous quarters in unsettled weather. Even with westerly winds there is sometimes swell entering the anchorage from the south. Take soundings to find best position to anchor, approximately midway between the south breakwater and the middle of the island.

138. Mousehole harbour at low water. (Photo: Aerofilms Ltd.)

Facilities Water and petrol. Three small hotels, several shops. EC Wed. Launching site: slipway in harbour. Car park near by. Buses to Newlyn and Penzance.

Admiralty Chart No. 34

High Water *(St Mary's Pool)* +05 h. 52 m. Dover.
Heights above Datum *MHWS 5m7. MLWS 0m7. MHWN 4m3. MLWN 2m0.*
Depths *Up to 2m1 in St Mary's Pool. 2m4 to 11m0 in anchorage north-west of New Grimsby harbour (Tresco) or 15m0 in Crow Sound and St Mary's Sound.*

THESE islands—some forty-seven of them—have a charm that only a personal visit can reveal, they are an eclectic of ingredients from England, Scotland, Brittany and the tropics.

Only five islands are inhabited, each so different from the others—St Mary's, Tresco, St Martin's, Bryher and St Agnes; of these St Mary's is the biggest with Hugh Town built around the harbour as its 'capital'.

Any yacht exploring these islands should not do so without Admiralty Chart No. 34 nor, if it is planned to explore the islands in detail, a splendid little paperback guide obtainable locally: *A Yachtsman's Guide to Scilly*, by Norm. The charm of this archipelago may lull the navigator into a false sense of security, as there are many hidden dangers in the form of pinnacle rocks with strong tidal eddies around them. Local knowledge is very desirable if any intricate passages between the smaller islands are contemplated. Here only the safest four, of the six, approach channels to St Mary's Road will be described.

Off-lying Dangers These are numerous and clearly marked on the Admiralty Chart. All rise suddenly from deep water; mentioned here—only because of their isolation in the extreme west—are the Crim Rocks (2m0) and others near them lying

223

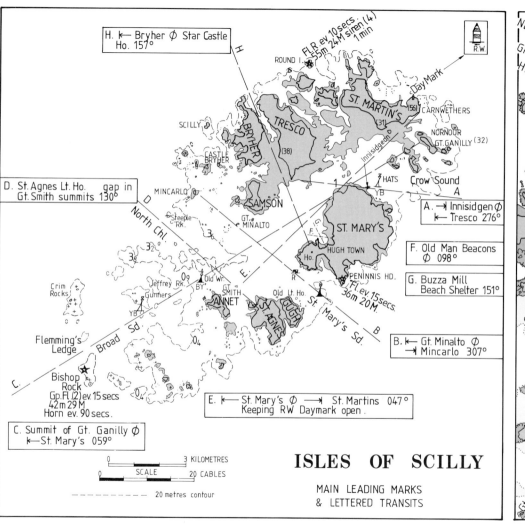
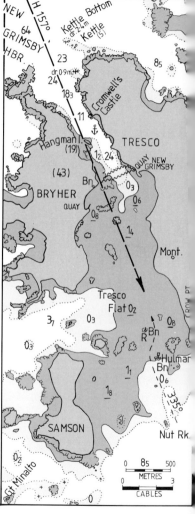

ISLES OF SCILLY

MAIN LEADING MARKS & LETTERED TRANSITS

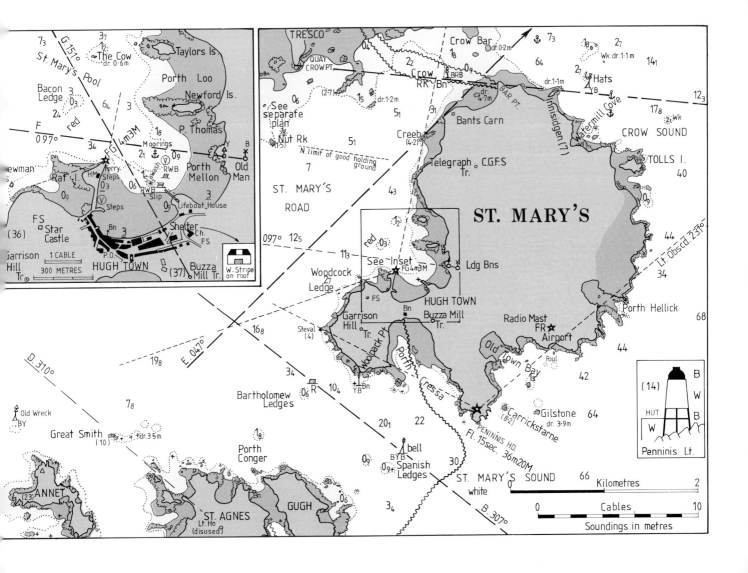

139. Round Island. This island, situated on north side of the Scillies, is conspicuous by its shape and white lighthouse at its summit. (Photo: Aerofilms Ltd.)

about $1\frac{1}{2}$ miles north of the Bishop Rock. Approach into these islands in thick weather is extremely dangerous, and the greatest caution is needed if the distant leading marks cannot be seen. If in doubt lie off. The approach to St Mary's Road from the east, which is recommended locally, is by way of St Mary's Sound which is clearly marked. Alternatively approach can be made in suitable weather to Crow Sound from the south-east provided the wind is offshore, the bar is not crossed and one anchors to the east of the Hats buoy. At night also, if seeking a lee on the east side of the islands, it may assist to note that Peninnis light becomes obscured on a bearing of about 231°. However, the navigation at night is not recommended in the absence of local knowledge.

Approach Channels from the East

Crow Sound (Transit A)   The flood tide flows into here, thus the Hats buoy (YB south cardinal) is left close to starboard, after which Transit A is left to give the rock of Innisidgen Island (7m high), which dries 0m6, a clear berth anywhere near LW. The Crow Bar Sands, formerly 0m9, have moved and increased. From the Hats buoy steer 289° heading for Green Island, a rock off the nearest (SE) corner of Tresco. With Bar Point (the northernmost point on St Mary's Island) abeam, course should be altered to 250°, so as to leave the R Bn marking Crow Rocks one cable clear to port. At this point it is safe to alter to port to SW and the deep waters of St Mary's Road. Entry should not be attempted at springs without ample tide; the best water will be found where sand and weed meet, which can usually be spotted in the clear water.

St Mary's Sound (Transit B)   Approach from the SE to avoid Gilston (dries 3m9). The recommended leading marks for this Transit are often difficult to pick up, but there is deep water close to the south of Peninnis Head, with its white pepper-pot lighthouse on a black trellised base (Fl 15 sec. 36m 20M). The BYB east cardinal bell buoy marking Spanish Ledges should be left to port, whence the transit course of 307° will leave the R can Bartholomew Ledges buoy close to port. However care should be taken south of Garrison Hill not to get too close to the R Woolpack Bn, as there is a 0m7 patch $\frac{1}{2}$ cable west of it. Leaving the Bartholomew buoy to port, swing slowly round to the NNE. Deep-draught yachts may want to take Transit E clearing Woodcock Ledge with 2m7 over it.

Approach Channels from the West

Broad Sound (Transit C)   The leading marks are far away and may not be readily identifiable. However, the channel is buoyed starting with the YB south cardinal Gunner buoy, which is left to port. Next make for the north cardinal Old Wreck BY buoy, leaving it to starboard, taking care to keep clear to the SE of the

140. *Hugh Town harbour, St Mary's. The anchorage (often crowded) lies east and north-east of a line from well off the pierhead to just east of the lifeboat slip. (Photo: Aerofilms Ltd.)*

Jeffrey Rock (om9). The leading marks should now be picked up; they will take the yacht clear to the middle of St Mary's Road.

North Channel (Transit D) A cross-tide may be experienced in this channel, but the leading marks are good in reasonable visibility. The main danger is Steeple Rock (om4) which is over 6 cables SW of Mincarlo and is left less than 2 cables on the port hand when on the transit of 130°. Stay on it until picking up the Broad Sound Transit C, when course should be altered to 059° into St Mary's Road.

Entrance to St Mary's Pool and Harbour Once in St Mary's Road, most yachts will wish to bring up in the pool. The only danger is the Bacon Ledge (om3) or Pool Ledge. The former is

227

141. *Transit F. Entrance to Hugh Town harbour—Old Man beacons in line: front white pole and triangle top, rear white pole and St Andrew's Cross. (Note lifeboat slip on right.)*

142. *Transit G. Entrance to Hugh Town harbour—Buzza Mill Tower in line with white-roofed shelter on the esplanade.*

flanked on the NE by the Cow, which dries 0m6. The most commonly used entry in Transit F on course 097° which brings into line two beacons north of Porth Mellow, with a triangular topmark on the front one and a cross on the higher rear one. (Note: although the chart shows these to be W, alternative colours are under trial and they are currently painted yellow.) Transit G is from the NW on course 151° between the Cow and Bacon Ledge. It is straightforward, bringing the squat Buzza Mill tower on the rising ground behind Hugh Town into line with a small shelter on the esplanade, with a white roof and white vertical stripes on either end of its front elevation.

The limit of the anchorage for yachts is roughly a line from the outer quay steps to Newford Island. Yachts should anchor to the SE of this line, clear of the launching area for the lifeboat, leaving plenty of room for the ferry *Scillonian* to turn through 360° after slipping.

An Alternative Anchorage If a blow from the SW is imminent, larger yachts can anchor in Crow Sound ESE of the Hats buoy off Watermill Bay in the NE of St Mary's Island.

Facilities Although the smaller inhabited islands have little village stores, Hugh Town on St Mary's offers every facility to be found on the mainland, such as a PO, chemist, hospital, provision stores, banks, hotels and bistros. Water and fuel are obtainable on the quay. There are chandlers and boat repairers. Customs are on the quay. Frequent daily helicopter service to Penzance, with connecting bus services from downtown. Ferries leave every afternoon in the summer for Penzance. The HM's telephone is Scillonia 22768. Yacht club: Scillonian Sailing and Boating Club.

New Grimsby Harbour—Tresco See Admiralty Chart. This island is justly famous for its tropical gardens and many yachts like to bring up in the passage between the island and Bryher. The entrance from the north-west is a little tricky and

228

143. A view of Cromwell's Castle, Tresco, with St Mary's behind and Bryher with Hangman's Island on right.

should only be attempted for the first time in favourable weather conditions with a leading wind or under engine. Clear of the north-west entrance a flood tide, north-east going, of 2 to 4 kts may be experienced. Keep on Transit H and give particular attention to the Kettle and Kettle Bottom Ledges which dry little over a cable to the north-east at the entrance, and also to a drying rock which is inside the entrance but scarcely ½ cable to the north-east. There is a deep anchorage in 11m between Cromwell's Castle and Hangman Isle; after this the bottom shoals to 2m4 and then down to 0m3 in the channel opposite the quay at New Grimsby on Tresco, where a dinghy may be left in safety while exploring the famous tropical gardens at the south end or the luxurious hotel on the other side of the island at Old Grimsby. Note that a cable, marked by beacons on either side, crosses the channel just north-west of the quay. There is an inn and a small shop close to New Grimsby quay.

The passage from St Mary's to New Grimsby looks more formidable than it is. Leave to port the unmarked Nut Rock (2) and the B Hulman Bn close to starboard, Raggs Bn to port, Merrick Island close to port and thence straight to the anchorage. A useful transit between Hulman Bn and Merrick Island is to keep the latter in line with Hangman Isle, then leaving it close to port proceed as before to the anchorage. Tresco Flats dry out between Hulman Bn and the the anchorage but these can be crossed by vessels up to 3m draught at HW if precisely on course. On the first occasion a stranger might be wise to treat the flat as drying 1m4. Alternatively, make a reconnaissance by dinghy or in one of the tripper boats which ply between the islands—then consult Norm's book.

United Kingdom

Aberdeen	Kelvin Hughes	21 Regent Quay
Aberdovey	Dovey Marine	Copperhill Street
Abersoch	Abersoch Boatyard Ltd	The Saltings
Alderney	Mainbrayce Ltd	Inner Harbour, Braye
Aultbea	Bridgend Stores	—
Axminster	Axminster Chandlery	Chard Street
Barmouth	"Seafarer"	Church Street
Belfast	James Tedford and Co Ltd	5 and 9 Donegal Quay
Birmingham	Hollywood Marine Ltd	15 Highfield Road, Hall Green
Boston	Boston Marina	5/7 Witham Bank
Brightlingsea	L H Morgan & Sons (Marine) Ltd	The Boat Centre, 32-42 Waterside
Brighton	Brighton Marina Co Ltd	The Brighton Marina, Black Rock
Bristol	W F Price & Co Ltd	24 Gloucester Road, Avonmouth
Brixham	Brixham Yacht Supplies	72 Middle Street
Buckie	Thomas Garden	Harbour Office, Commercial Road
Burghead	Burghead Boat Centre	Burghead Harbour
Burnham-on-Crouch	Kelvin Aqua Ltd	The Quay
Cardiff	T J Williams & Son Ltd	19 West Bute Street, Docks
Cardiff	Blair's Nautical Supplies Ltd	20 James St Docks
Chatham	Gransden Marine	10 High Street
Chester	Deans Marina	Rowton Bridge Road, Christleton
Chichester	Yacht & Sports Gear	13 The Hornet
Christchurch	Purbrook Rossiter Ltd	Bridge Wharf, Bridge Street
Cowes	Pascall, Atkey & Son Ltd	29 High Street
Crinan	Crinan Boats Ltd	—
Dale	Dale Sailing Co Ltd	—
Dartmouth	The Bosuns Locker	24 Lower Street
Douglas	Manx Marine	35 North Quay
Dover	Dover Marine Supplies	158-160 Snargate Street

Dundee	Allison-Gray	59-63 Dock Street
Edinburgh	Chattan Shipping Services Ltd	5 Canonmills
Exeter	Eland	22 Bedford Street
Exmouth	Dixon & Sons	The Pier
Falmouth	Marine Instruments	50 Arwenack Street, Hulls Lane
Felixstowe	Outdoor Life	34 Orwell Road
Fishguard	Fishguard Yacht & Boat Co Ltd	1 Wern Rd. Goodwick
Fleetwood	The Fleetwood Trawlers Supply Co Ltd	240/244 Dock Street
Folkestone	Forepeak, Folkestone Marine Ltd	Fish Market
Fowey	Troy Chandlery	10 Lostwithiel Street
Glasgow	Kelvin Hughes	375 West George Street (Enter by Holland Street), G2
Glasgow	Christie & Wilson	44 York Street, G2
Gorleston on Sea	Gorleston Marine Ltd	Beach Pavilion Road
Gosport	Hardway Marine Store	95-99 Priory Road, Hardway
Grimsby	Grahams Ship Services (Grimsby) Ltd	Humber Bridge Road, Fish Docks
Holyhead	Holyhead Chandlery	Newry Beach Road
Hull	B Cooke & Son Ltd	"Kingston Observatory" 58-59 Market Place
Ipswich	C H Fox & Son Ltd	The Strand, Wherstead
King's Lynn	Reynold Riggers Ltd	John Kennedy Road
Lerwick	Hay & Co (Lerwick) Ltd	106A Commercial Street
Liverpool	Dubois Phillips & McCallum Ltd	8A Rumford Place, L3
Liverpool	J Sewill Ltd	36 Exchange Street East, L2
London	J D Potter Ltd	145 Minories, EC3
,,	Kelvin Hughes	100 Leadenhall Street, EC3
,,	Capt O M Watts Ltd	45 Albemarle Street, W1
,,	London Yacht Centre	13 Artillery Lane, E1
,,	Brown & Perring Ltd	7 St Botolph Street, EC3
,,	Boat Showrooms of London Ltd	288-290 Kensington High Street, W14
,,	Thomas Foulkes	Lansdowne Road, Leytonstone, E11
Lowestoft	Charity & Taylor (Electronic Services) Ltd	4 Battery Green Road
Lyme Regis	Sails Marine & Sports Centre	14 Broad Street
Lymington	Haven Boatyard	Kings Saltern Road

Maldon	Dan Webb & Feesey	Shipways, North Street
Milford Haven	Jenkins Boats Ltd	Burton, Neyland
Newhaven	Cantell & Sons	The Old Shipyard, Robinson Road
North Shields	John Lilley & Gillie Ltd	Clive Street
Oban	Nancy Black	24/25 Argyll Square
Pembroke Dock	Kelpie Boat Service	Hobbs Point
Plymouth	A E Monsen	Vauxhall Quay
Poole	H Pipler & Son Ltd	The Quay
Portmadoc	Glaslyn Marine Supplies Ltd	3 Oakley Wharf, The Harbour
Portsmouth	Gieves & Hawkes Ltd	22 The Hard
Pwllheli	William and Partingdon Marine Ltd	The Harbour
Ramsgate	Seagear (Ramsgate) Ltd	54 Harbour Parade
Rye	Sea Cruisers Ltd	Winchelsea Road
Salcombe	Salcombe Chandlers Ltd	19 Fore Street
Salford	International Marine	249 Ordsall Lane
Saundersfoot	Jones & Teague Ltd	The Harbour Yacht Yard
Sheerness	William Hurst Ltd	19 West Street, Bluetown
Sheffield	Peter Copley Marine Ltd	The Sailboat Centre, 3-11 Edgedale Road (off Abbeydale Road)
Southampton	Camper & Nicholsons Marine Equipment Ltd	Royal Crescent Road
Southend-on-Sea	Shoreline (Yachtsmen) Ltd	36 Eastern Esplanade
Southwick	A O Muggeridge Ltd	102 Albion Street
St Helier	W H Coom	South Pier Shipyard
St Leonards-on-Sea	Sussex Marine	48 Marina
St Mary's	South'ard Sailing	The Quay
St Peter Port	David G Bowker Ltd	Pier Steps
Stornoway	Duncan MacIver Ltd	7 Maritime Buildings
Swansea	Cambrian Small Boat & Chandlery Co Ltd	14 Cambrian Place, South Dock
Tarbert	W B Leitch	—
Topsham	The Foc'sle	32 Fore Street
Wells Next the Sea	Charles Ward	Standard House, East Quay
West Mersea	Clarke & Carter Ltd	110 Coast Road
Weymouth	W L Bussell	11 Nothe Parade

Whitby	M R Coates (Marine)	The Boat Yard, Esk Terrace
Whitstable	Roy Rigden & Partners	The Dinghy Store, Sea Wall
Woodbridge	Small Craft Deliveries Ltd	12 Quay Street

Irish Republic

Cork	Union Chandlery Ltd	Andersons Quay
Cork	J B Roche Ltd	1/2 Cornmarket Street
Dublin	Windmill Leisure & Marine Ltd	3 Windmill Lane, Sir John Rogerson's Quay
Galway	Galway Maritime Services	New Docks

NOTES

NOTES

NOTES

NOTES

NOTES

NOTES

NOTES

IALA/IAPH/PIANC International Unification of Port Movement Signals – 1982

● ● ● (red quick flashing)	**QUICK FLASHING** Serious emergency. All vessels stop or divert according to instructions	● ○ ●	A vessel may proceed when it has received specific orders to do so
● ● ●	Vessels shall not proceed	○ ● / ● / ●	Vessels shall not proceed. Vessels outside the main channel need not comply
● ● ● (green)	Vessels may proceed. One-way traffic	○ ● / ○ / ●	A vessel may proceed when it has received specific orders to do so. Vessels outside the main channel need not comply
● ● ○	Vessels may proceed. Two-way traffic		**NOTES:** 1. Other than the Quick Flashing red lights indicating a serious emergency, all other light signals are fixed or slow occulting. 2. Adoption of this system in the UK is at the discretion of local Harbour Authorities any time from 1982 onwards.